CREATURES OF WANT AND RUIN

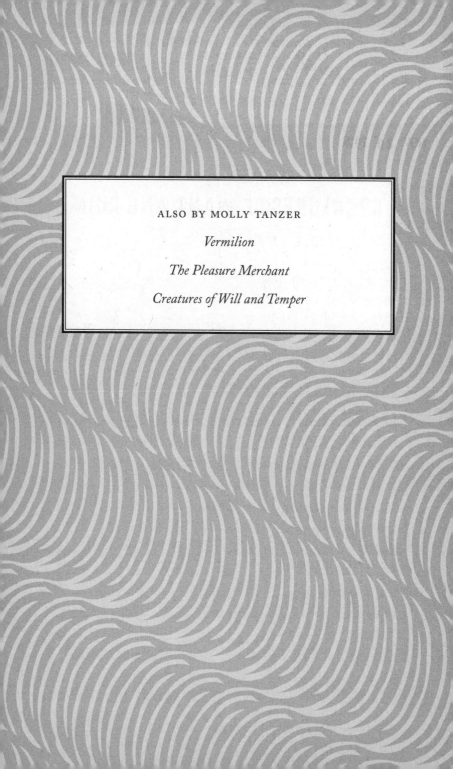

ALSO BY MOLLY TANZER

Vermilion

The Pleasure Merchant

Creatures of Will and Temper

CREATURES

OF

WANT

RUIN

Molly Tanzer

A John Joseph Adams Book

MARINER BOOKS

HOUGHTON MIFFLIN HARCOURT

BOSTON   NEW YORK

2018

For my grandmother
and for my mother

For information about permission to reproduce selections from this book,
write to trade.permissions@hmhco.com or to Permissions,
Houghton Mifflin Harcourt Publishing Company,
3 Park Avenue, 19th Floor, New York, New York 10016.

hmhco.com

Library of Congress Cataloging-in-Publication Data
Names: Tanzer, Molly, author.
Title: Creatures of want and ruin / Molly Tanzer.
Description: Boston : Mariner Books, 2018. | "A John Joseph Adams book." |
Identifiers: LCCN 2018012227 (print) | LCCN 2018014274 (ebook) |
ISBN 9781328710352 (ebook) | ISBN 9781328710253 (trade paper)
Subjects: | BISAC: FICTION / Fantasy / Historical. | FICTION /
Occult & Supernatural. | FICTION / Horror. |
GSAFD: Occult fiction. | Horror fiction.
Classification: LCC PS3620.A7254 (ebook) |
LCC PS3620.A7254 C73 2018 (print)|
DDC 813/.6 — dc23
LC record available at https://lccn.loc.gov/2018012227

Book design by Chrissy Kurpeski

Printed in the United States of America
DOC 10 9 8 7 6 5 4 3 2 1

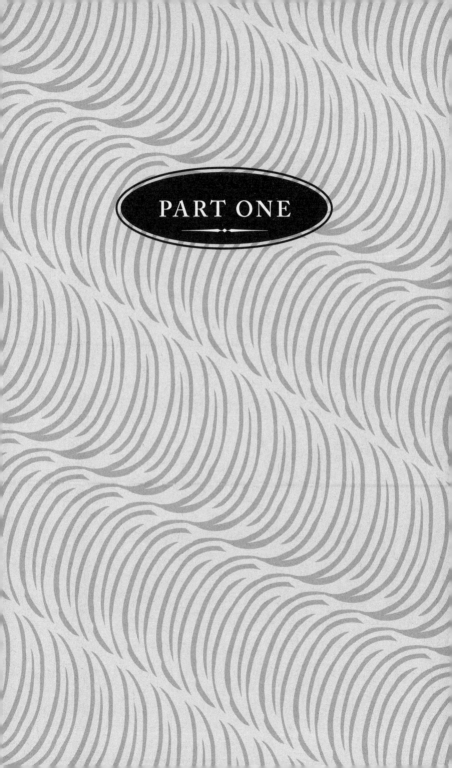

PART ONE

The Demon in the Deep
by G. Baker

S USAN WAITED AND WAITED for Miss Depth to walk through the door of the Calico Cat and join her for tea, but after an hour she gave up. The cake had dried out on their plates, the Earl Grey had gone cold in the pot, and Susan was too cross to enjoy either.

Cross, but also worried. Miss Depth had been quite troubled after her sister's death. It had been difficult to get her to agree to come into town at all, so Susan decided it would be best for her to go and check on her friend.

It was drizzling, and cold, and late enough in the year that the skeletons of autumn's glorious leaves had all been whisked away on the wind. Twilight had fallen by the time Susan approached the little house by the sea, making the light in Miss Depth's window shine the brighter. She was there, at home ... but when Susan peered in through the window, her friend was not reading in her chair or writing letters at her desk. She was in her parlor, kneeling before what could only be described as a small altar in the center of a circle drawn in chalk on her Turkish carpet.

Miss Depth's sister had brought that carpet back from her travels abroad; Miss Depth had always taken such good care of it. Usually, she wouldn't let anyone bring a glass of lemonade or iced tea into her parlor, but Susan saw she had a little cup set on the altar and candles burning, too.

At first Susan thought Miss Depth was praying, but the longer she watched, the more it seemed like her friend was talking — talking to someone Susan couldn't see. It made all the little hairs on her neck and arms stand up.

Then her friend cried out, and Susan watched in horror as Miss Depth went white as a sheet — not in the way that people usually meant when they used the expression, but actually *white*, from her skin to her hair — all except her eyes, which turned completely black before a dark fluid began to drip down her cheeks.

Susan fled into the wet night, running all the way home, but only after she'd locked the door behind her did she wonder if she should have tried to help. It hadn't occurred to her at the time, as Miss Depth had been smiling.

1

THE WIND WAS EAST and the tide was running high by the time Ellie West finished jamming all the crates of moonshine liquor into the smuggler's hold of her skiff. Leaden bands of clouds were thickening on the horizon, and the air was so hot and wet that breathing felt a little like drowning. Any seasoned bayman could see that they were in for a storm, but Ellie's customers were expecting her, and she didn't like to disappoint them.

Mopping her brow with a threadbare red handkerchief, Ellie frowned at the sky. She figured she'd probably be all right. She wouldn't be out of sight of land for most of her delivery run; save for crossing the Great South Bay to get over to Jones Beach Island she'd be darting in and out of slip and cove the whole time, and it hadn't even begun to rain.

The humidity really was something else that night, even for summertime on Long Island. Ellie swept her bobbed hair away from her sticky forehead, tucking the lank strands behind her ears. She'd lopped her braid off a week or so ago, and she still wasn't sure how she felt about showing the world the back of her neck, even if it was undeniably cooler on nights like this.

Ellie looked up. At the top of the slight rise she saw her supplier, SJ, silhouetted in the doorway of the shack that housed her small moonshining operation. White steam puffed out of the chimney behind her. She too was watching the sky.

"I'm heading out," called Ellie, raising her hand in farewell. "I think I'll be all right!"

SJ might have nodded her head once—at least her big thick glasses flashed, reflecting the golden light inside—but Ellie couldn't be sure.

"Thanks ag—"

SJ shut the door.

Ellie wasn't offended by this brusque dismissal. SJ was a woman of few words, and even fewer friendly ones. She'd been like that as long as Ellie had known her . . . and that had been a very long time.

Ellie untied her skiff, hopped on board, and rowed herself beyond the pines, sycamores, and low brush that concealed SJ's operation from prying eyes. Only when she was a good ways away did she start the motor.

The little boat sat low in the water as Ellie navigated the choppy bay past darkly wooded shoreline and pale spits of stony beach, past fine homes with shiny new runabouts tied up to private docks and boatyards cluttered with shabbier vessels. Her small engine puttered in pleasant harmony with the drone of the insects and the last few cries of the gulls; a light rain added some gentle percussion just after her first handoff, where she exchanged two full swing-top bottles for two empties—and some cash, of course. The Widow Hawkins might be a shut-in, but she didn't mind getting a bit of fresh air whenever Ellie tied up in the shadows beneath the trailing branches of the old willow at the edge of her property.

Undeterred, Ellie pulled on her oilskin; a little rain didn't bother her. In fact, the changeable nature of Long Island's weather was a source of continuous joy to her. While ominous, the churning sky above her was beautiful, and the first line of a new poem came to her as she dropped off more bottles along her route. "The wind is east and the sky is gray," she said aloud as said wind gusted under her hood, knocking it back off her head. "There's going to be a shower tonight!"

She stopped composing when the rain began to fall in earnest. Her handoffs, which usually entailed an exchange of gossip as well as goods, became brief and hurried, with no more than a "Stay dry!" shouted at her over the worsening downpour. More than one customer offered to let her tie up and wait out the storm inside, but she decided it was safe enough to make the crossing over to Jones Beach Island. Rocky was expecting her.

Todd "Rocky" Rockmeteller was Ellie's last stop on her usual route. A poet by trade, he'd moved to the area after he'd "cracked," to use his word for it—life in the city had stressed him to nervous exhaustion. He'd used the last of the advance from his first book to buy a derelict bungalow between Gilgo and Oak Beach in the hope that peace and isolation would help him finish a second. He had, and in record time; he'd been so inspired by his far-flung paradise that he now lived there year-round, and in all but the very worst of weather.

The crossing to get to Rocky's house was typically quick and easy, but halfway there the rain switched direction and the final leg of the trip got soggy. Though Ellie had intended to say merely a brief hello, by the time she pulled up at the dock and trekked across the rickety boardwalk to his little house on the ocean side of the island, she was more than happy to accept his invitation to come in, dry off, and warm up with a bit of what she'd brought him.

Wrapped in a towel, her clothes dripping and steaming by the cast iron woodburner, Ellie shivered as Rocky bumbled about, unable as usual to remember where he'd left the poker, or the kettle, or the tea. The place was so small there were a limited number of places any of it could be; even so, he never seemed able to put anything in the same place twice.

Ellie had met Rocky when he'd been wandering around a fish market looking bemused by the bright-eyed hauls of snook and flounder. They'd hit it off quickly. Ellie had been pleased to befriend a "real poet"—and then had been pleased to be seduced by one.

Rocky hadn't been the first to make Ellie moan that way as he pawed her small heavy breasts, but he'd certainly been the most glamorous. At least she'd thought so at the time. Having gotten to know him better over the years, she couldn't help but smile ruefully when he found the poker by stubbing his toe on it, and then burned his finger putting the kettle on to heat. Rocky might possess a strange grace while speaking about poetry or making love to her — or her favorite, both at the same time — but otherwise, he was hopelessly clumsy.

"I can't believe you went out in this," he said, his faint English accent accentuated by his concern.

"Booze doesn't deliver itself," said Ellie.

"And you can't deliver booze if you"—he handed her a mug of tea laced with SJ's potato spirit—"capsize."

"Capsize!" Ellie chuckled as he settled in beside her on his worn leather sofa. Rain lashed the windows, a tattoo wilder than a jazz drum line, and the wind howled; Ellie could see tree branches swaying in the darkness beyond the windows. "It's not *so* bad out . . . at least, not on the bay side."

Lightning flashed. Ellie's confidence flickered as Rocky's hurricane lantern guttered in the draft; after the thunder rolled by and no more came, she shrugged it off. "I'm sure I can get back."

"Back across? Tonight?"

"Sure."

"You're welcome to stay," said Rocky, threading a slender arm around her waist and snugging her closer to him.

"I'm sure it'll let up soon," said Ellie, settling against his warmth in the meantime. Truthfully she was extremely tempted by his offer, but she was expected elsewhere. "It seems like it's letting up. I'll finish this and then be on my way. But next time . . ."

"Next time," he agreed, and kissed her on the neck, just under her ear. His soft, long-fingered hand wormed its way down the front of her towel, and then under the band of her knickers, where he began to casually toy with her hair there.

Ellie sighed happily. She was warm, almost dry, and feeling

pretty loosey-goosey from the white dog in her tea. But when the storm showed signs of abating she pulled herself away from Rocky's caresses and donned her damp togs. Though almost too hot at first from the stove, they quickly turned clammy against her skin.

At least she had a thick roll of bills in the pocket of her coveralls. They'd provide a bit of extra warmth, even if it was only psychological.

"Are you sure about this?" Rocky stared out the door, dark brow furrowed.

Ellie also had her doubts, but no more thunder boomed and no lightning brightened the night.

"Don't worry," she said. "I know what I'm doing."

"My little water rat doesn't mind rain on her pelt," said Rocky admiringly.

Ellie smiled to hear her nickname. That's how he'd inscribed the copy of his duology, *City Songs* and *Sea Songs*, that he'd given her as a birthday gift—"To my little water rat."

"Thanks for the pick-me-up," she said. "It was nice to get warm."

"A sensation I fear will be all too fleeting," said Rocky.

Oh, she liked it when he lapsed into formal language like that! She kissed him one last time on his luscious, too-big mouth and headed out into the night.

THE BOAT'S MOTOR STARTED RIGHT UP in spite of the damp, but too quickly Ellie realized she ought to have listened to Rocky instead of trying to out-bluster the storm. The bay had become wilder as she'd relaxed indoors; apparently the squall had only been drawing its breath before really starting to howl.

Ellie wasn't sure what to do. It'd be risky to increase her speed while the bay was so choppy, and the rain made it difficult for her to see much beyond her bow, but when a streak of lightning split the heavens right above her Ellie decided a bit of salt never killed anyone. She needed to get somewhere safe, and fast.

She could barely hear the motor over the downpour as she sped along the coast of Jones Beach Island, her skiff skipping on the waves, her mouth shut tight against the spray. She hadn't yet risked the crossing, but staying on this side had its dangers, too. There was no shelter here, nor were there any docks, but Ellie knew there was a cove close by where she could hunker down and wait this out. And indeed, after a few more moments, she saw the inlet where she could turn out of the wind.

As a child, she had come here, to this secret place. Her father had shown it to her before the war, back when they used to go out digging for clams together. It had changed over the years—high tides and hurricanes had taken their due, old trees had fallen and younger ones grown, and the bit of sand on one side where a boat could be pulled up was a different shape and size—but it was still basically the same.

Lightning flashed again. To Ellie's surprise, she saw that another boat had also sought refuge here—but its sole passenger lay lifelessly draped over the bow.

Ellie had no idea if the dark lump of a person was dead or in need of a rescue, but either way she couldn't just leave him there. Not in this weather. She sighed, but her small protest was swallowed by the wind and rain.

A rescue wouldn't be easy—or safe. While the secret cove was calmer than the bay, lightning was now bursting across the sky in jagged flashes, dangerous and bright, and the wind and rain continued to make it difficult for her to see and steer.

Doing the right thing doesn't always mean doing the easy thing. That was something her father used to say to her, back when Ellie was young. Then as now she'd found it a hard adage to argue with.

She put her skiff's motor in neutral as she drew near the drifting craft, using the rudder and her momentum to ease up alongside the other's stern. Grabbing it, she tied off her bowline to the cleat. It seemed wisest to board the other craft and secure its passenger, whatever his fate, before trying to tug it to the beach. On the off chance the man was still alive, Ellie had to make sure he didn't fall into the bay and drown.

Ellie killed the motor, and mindful of the treacherously slick wood and choppy surf, she made her way carefully to the bow of the other vessel. She couldn't tell if the man was breathing, but she could see that he was half-draped over his open smuggler's hold. Another moonshiner like her. Most likely he'd slipped and knocked himself a good one to the head. She reached out gingerly, expecting to touch a cold corpse, but his neck was warm.

She pressed deeper into his skin to feel for a pulse. There it was, faint but present. Lightning flashed again; in that bright moment she saw he was bleeding freely from the temple. She also recognized him: it was Walter Greene, who stocked the shelves at the feed and hardware stores. She didn't know him; he wasn't one of her clients and he wasn't much of a bayman. So what was he doing out on a night like tonight?

Greene was a large, heavy man. Moving him wouldn't be easy. Ellie braced herself, but when she grabbed him by the collar and the waistband of his pants to haul him away from the edge, his eyes shot open. The whites of them glowed unnaturally, bright as two lamps.

Greene howled like a mad dog and sprang at her, punching Ellie square in the nose. The night exploded into white light that was not another streak of lightning as Ellie staggered back. The warm rush of blood filled her mouth, the metallic taste mingling with salt spray and rainwater.

A lifelong boxing fan, Ellie had once taken some lessons from a prizefighter who'd been part of a traveling carnival. He'd told her if she could get her hands up, keep them up, and stay light on her feet she'd do all right in just about any fight. The few times she'd needed to defend herself, his advice had helped; even though she couldn't land the hardest punches, she'd still done okay. Since she couldn't easily stay light on her feet on a rocking boat in a storm, Ellie did what she could, guarding her face with her balled fists.

"Wait!" she cried. "I'm not—"

He did not wait. Greene fell upon her, knocking the wind out of her as he brought her to the deck, pinning her with his substantial bulk. He landed another punch, this time to her ribs, and then a third to her gut.

That was when Ellie's instincts kicked in. She got in a punch of her own to Greene's barrel-like stomach. It wasn't a hard one, but when more lightning lit the sky she saw his face contorted, furious. He got his big hand around her neck and began to squeeze.

Ellie thrashed, panicking; he stayed atop her, but she felt his foot slip on the wet wood of the deck. As he struggled to keep his balance she got her knee up, catching him in the groin. Then, at last, Greene's grip on her throat loosened and she managed to shimmy out of his grasp, catching him on the chin with her other knee as she got to her feet.

As he shook his head, spraying water like a wet dog, Ellie cast around to see if there was anything she could use to defend herself. Two oars were nestled along the edges of his boat. She grabbed one.

"Hey!" she shouted as she brandished it at him. "I was trying to help you!"

Maybe he couldn't hear her; maybe he was past caring. All she knew for certain was that Greene had a bottle in his hand, and while at first Ellie thought he might use it as a weapon, instead he flipped the swing-top with one strong thumb.

He drank deeply of it as Ellie watched, oar in hand. She couldn't make sense of what she was seeing; it seemed like when he swallowed, his eyes glowed brighter, and when he wiped his mouth with his sleeve, it left a rainbow smear behind. His tongue too was coated in something bright, though the liquid in the bottle remained clear. But that was impossible . . .

Regardless, Ellie had no time to marvel. Greene cast the bottle aside and came at her, his footfalls rocking the boat hard enough that Ellie could barely keep her heavy oar up, much less swing the makeshift weapon at him.

Greene grabbed the paddle with both hands and ripped it out of her grasp. She fell to one knee, barking it sharply as he hurled the oar to the deck. She flung her hands up again; Greene had the high ground now, and once again he pressed her down onto the deck and got his hand around her throat.

The night seemed to contract around Ellie as the clouds beyond Greene's head turned impossible colors like the coral of a sunset, egg yolk yellow, robin's egg blue. The rain felt colder as it struck her skin, but his hand burned like a fire around her neck, another torment as he tightened his grip. She thought it was just her imagination, but no—the skin of Greene's face and neck had turned red as a boiled lobster, and the rainwater dripping down his forehead and cheeks turned to steam and billowed away into the night. The spittle that flecked his lips and bared teeth was rainbow-hued, and in his eyes she saw writhing fire and boiling earth. Ellie went limp in wonder, unsure if what she saw was real or she was merely dreaming as she died.

The air grew thick and electric as she gave up struggling to breathe. Ellie wondered if they'd been struck by lightning, but when another flash revealed his face, Greene looked confused, as if something he'd expected to happen hadn't, and his grip on her neck relaxed a little.

Ellie got some air back into her lungs, and drawing from some deep well within her, she slung herself off the deck and into his midsection, grabbing him around his waist. He slipped, and when he fell backwards, he fell hard. Ellie heard the sickening crack of his head as it hit the deck, even over the rain. She scrambled off him. Greene did not stir as his bright eyes dimmed and a black stain spread out from the back of his head all over the deck, thinning at the edges to a sickly gray as it mixed with all the rainwater.

She sat still for a moment, getting her wind back, waiting to see if Greene moved. He did not. Her gut said he was dead, but she made herself get up and check; she didn't want him waking up again with her on board. This time, his pulse faded under her touch.

She retrieved her handkerchief and dabbed at her nose—it was still bleeding. Her ribs were on fire; her throat was sore; her knee throbbed. Ellie sat down again, thinking about Greene's burning hand on her neck, his eyes, the steam clouds surrounding him like a horrible halo as he spat impossible color onto her. One sob escaped her before she bit it off. Long ago she'd vowed she was done with crying, and she wasn't going to start now—not for him. Not for anyone.

Reason reasserted herself as she rested. What she'd seen . . . That had all just been a fever-dream as he'd cut off her air. People could not suddenly become hot enough that rainwater would steam off their skin; people's eyes couldn't contain visions of the end of the world. And yet, it hadn't felt like a dream . . . It had felt real.

Furious, Ellie pulled herself to her feet and kicked Greene's corpse in the side with her good leg, once, and then she couldn't stop kicking him. Eventually, she calmed down. After wiping yet more blood from her nose, Ellie stepped over the dead man. Her foot nearly came down on the bottle he'd drunk from. She picked it up and sniffed it.

All this for some moonshine. How stupid.

Not all the booze had spilled out of the bottle when he'd cast it aside. Ellie toasted Greene's body and then took a long pull. It was raw, harsher than SJ's potato spirit, and had a strange flavor Ellie couldn't place. Musty, earthy, greasy.

Whatever it was, it did the job. Her aches eased a bit; her muscles loosened up. She felt the power of motion returning to her limbs, and took another swig for good measure.

She peered into his smuggler's hold. There she discovered two items nestled in the darkness: a burlap sack, and a crate of bottles with one missing. She dragged both out onto the deck to look at them more closely.

The sack was full of soil. Ellie sifted through it with her fingers and found a dark chunk of something spongy and unpleasantly oily to the touch. What little light there was shone strangely on it, playing with Ellie's eyes. She couldn't tell if it was round like a ball or indented like a bowl. Running her fingers over its slick surface just made her feel nauseated. She hurled it into the bay, and out of spite tossed the rest of the sack overboard too.

It was so senseless. Greene had attacked her while she was trying to help him, and for a few bottles of rotgut and some nasty dirt.

She knew well enough she'd been defending herself; knew her intention had been to help. It didn't make her feel better about how it had ended. He'd frightened her, hurt her, and she'd killed him — or at least, he'd died.

Ellie replaced the loose board that hid the smuggler's hold. Of course it was at that moment that the rain chose to let up; it was barely drizzling after she got the rest of Greene's booze onto her skiff and untied her craft from the other. The moon even came out a bit as she sped away, leaving him and his boat to drift where they would.

The stupidest part was, she didn't even have very far to go to get home.

No, the stupidest part was if she'd stayed with Rocky for an hour longer, she wouldn't have needed to pull into the cove at all.

She'd killed a man. And robbed him, too. The second crime didn't weigh too heavily on her heart, but the first . . . It was terrifying. At least the consequences were. The act itself had been necessary.

And then there was what she'd seen, what she'd felt . . . Even though she knew she'd been deprived of air and hallucinating, it nagged her. It had all felt so real.

She wondered if she should tell someone.

No. If she did—if she told anyone what she'd seen and done —they'd send her to jail, or to the Long Island Home for some "much needed rest." She couldn't let that happen. Her family depended on her, on the fish she brought them to eat and the cash she earned.

And, of course, there was Gabriel.

He'd waited up for her. A light burned in a window of the colonial saltbox he was restoring for them both to live in one day. It looked so snug as Ellie pulled up to the dock, the clean straight lines of the house contrasting with the muslin curtains that twisted as if they were alive as the cool, wet breeze blew in through the windows. When the house was done, they would be married. By then, hopefully Ellie's younger brother Lester would have gone off to school, and Ellie could move out of her parents' house with a clear conscience.

Exhaustion set in as she tied up. She tried to lift the crate of moonshine out of the hold, but her arms failed her. She couldn't even shift the remaining few bottles of SJ's hooch. Well, it had to come in. She'd just have to ask for her fiancé's help. She couldn't leave it outside overnight.

Weaving and stumbling, she picked her way up to the house and fell against the back door. Her hands were now shaking too badly to turn the knob, but after a minute or so of fumbling with it, it opened. She swooned into Gabriel's strong arms, looking up at his wide, handsome face; the bright blue eyes behind the thick lenses of his tortoiseshell glasses. She'd never seen anything so wonderful in all her life.

"Ellie!" he said, touching the crusted blood on her face. "What happened?"

Ellie chose to focus on her immediate concerns, rather than her esoteric ones. "I think my nose is broken," she said. Her voice was so scratchy it barely sounded like her own.

"Jesus Christ." He was so strong he just picked her up and carried her inside. His broad chest and powerful arms warmed her better than any blanket or fire.

"Will you please bring my things in?" she rasped as he set her down on the sofa.

"Your things can wait."

"No," she said, her throat burning. "Really!"

"Ellie, I'll get everything inside, I promise, but I'll get to it after I help you out of these wet clothes."

Gabriel was always so mild in his ways; his firm tone brought Ellie up short. He was right, too; it had been so hot earlier, but she was shivering now; her clothes gave her gooseflesh where they clung to her skin. He helped her out of her boots and socks and then peeled off her coveralls; that felt good. The dry blanket he wrapped around her felt even better.

"I'm going to put some water on to heat—yes, first," he said, in that tone that brooked no argument, "and then I will unload your boat. You just sit still." When she tried to sit up, he gently pushed her back down onto the sofa, where her body welcomed the comfort and rest even if her spirit rebelled against it.

"There are two cases," she croaked. "A full one and a partial."

"I know you don't think I'm ready for the responsibility, but I'll take care of it." Gabriel sounded amused, but Ellie took the hint.

She stretched out after moving aside the latest issue of *Weird Tales* that Gabriel had left open on the couch. She studied the garish cover of her fiancé's favorite magazine for a moment but then set it aside, feeling sick. The image of a terrified girl, presumably the advertised "Bride of Osiris," being loomed over by a shadowy figure reminded her too much of what had happened to her that night.

There were so many things Ellie loved about Gabriel, and his ability to let her talk in her own time was one of them. He asked her no questions after bringing in the booze and helping her into their small tub; instead, he made gentle small talk with her while cleaning up her face. She'd missed the fight between Jack Dempsey and Jack Sharkey, but he'd listened for her and gave her a bit of play-by-play of what he'd heard on his beloved wireless. Normally, Ellie appreciated his recaps; tonight, however, the idea of punching people for sport made her feel queasy. Thankfully her injuries gave her license to just close her eyes and listen to the sound of his voice instead of responding to the details of what he was saying.

After Gabriel had finished his ministrations he said it didn't look like her nose needed to be set—that was good news. Then he washed her hair and wrapped her in a clean towel before concluding his doctoring by dotting her cuts with some iodine and helping her into bed.

"So what happened?" he asked as he slid into bed beside her.

She didn't want to tell him the truth. Ellie loved Gabriel, and she didn't want him to see her as a killer; didn't want him to look at her any differently because of something that wasn't her fault. And while her fiancé was a fan of the works of H. P. Lovecraft, William Hope Hodgson, M. R. James, Clark Ashton Smith, and similar, she didn't want to talk to him about whether she could have seen something supernatural. He just liked to read about that stuff. He didn't believe in it.

"It was the storm," she rasped. "I shouldn't have risked crossing the bay. I got tossed around bad, and fell on my face." She considered what else she needed to explain away. "I got tangled in a rope; it got around my neck as I struggled."

"Poor thing," said Gabriel, and wrapped her gently in his arms. She melted into his embrace, softening against him like butter on warm bread. "Well, all's well that ends well."

She shuddered, overwhelmed with the sensation of being warm and cared for. He told her it would all be all right—that she'd feel better in a few days. That she'd be sore, but she'd heal. That she was safe, and it was all over now.

Ellie wondered if that would really turn out to be the case.

2

GABRIEL HAD GROWN UP on a duck farm forty miles east of Amityville, in Center Moriches, and a childhood spent alongside flocks of those quacking, stinking birds had left him with a lifelong aversion to duck meat and the inability to sleep past five in the morning. When she stayed over, Ellie usually got up with him so they could enjoy a cup of coffee or tea together as the sun rose, sitting on the porch in good weather, or in front of the little woodstove when it was cool.

The morning following her misadventure, however, Ellie did not get up. She tried, but she was so sore she could not make herself move, and she fell back asleep after he tiptoed out of the bedroom.

Her dreams were unpleasant. A dark figure gripped her with bruising fingers so hot they burned her skin. She pushed him away, but they were at the edge of a cliff and he fell, screaming, off the edge into a dark abyss full of fire and water. She crawled to the edge and peered over only to have two hands grab her and pull her down, too.

She awoke with a gasp. Gabriel was standing there in a halo of bright sunlight, holding a cup of coffee that steamed in the warm morning air. The smell of it brought her to her senses.

"Hey," he said. "You okay?"

"I had a bad dream," she said, and with a groan she pushed herself up to lean back against the headboard of their bed to accept the mug. "That's all." Her voice sounded even worse than it had the previous night.

Gabriel sat down on the edge of the mattress. "You look better," he said. Ellie was sure that was not the case.

"Did you put the booze down in the cellar?" she asked.

"Yes ma'am," answered Gabriel, with a faint smile.

"Don't you 'Yes ma'am' me," she said irritably.

"Yes ma'am." Gabriel's smile deepened, and she felt her annoyance melt away.

With that fair hair and jawline, Gabriel had missed his calling—he ought to have posed for army recruiting posters instead of restoring houses. The photographers could have taken pictures without him having to wear the glasses that had kept him out of the service.

"Looks like you came back with more booze than usual. People not show up because of the weather?"

Ellie frowned, displeased to have to come up with another alibi. "Nah, SJ had more than she needed."

"Nobody wanted to buy it?"

"Maybe next week," she said, though truth be told, she wasn't sure if she ought to sell it at all. SJ might run an illegal still, but she did things the right way; other operations couldn't be counted on to do the same. Selling unknown moonshine could mean a quick profit and then a big loss if something went wrong and word got out she was selling liquor that made people sick, or blind. Sure, she'd had a sip or two, but that didn't mean much. Consistency was one of the main issues with moonshining, and there might be two or even three different batches present in that one case.

Gabriel pushed his glasses up his nose and peered at her. "We could always keep it for the wedding ... or even better, *after* the wedding, once we send everyone home ..."

Even worse than selling questionable moonshine would be serving it to her guests. "It'll be better to get rid of it, if I can. I'll need every penny I can make if I'm going to be able to send Lester off to college this fall." Seeing her fiancé's expression, she added, "And I already had SJ hold back some of her private reserve for our wedding. You know, the stuff she actually ages. I paid through the nose for it, but I figured it was worth it."

Gabriel's good humor was restored by this, but Ellie's mind strayed to the dead man to whom the liquor in question had belonged in life. She imagined Greene's corpse staring up at the same sun that streamed in through the glass of her bedroom window; saw him in her mind, adrift, undiscovered. She wondered if the body had begun to smell yet. How long did that take?

She also wondered if Greene could be traced back to her. She had no idea what would be better—for her to confess before that happened or wait to see if her crime was discovered.

"Ellie?"

"Sorry." She tried to play off her momentary inattention like nothing was wrong, but her smile turned to a wince when the motion made her nose ache. "Got lost in my own thoughts."

Gabriel took her coffee away and set it down on the nightstand—he'd built that, along with the bedstead and any number of chairs about the place, all out of scraps he'd sanded and stained—and kissed her. "Let's turn your mind to other matters," he said.

It was as if she'd been holding her breath ever since last night, as if her heart had stopped—and then the feel of his lips on her made her blood started to flow again, and she got her first taste of air. She started pulling off Gabriel's shirt, her aches and pains be damned. She was alive. She'd won. No one would connect her to Greene—how could they? Even more important, why would they?

She was safe, Gabriel was here, and he wanted her.

She could have eaten a steak right then, a whole one, with extra horseradish. Could have drunk an entire bottle of champagne, and one of real Scotch whiskey. She would have agreed to satisfy an entire roomful of men. She was alive; she wanted to celebrate that—wanted to appreciate her body, to live in it.

Once Gabriel had shed his clothes, he joined her beneath the thin coverlet. His big hands roved over her, mindful of her bruises but still eager. She gasped as he slid a finger inside her.

"Did you stop at Rocky's last night?" he asked, working her as she writhed.

"I did," she said, "but we didn't . . ."

He paused. She wriggled urgently, begging him with her body. Gabriel resumed his attentions, but she could tell he was disappointed.

When she and Gabriel had gotten serious, she hadn't broken things off with Rocky—at his request. He liked to hear about it. It got him hot.

"I wanted to get home to you," she said as she reached for her cervical cap. "So I left early."

"Is that so?"

"It is, it is . . . But I was thinking about the first time he had me—Rocky, I mean."

"Oh?" She heard the interest in his voice as she inserted her contraceptive.

"Yes," she said, reaching down and bringing his hand back to her. "He had a flask, so we bought two coffees on the street and poured it into the cups." She elected to redact the conversation they'd had when she found out he was a poet, jumping straight to the good stuff. "He asked if I'd like to have another drink, back at his bungalow, and I told him I had a skiff."

Gabriel grinned. "You easy little slut," he said affectionately. "What happened then?"

"We didn't make it to his house," said Ellie. "He took me on his front steps. Didn't even take his pants off."

Gabriel could wait no longer. She came immediately as he entered her—which wasn't her usual way, but she didn't usually feel like her whole body burned with some sort of living fire beneath her skin. After that, their communication became wordless until they fell apart, sweaty and satisfied in the warm morning air.

SHE DIDN'T HAVE A STEAK AFTER, or horseradish, but she did fry up an enormous quantity of bacon for them—only burning some of it—and then fried some bread in the drippings. That and coffee put her right, as did seeing her latest poem, "Sunset on the Bay," in the *Record*. She wondered if Rocky would see it. He couldn't be counted on to mention her publications until she brought them up, and then had only the vaguest of remarks, though he assured her he read every one he saw.

It was a lot harder to believe in a man with hot hands and colorful spit and eyes that held fire and water and cracking earth within them as she drank coffee and read the paper in the morning's bright light. Given the number of baymen she'd known who'd told crazier stories, and seemed to really believe them, her senses had likely been playing tricks on her in a confusing and desperate situation.

Pleased to have banished her air-starved brain's doubts from her well-fed, well-rested mind, Ellie dawdled over dressing before going down to inspect the windfall booze in the cellar. Once she ambled down there, she sniffed at the bottles—they all had that distinctive vegetal funk—and then scooted them behind some other crates.

After assessing her stock, Ellie felt good enough to take a few practice swings at the heavy bag she'd saved up for after taking those boxing lessons years ago. She still practiced on it when she had the time—and energy. When Gabriel had hauled it over here and hung it up for her, it had finally hit her that they would marry, and she would really live here one day.

It felt good to stretch her muscles with a few jabs, but when her knuckles collided with the leather she winced. The pain reminded her of Greene with his lamplike eyes, his strange rainbow spittle. . .

The memory asserted itself with surprising potency in the gloom of the cellar, and when Ellie went back upstairs to look for Gabriel, her mood had substantially soured.

"I gotta go," she said, finding him in his work shed, sanding down a wooden beam.

"You sure?" said Gabriel.

"Can't stay with my crab traps waiting for me."

Perhaps it wasn't the greatest of her obligations, but it was an important one. The money she brought home from running booze wasn't the only thing her family relied on her to provide.

Gabriel slid his glasses down his nose and looked at her like a disapproving schoolteacher. "I know you can't. I just wish you could is all."

"Sorry. Me too," she said. "Soon, though."

The breeze off the bay was cool that morning, but even so, she could tell it was going to be yet another hot one. Usually, Ellie was ready for fall before the weather broke, but not this summer. She'd need every day to make enough money to send Lester off to school.

Ellie tied up at the little boatyard at the end of Ketcham Avenue, a bottle of liquor tucked deep into her bag. Even if plenty of people ran booze all over Long Island, from her Uncle Jimmy to Al Capone, there was no need to advertise what she did for a living. Some stranger might see, and be scandalized enough to report her to someone who might do something about it.

One who would *not* do something about it was the person for whom Ellie's bottle was intended. Officer Hector Jones of the Amityville Police Department was ostensibly in charge of filing any and all reports on illegal distilling operations and clubs accused of serving drink, but unless somebody really stepped out of line (or failed to pay their bribe), those citations seemed to get lost in the shuffle.

Several years ago, Jones had been deputized by the feds in a case involving an Italian grocery store clerk who'd purchased three hundred pounds of sugar a few days before an illegal still exploded in the woods behind the Powells' barn. Jones, a decorated veteran of the Great War, hadn't wanted to be deputized—hadn't wanted the subsequent promotion and responsibility, either—but his superiors felt this addition to his resume made him the ideal man for the job. Amityville residents felt the same way about his eagerness to overlook their efforts to obtain and consume spirits.

Officer Jones had an arch sense of humor that Ellie liked. She liked his looks, too, even if she wouldn't quite call him handsome. At one time she'd thought he might enjoy her humor and her looks, but he'd never asked her out—a shame, for at one time she'd have said yes to him in more ways than one.

Ellie typically looked forward to her visits with Officer Jones, but that day she dreaded their rendezvous. Her fresh injuries looked bad enough that the men who perpetually haunted the boatyard had not believed her when she assured them she was not in need of a doctor's attention. Mercurial and detached as Jones might be, he wouldn't be pleased to see her walking gingerly, a black eye blooming and her neck all bruised and red.

She was right.

"Who did this to you?" he demanded after quickly ushering her inside his office. His sharp tone alarmed his faithful companion, a leggy brown mutt called Cleo.

"I'm all right," croaked Ellie, trying not to wince as she lowered herself into a chair. Cleo stood and padded over to her.

"Was it that Polack you took up with? Did he beat up on you after drinking too much *po-tah-to wodka*?" asked Jones, with a terrible imitation of a Polish accent.

"*No,*" she said, and lowered her hand so that Cleo could lick it. "You and I both know Gabe's gentle as a lamb. And don't call him a Polack."

"Fine, fine, but it's my job to ask," said Jones with a shrug. "So what happened?"

Ellie had already decided not to tell Jones about her night. It had taken a lot of deliberation on her part—she figured as a veteran he'd understand taking a life in self-defense. But at the same time, he was a cop. He might look the other way about her running booze . . . but killing someone was a different matter entirely.

"I was out last night in the storm." He quirked a thick eyebrow at her, and she sighed. "Misjudged the weather badly; I admit it. Hit my ribs, fell on my face, got my neck tangled in the lines. That's why I don't look so pretty this morning. Satisfied?"

"You look fine," said Jones, surprising her. "Just take care of those ribs and your awful neck, all right?"

"All right."

"So where's my booze?"

There was the Jones she knew. After apologizing to Cleo for moving, for the dog had pressed her narrow body against Ellie's left leg, she fished the bottle out of her bag and passed it over. Another surprise: Jones handed her some cash for it. She accepted it without comment.

"Was it your father?" he guessed, gazing at her.

"I slipped. End of story."

"I don't believe you." There was no threat behind his words, no menace. It was just a simple statement of fact. That's what worried Ellie. She tried not to react, but she felt her cheeks grow hot. She didn't know what to do—play it off as annoyance that he was pressing her? Confess to killing Walter Greene?

Thankfully, Jones took care of the situation for her. "Look, Miss West . . . there've been some recent incidents around Amityville. Attacks, mostly, but some disappearances, too. If you ask me, I think they're all related, though I haven't voiced that suspicion to any of my fellow officers."

Ellie went back to petting Cleo, trying to play it cool. "Why not?"

"Because I think a group is responsible, not an individual." Ellie was confused; Jones must have seen it, because he explained, "Individual killers, Ripper-types—they tend to have a pattern, but there's no pattern here, except that all the victims are either immigrants, *entrepreneurs* like you, loose women, artists . . . or Negroes, of course."

"So it's the Klan."

"Actually, *Detective West,* I'm pretty sure it's *not* the Klan. These people, their pattern is different. They're more aggressive than our usual band of bigots, but it's definitely some group with similar . . . ideals, if you can call them that. It's frustrating—I don't have a lot to go on. The survivors come away pretty shaken up, sometimes roughed up, but all unwilling to talk."

"So why haven't you told the other officers?"

"Because half are in the Klan already, and as for the rest . . . I don't trust them." He shrugged irritably. "Haven't been able to do much, as I don't have a lot to go on. Yet."

"It's strange I haven't heard anything about this."

"Well, disappearances are tricky. We don't like news of those to get out for a few reasons. And as for the attacks, well, I've wanted to keep those hushed up too. So I'm just telling people to be careful where I can, since I really don't know what's going on, or if I'm even hearing about everything."

"I'll think on it and advise some friends, too," said Ellie, thinking about SJ.

"Good, and let them know that if something happens they can always come to me. If they're willing. Whoever's doing this, they're doing a real job on their victims. No one's coming forward. The only reason I know anything at all is due to a black kid who went to the hospital two weeks ago. He was roughed up bad enough that a nurse called me in to check him out. He wouldn't talk—too scared. My only lead is that apparently he woke up from the ether

screaming about *masks,* and some farm-girl said something similar when I went to check out a report of a fire a while back. The
family had already put it out—nasty, greasy thing, we're not sure
what happened—and before the girl said more they hushed her
and sent her inside." He sighed. "*Polish* family," he added, eyebrows
all the way up.

"That's terrible." Ellie was struggling to keep her voice neutral
as her mind churned. She wondered if Jones would link Greene's
disappearance to these others.

"It is. So you see why I'd want to know if you'd experienced anything similar."

Greene hadn't been wearing a mask, no. "That's not what happened to me, Hector." Ellie rarely used his first name, but she
needed him to believe her . . . or at least to back off.

It worked. "All right," he said. "I still don't believe you slipped,
but that's your business."

"It is," she said, earning a grumble from Cleo as she stood, but
she couldn't get out of there quickly enough.

Jones also looked surprised that she was putting such an abrupt
end to their interview, until she said, "I'm running late today. My
family will be worrying."

He favored her with a rare grin. "What, didn't you make it
home last night?"

"Good day, Officer Jones," she replied, and headed for the door.

"Miss West," he said. She turned, surprised by the tone in his
voice. She couldn't quite decide what it was. Tenderness? Fear?
"Stay safe out there, all right?"

"I'll do my best," she said.

ELLIE THOUGHT ABOUT WHAT Officer Jones had told her
as she cut over onto County Line Road to make her way toward

her family's house on Cedar Street, glad she had a bit of a walk ahead of her before needing to be civil to anyone. She was furious.

It was bad enough that the Klan had a toehold on Long Island —more than a toehold in some villages. Hearing that some other group was trying to pick up where they left off was horrifying and enraging. Ellie didn't know what she could do beyond talking to SJ, Gabriel, and anyone else she knew who might be in danger . . . and keep a sharp eye out for herself, too. The Klan hated bootleggers. These newcomers might, as well.

It was a strange sensation for Ellie, walking down the street of her hometown and not feeling safe. But she also knew that the likelihood that she'd be attacked in broad daylight was slim, so it was probably better to prepare herself for whatever problems were awaiting her at home.

Ellie knew she couldn't understand what it was like to rush off to serve one's country only to be sent home permanently injured from a training accident, but—but at the same time, a body could make the most of things. It had been her dream to work on a trawler when she was a girl, back before she'd learned that women had a place in the world, and it wasn't on board a fishing boat. That wasn't the same thing—she knew it wasn't. But she'd found a way to be happy enough, and felt her father could too, if only he wasn't too proud to have it said he'd come down in the world.

Like how her father wouldn't go out on her skiff with her, as they'd used to do before he went off to war. It wasn't that he couldn't—he just needed a little help getting in and out was all, and a cushion or two to support his hip while they fished. They'd done it a few times, right after he'd come home, until one of the old men at the marina had cracked wise about what a shame it was. Ellie had snapped back at Fred that it would be better for him to mind his own business, but the damage had been done. Her father wouldn't go out again with her, even years later.

The house on Cedar Street looked homey enough, shaded by spreading maple trees and surrounded by a wild tangle of raspberry bushes, but Ellie did not anticipate any sort of happy domestic tableau awaiting her inside. She touched her pocket, taking comfort in her night's earnings nestled deep and safe there like some sleeping creature. Her mother would be pleased, at least.

Her father . . . he wasn't against sending Lester to the medical college, but neither was he excited by the idea of a doctor in the family, as Ellie and her mother were. He was too disappointed that his dream of a strapping son to follow in his footsteps had been thwarted twice, once by Ellie being born a girl, and the second time when Lester contracted polio.

Her father's attitude didn't let him see how fortunate it was that the disease hadn't affected Lester's mind. He was brilliant. He *had* to go to school, but the scholarship from New York Medical College only covered tuition; they wouldn't pay for his room and board, his books, the clothes he must have, and the other incidentals such as the pocket money that Lester would need to socialize with his peers, all of which had quickly become all too real once he'd been accepted. The "fees" in particular were astounding; that word didn't seem to mean the same thing to the college that it had always meant to her.

They didn't have enough to cover it all, even with her father's pension and what Lester brought home from working as the local veterinarian's assistant. The few dollars her mother brought in teaching piano helped—as did Ellie selling bait clams, bootlegging, and fishing for their suppers—but her hope that by scrimping and saving and hustling they'd have what they needed by this time in the summer had not come to pass. An unexpected doctor's bill had set them back, as had a leak in their roof. Gabriel had fixed it at cost, but that didn't mean *free*. It all added up so quickly.

"Oh, there you are." Ellie's mother didn't look up from chopping carrots and potatoes from their little garden when Ellie came in the back door. "I was beginning to worry."

"Sorry about that." Ellie knew she couldn't avoid a fuss any longer. "So, Ma—"

At Ellie's raspy voice, Harriet West looked up. "Oh my goodness," she cried, dropping her knife. Ellie pulled her mother out of the way of the shining blade as it bounced once and skittered across the wooden floor. "What happened to you?" she asked, taking in Ellie's black eye and bruised neck and other abrasions.

"I got caught in the storm and I slipped." Ellie tried to smile, but judging from her mother's reaction, she must look more ghastly that way. "Looks worse than it is, I promise."

"What's all the commotion?" Ellie's father's voice reached them from the living room.

"Nothing, Pop," called Ellie.

"He'll find out sooner or later," said her mother quietly as she picked up her knife and washed it off.

"So he'll find out later. Anyway, I finished my run." Ellie handed over the cash in her pocket.

"I was worried about *you*, Ellie, not the money . . . but thank you. You know it helps so much." Ellie flushed with pride as her mother immediately tucked the cash into the little leather wallet she kept in the top drawer of her desk.

"What's going on in there?"

Ellie's flush changed to one of annoyance. Her father *could* get up and come into the kitchen; he just chose not to. And yet Lester had managed to come down from his bedroom and into the kitchen to see what all the fuss was about.

"Ellie, you're hurt," he exclaimed. In a commanding tone at odds with his slender limbs and elfin features, he said, "Sit down; let me look at you."

As Lester delicately prodded her nose and around her eyes with his long fingers, Ellie felt certain he had a brilliant career ahead of him in medicine. He had a more sensitive touch than the local doctor — likely because his bedside manner had been formed working with spooked horses and hurt dogs.

"Nothing's broken," he declared, "but you'll look a fright for a good long while. And I think your windpipe must be bruised, but that'll fix itself with time, too. Do you have any other injuries?"

Ellie unbuckled her coveralls and pulled up her shirt to display her bruised side.

"Hmm." Lester felt around a bit more, but again was pleased to find no breaks or obvious fractures among her battered ribs. "Rest is what you need," he said, seemingly satisfied she was in no immediate danger. "What happened? Did you get into a fight?"

Ellie's mother peered at her, as if Ellie might confess to something now that her baby brother was in the room.

"I slipped when the storm got bad last night."

Lester reached across the bare kitchen table and patted her hand. "I'm glad you made it home safe. But don't go out in weather like that again. It's too risky!"

Ellie knew what Lester meant, but all the same his remark annoyed her. She had to take these risks — was taking them for his sake. They all did their part, and this was hers. But she repented of these sour thoughts immediately upon seeing her brother's expression fall. He knew he'd irked her.

"I'm sorry," she said.

"No, I'm sorry," he replied, reaching out to squeeze her hand.

"Sorry for what?" asked their mother, confused.

"Nothing," said Ellie. "Never mind." Then she and Lester collapsed into giggles, as if they were fourteen and seven again, not twenty-five and eighteen.

They'd always been like that — able to have an entire conversation without using any words at all. Their mother shook her head, baffled, which just made them laugh harder. It was nice, like old times, when the world had weighed less heavily on everyone.

"Why do I have to ask more than one time what's going on under my roof?" Ellie's father loomed in the doorway, filling it with his bulk. Never a small man, Robert West had at least been fighting trim during his army days. His sedentary life had taken its toll, muscle giving way to fat, but he was still imposing.

"Hello, Pop," said Ellie, gingerly getting up from the kitchen table. Her mother didn't even glance their way; her eyes were back on her carrots and potatoes.

"What happened to you?" he said. His tone was the one that had made Ellie straighten up and fly right as a child—not that he'd had cause to use it much. As a girl, she'd never found much reason to disobey. Nowadays, she was very practiced at it, and lied smoothly.

"It was a wet night," she said. "I slipped and fell, got tangled up in my own ropes."

Ellie wondered if she kept claiming she'd slipped if she'd start to believe it herself—a falsehood made true by repetition.

"Is she all right?" This was directed at Lester.

"She's pretty banged up, sir, but it's all bruises. Nothing that won't heal soon enough," said Lester.

Their father nodded, satisfied, and Ellie relaxed a bit. His approval of his son was as rare as it was desired. It was worth the beating to have made her father see how useful and worthwhile Lester was.

"Saved me a trip to the doctor's," she said, in the hopes of keeping the mood going. "I was worried about my ribs."

"Good, that's good," he said. "But of course, he'll be doing more than just poking at bruises when he's in medical school."

"I'd hope so, at least," said Lester.

"You do?" said their father. "It'll be demanding physically as well as mentally, you know. I hope you're up to it, after all everyone's doing to help you get there."

Ellie had never been so furious. While she'd had the same thought a time or two, she also knew what her brother lacked in strength he made up for in determination. The shame of saying such a thing to his face! Ellie was glad she was so sore; the pain kept her from flying at him to spit in his face or do something even worse.

"The crabs," said Ellie's mother, staring at the ingredients for the chowder. "Ellie, where are the crabs?"

Lester used this distraction to depart from the kitchen, his back horribly straight and chin held proudly aloft. Their father didn't stop him.

"The crabs?" he asked.

"For the chowder."

Ellie was shocked to realize she'd failed to check her traps—she'd meant to, but it had slipped her mind. "I'm sorry," she said. "I forgot."

Ellie's parents stared at her like she'd grown another head. Their astonishment was both flattering and frustrating. While it was unusual for her to forget something like that, they knew she'd had a rough night.

"Oh no," said their mother, as if some shocking news had just been delivered. "Whatever will we do?"

Ellie managed not to sigh; instead, she said, "I can go out now . . ."

"That'll put dinner off for hours," said her father, before slouching out of the room shaking his head, as if he was so disappointed he could no longer be a part of the conversation.

"Then I'll go and buy something from the butcher," said Ellie desperately. "He'll still be open."

"I suppose we'll have to." Her mother sighed. "I was counting on you, Ellie . . . Meat's expensive, and—"

"You think I don't know that?"

"Ellie!"

Ellie hadn't raised her voice to her mother since she was a teenager, but this was too much to endure, not while she was in pain, not after seeing Greene breathe out his last in a boat in the middle of a storm. "Don't you 'Ellie' me," she said. "How dare you imply I'm careless. I forgot *once!* People are allowed to forget things every once in a while when they're busy and—"

"Will you two hens stop squawking at one another!" bellowed Ellie's father, and the two women went quiet.

A knock at the door broke the silence. Ellie considered following her brother and running upstairs, but as neither her father nor her mother moved to answer the summons it fell to her to go and do so.

Down the way from the Wests lived a fairly well-to-do family called the Hunters. The patriarch, Joseph, was a recent widower, a solemn man whom all spoke well of but few invited over for dinner. He had seven children, but Ellie had a hard time telling all but the very youngest girls apart. The family were all brown-haired, blue-eyed, and rosy-cheeked, but only the two boys went to school as far as Ellie knew.

Three girls stood there now. They could have been copies of one another save for their height and slight variations in the calico of their dresses. Their similarity to one another was uncanny, and they all shared the same milk-white, almost lustrous skin.

The middle one, both in height and position within the trio, held a covered dish of some sort, her hands protected by a dishrag. To their credit, none of them reacted to the sight of Ellie's nose, black eye, or bruised neck.

"Hello," croaked Ellie, after an awkward moment. "Can I help you?"

"Our sister made too much pot roast," she said. "Father had the idea that we ought to send some over, just to be neighborly. Her pot roast is very good."

Ellie stared at the girls. She had many questions for them that good manners prevented her from asking, such as: Had they heard them all fighting? Were the Wests believed to be in need of help? What had inspired this generosity, and why today?

"Thank you," she finally said, when her mouth would work again. The girl extended her arms, and Ellie took the dish automatically.

"I'm sorry, but we can't accept this." That was Ellie's mother, her mouth a thin line of pride and disapproval. Ellie still clutched the dish. Here it was, the answer to their problems. At least, the ones they were having tonight. No need to waste money on food that should go to Lester's college fund; no need for Ellie to get pinched and snapped at by a grumpier group of crustaceans than even those in her home. Why couldn't they accept the gesture of neighborly affection? Next time she brought in a haul of snook or a mess of clams they could return the gesture proudly, for Ellie's mother was a good cook.

"You go tell your old man we're not interested in charity." Ellie's father had also joined them at the door. It was practically a party.

"We beg your pardon, Mr. West," said the tallest girl, "but he told us not to come back with it. We're to leave it at your doorstep if you won't take it. He said you might be offended, but really, she just made so much. Our aunt was supposed to come into town for a big dinner, but she took ill and can't make it."

"Rather than let it go to waste, we brought some over. It doesn't keep well," the shortest added.

"Thank you," said Ellie firmly. "We'll enjoy it, and we'll return the dish full."

"We look forward to it," said the middle girl, the picture of polite, sincere femininity. There was nothing condescending or disrespectful in her manners; nothing that Ellie's parents could be offended by.

And, miraculously, they weren't.

"Yes, please thank your father for us," said Ellie's mother, thawing a bit. "It's very . . . very neighborly of him to think of us."

"We will. Good afternoon," they said, almost in unison, and Ellie again felt that mild disgust for how alike they were. She quickly pushed it away. They'd done more than they knew for the Wests that day.

"That was lucky, I suppose," said Ellie's mother, after the door was closed and shut.

To Ellie's relief, her father now seemed resigned rather than angry. "It won't be your home cooking."

"No, but I'm sure it'll be delightful."

Ellie's father frowned. "Even if it is delightful, I'll be sure to impress upon Hunter that we're not in need of charity when I return his dish, though."

Crisis averted, Ellie left them to it. She went upstairs to check on her brother and maybe get in a bit of time with the *Vanity Fair* she'd borrowed from Rocky, which he'd said had a top-notch poem in it by Helene Johnson.

She found Lester sitting at his desk, his books open in front of him, but it was clear he wasn't studying.

"Don't," he said when she came in. Not for the first time did she marvel at the tidiness, the precise organization of his bedroom. A future doctor's bedroom, she thought to herself.

"Don't what?" She sat on his bed, making creases in the smooth comforter.

"Defend him."

"When have I ever?" Ellie was genuinely offended by the idea that she might.

"I don't know. I just don't want you to tell me not to pay attention to him, or never mind what he says."

"I'm not our mother. I was ready to sock him."

"Well, good. Because I can't not pay attention to him, and I *do* mind what he says. I've been working so hard—I'll be ahead, if I get to go to school, and—"

"*When.*"

"It doesn't feel like *when.*" Lester shook his shock of dark curls. Their father said his hair made him look like a girl, but Lester wouldn't cut it, much to Ellie's joy. He was a bit vain of his lustrous mane, and he should be, as even sisterly affection would not allow Ellie to describe him with sincerity as handsome or robust. One day a girl would notice that hair, Ellie was sure, and then the whip-smart boy beneath.

"You can believe me that it's *when,*" she said, even though she didn't believe it herself.

"Thank you. I'm sorry. It's just hard sometimes." His voice got a bit tighter in his throat. "I hate it here."

"Move then—in with Gabe and me, I mean."

"I can't."

He scooted his chair back from his desk and came to sit beside Ellie. She leaned her head on his narrow shoulder.

"Why not?"

"You know why."

Ellie thought of all the excuses he'd made since Ellie had accepted Gabriel's hand—that getting him back and forth across the Great South Bay to work with the veterinarian would be a huge hassle, that the damp of an unfinished house would get into his books, that he couldn't leave their mother and still take her money, that he would "be in the way," a phrase he said with a blush, making it immediately obvious what he was thinking about.

"Well, it'll only be until the semester starts," she assured him. "Not too much longer for us to stick it out. We'll drop you off at college and you won't have to see Pop again until you're Dr. Lester West—and not even then, if you don't want to. I'll come have Christmas with you in the city."

"I don't know why you insist on staying here when you have a much nicer place to go," said Lester.

"You know why," she said, imitating his voice. They giggled like they were kids again.

"Ellie. Lester," their mother called. "Time for dinner."

Ellie suppressed a sigh as she and Lester stood. There was always something she needed to do, somewhere she needed to be.

Maybe after dinner she'd find some time for her poetry.

3

WHERE SHOULD WE PUT THIS, ma'am?"

Fin was asked this question by one of the movers as he and another man shifted a lavishly carved mahogany armoire as she passed through the foyer of the house on Ocean Avenue that she and her husband and several of their friends had rented for the season. It was a fine house, with large windows that let in light and the warm summer breeze, many big white rooms, and a large cool green lawn that ended in a private dock; they would be able to do the sort of entertaining they wanted to here.

Or at least the sort of entertaining her husband Jimmy and their friends — Lily and Duke Freemont, Edgar Bishop, and Bobbie Brennings — wanted to do. Fin never really felt at ease at parties, and definitely not the sort they'd be having here, without even the pretense of a meaningful impulse like a charitable fund-raiser behind them.

Amityville was a tourist destination in the summer, especially for the rowdier element within "the smart set." Lily had even boasted to one of their acquaintances back in Philadelphia that they'd be "free of those tiresome benefit luncheons and charity balls" for an entire season. Fin had overheard Lily say this at the grand gala Fin had organized on behalf of Philadelphia's needy mothers; it did not do much to increase her confidence that she'd be spending a pleasant summer on Long Island. For her part, Fin loved organizing and attending fund-raising events; it gave her a sense of purpose — a feeling that she was part of something larger than herself, and doing some good in the world. Dressing up for no reason just to drink to excess with "the beautiful and the damned" seemed like a good way to end up in a similar situation.

"Ma'am?"

Oh, right. Fin was supposed to be telling the movers where to put that armoire. The trouble was, she didn't know, and she was the only one around right now. The others had gone out; Fin didn't know to where. She hadn't been listening while they settled on their plans; she'd been reading more of *To the Lighthouse*, which she had shifted to the top of her to-be-read pile when they decided on Amityville as their destination instead of the Catskills. Edgar had asked if it was a travel guide to the area. No one had laughed when she'd said she certainly hoped not.

"That ought to be put in Mr. Bishop's room," said Fin with authority. If it turned out she was wrong, she could claim she'd told the movers no such thing, and who would ever know what the truth really was?

"Yes ma'am," one of the men replied, and they went deeper into the house with it.

Fin left the entryway to avoid the risk of being asked further questions. Fortunately for her, getting lost was easy to do. The house was so large, and all the rooms were so white and had come furnished with such unrecognizable furniture, that she quickly had no idea where she was. In the whitest, largest, most unfamiliar of the rooms she plucked a cigarette from a cigarette box and lit it on a cut-crystal table lighter; then she wandered outside while inhaling a few healthy lungfuls of the soothing smoke.

Too restless for her book, Fin thought to go to the simple gazebo that slouched at the edge of the property like a poor relation in a family photograph. Cooled by the water, shaded by trees, and out of earshot of the house save for the dinner bell, it was the only place on the property Fin really liked.

As she traversed the lawn, she mused on how it was really too bad that Jimmy's uncle had died — not only for the usual reasons, but for the unexpected damage it had caused to her marriage. Fin and Jimmy might have been content if not happy together had the fool not gotten drunk as a lord at his own birthday party and choked on his cake. It had been a real surprise to hear he'd made Jimmy his heir, and while at first the news had been exciting and the possibilities seemingly limitless, Fin had quickly realized the changes to her and Jimmy's lives were not destined to be good ones.

It had dismayed Fin to discover that her husband's interest in practicing law had been financial, not humanitarian. He only looked the part of the strong-jawed, broad-shouldered public defender destined one day to become district attorney. The estate had not even been settled before his ambition had turned to idleness and his interests had shifted from helping others to helping himself. He left his job in order to apply himself to a different occupation: being wealthy. And it did occupy him, whether he was buying new clothes he didn't need or new furniture to clutter up their home, finding new entertainments to pass his newly unoccupied hours, and making new friends at the new parties they attended.

It was at one such party, back in Philadelphia, where Fin encountered her old school friend Bobbie Brennings, née Jordan. Bobbie was in a bit of a pickle, as it turned out—Philadelphia's elite had all but given her the cut direct for having the most outrageously public affair with a famous tennis player, and no one had talked to her the entire night. High society always loved a scandal, but not an ugly one—and this one had gotten ugly. Not only had Mr. Brennings turned to drink, the tennis player's wife had been pregnant with their second child when the news broke.

A former suffragette and member of the American Birth Control League, Fin had been torn between wanting to support a sister in her struggle to free herself from the twin chains of marriage and social expectation . . . and feeling it was hard cheese on Mr. Brennings and the tennis star's wife. But in the end she had let Bobbie take her aside, for she had been lonely in the crush, and listened to what her childhood friend had to say. She hadn't wholly believed Bobbie's version of events, given that they required dismissing a few highly creditable reports on her behavior as slander, but what could Fin do but humor her old school chum?

And really, while Bobbie might be scandalous, she was *interesting*.

Given her reputation, Jimmy had resisted the idea of incorporating Bobbie into their set, but soon Bobbie had thoroughly charmed him and everyone else. Good thing, too, for when Bobbie's husband kicked her out of his house and hired the best lawyer in Philadelphia she'd needed somewhere to stay. The tennis player had quickly gotten cold feet and gone back to his wife.

Bobbie had made herself at home faster than a stray cat in Fin and Jimmy's spare bedroom. At first Fin had been pleased to have her there. Jimmy was often led by the opinions of the Freemonts and Edgar—and Bobbie could be counted on to side with Fin when there was disagreement. But as Bobbie became chummier with everyone she began to take *their* side, and Fin once again felt like the perpetual odd one out.

Standing on the cool green lawn of their new house, Fin took another long drag on her cigarette as one of the movers dropped an expensive-looking vase on their gravel drive. It shattered with the unmistakable, almost beautiful ring of breaking porcelain. Surprised insects stopped their droning for a moment as the mover looked her way, clearly worried, but Fin, who had never seen that vase before, turned away and headed for the gazebo.

She could not shake her sense of melancholy, even though she knew it was in her best interest to learn to like this new house, in this new town.

It was a nice house, and a nice town.

"There she is! Kid! Hey, kid!"

Kid was the nickname Jimmy had called her during their court-
ing days. Fin turned; the daring but silly mustache Jimmy had recently grown was the first part of his face she could make out as
he jogged up to meet her from the dock, entourage in tow. "Hey!
Fin! Come and see!"

They all seemed so happy; Fin couldn't imagine what had plastered those smiles all over their slightly sunburned faces.

"It's here! Look!" said Jimmy.

Fin looked where he pointed and saw a boat floating by the private dock. It looked very new and very expensive.

"Do we have visitors?" she asked.

"That's Fin for you, isn't it?" remarked Edgar. Lily Freemont
tittered at this wittiness, tossing her new-penny curls. Jimmy
laughed too, for a moment, but after seeing the look on Fin's face
he sobered.

"No, kid," he said, now horribly unctuous. "We just bought it!
It's ours!"

Fin wondered who this "we" was—her and Jimmy, or had everyone chipped in? She suspected the former. Bobbie's money was
all tied up in the divorce, Edgar was always claiming poverty, and
the Freemonts seemed to feel Fin and Jimmy ought to pay the li-
on's share based on some math that seemed surprisingly Commu-
nist given Duke's opinions of the Bolsheviks.

Fin didn't get a chance to ask.

"Isn't it just the bee's knees?" enthused Bobbie. "That's what we
were thinking of calling it. What do you think of that? *The Bee's
Knees!* Isn't it swell?"

Jimmy was still looking at her eagerly.

"So?" he asked. "What do you think?"

"When did we buy it?" asked Fin.

Jimmy's eagerness turned to mild annoyance. "Yesterday after
breakfast we all talked about it, don't you remember? We were sitting on the patio, and Duke made the point that it just made sense

to buy a boat if we already had the dock, and I said that sounded like a real wheeze, and you . . ." He furrowed his brow. "You said . . . well, I can't recall what you said."

Fin often brought a book to the table—a girlhood habit her mother and finishing school had never managed to break. Usually she kept one ear out for the conversation, but she couldn't remember ever discussing buying a boat.

As she thought about it, she recalled that she'd left after breakfast to go into town—to the Amityville Free Library, which was supposed to be a local attraction. She had also had business there. While researching Long Island she had come across a volume of poetry called *Sea Songs* by a local poet, Todd Rockmeteller. The companion to a book called *City Songs* that was all about New York, the second was concerned with his life on Long Island. Fin had always loved reading about the sea, and she had been captivated by the poet's simple but evocative descriptions. His obvious love for the area had made her feel better about the move. She'd been eager to see if the library had more of his work.

And they did—a book-length poem called *The Ginger-Eaters* and something even better than that: a flyer stating that the poet himself was soon going to do a reading from his latest unpublished collection, right there in Amityville. She'd opened an account at the branch, signed up for the event, and come home substantially more chipper.

She was just about to say this when Bobbie piped up.

"I think you said that you didn't know a lot about boats, so you'd trust Jimmy and the rest of us to take care of it all."

Fin stared at her friend. She didn't know whether to be shocked by this falsehood or concerned for her own sanity. Mostly, she just felt lonely—incredibly, crushingly so.

Bobbie seemed so completely certain that Fin looked to the Freemonts to see what they had to say about all of this, but they were softly bickering over some other matter. As for Edgar, he wasn't paying attention either. His eyes were on his cigarette; Fin had never seen anyone so bored in her life. Either that, or he had been wrongly denied many a role in favor of lesser actors.

It was beyond Fin why Bobbie would lie or why Jimmy would go along with it, but before she could object, he'd moved on.

"It'll be a gas," he said. "We'll have fun!"

Not wanting to cause a scene, Fin nodded. "So who will be our captain?"

Jimmy looked to Duke. "The man who sold it to me said it was easy enough to learn. Just don't flood the motor."

"Hard cheese, it's already sitting in the water then," she said, making a bit of a joke.

"Flood it with *gasoline*," said Duke.

"Please come and see it, Fin," Jimmy urged her. He awkwardly offered her his arm, but she could take no pleasure in his touch or the gesture. He hadn't been oblivious to the seething tensions underlying that conversation; he'd merely been pretending to be for some reason Fin could not yet perceive. Regardless, she accepted his invitation, and managed a smile in spite of feeling about as unhappy as she could ever remember.

FOR PERHAPS HALF AN HOUR Fin looked at the runabout she now owned, admiring whatever she was asked to, from the stitching on the leather seats to something her husband called its "lines." When she asked what those were, Jimmy didn't seem to know; he said it was the straightness of the planks of the deck and Duke the ropes that tethered it to the dock, until an exasperated Bobbie informed them that it was the shape of the hull.

"Let's take her out," suggested Lily. "The movers are still hurling the furniture around everywhere; they don't need us standing around, getting in their way."

Fin didn't reply; instead, she watched one of the hired men approach from the rear as Lily spoke. When he cleared his throat

Lily almost jumped out of her pale green dress. Fin couldn't help but smile, though she hid it by pretending to cough.

"Yes, what is it?" asked Lily, annoyed.

"We need you to tell us where a few more things should go," said the lad. He was clearly a local, with that accent and that abrupt, efficient, almost rude brusqueness.

"What a drag!" said Bobbie.

"You know, what we really need is a butler," said Duke.

Fin wasn't sure she wanted to go out on a boat when it seemed that no one knew how to pilot it, anyway.

"You go," she urged them. "I'll handle it."

"You sure?" Jimmy seemed surprised. "It'll be a lot on your shoulders, kid."

"It's not all *that* much to do," said Edgar.

Fin hadn't expected any gratitude, so she said, "Edgar's right. It won't be any trouble."

The truth was she had no intention of supervising these movers any more helpfully than she already had. It was just a reason not to go out with all of them, where there could be no escape but hurling herself into the bay.

If she was going to feel lonely, she'd rather it be because she was actually alone.

"All right then. We'll see you in a bit. We won't be out long, okay?"

Fin walked off with the boy, who led her around the side of the house, toward the front door. The moment they turned the corner, she stopped him.

"All right, listen to me," she said, the sound of the runabout's engine firing up a distant rumble. "I really don't give a damn where you put anything in this house. Pile it up in the foyer for all I care." The boy's mouth hung open stupidly as she continued. "There's cash for you all in an envelope on the kitchen counter when you're done. I don't wish to be asked any more questions."

She left him with his mouth hanging open, but she was no longer interested in the gazebo and its cool, relaxing pleasures. Threading her way among the movers, Fin made her way up to the master bedroom.

Fin had learned archery at school. What had started as an elective had become a passion for her, and she'd kept up with it since leaving behind her beloved school's ivied walls and manicured lawns for the ivied walls and manicured lawns of less enjoyable places.

She hadn't liked the idea of packing her gear into a crate; instead, she'd taken it all with her in the car on the drive, inconvenience be damned. She was glad she had. Her light Mongolian bow and the quiver that held her birch arrows had poked her during the whole way up from Philadelphia, but now they were right there in her closet, waiting for her when she needed them.

She changed out of the gauzy white gown she'd selected that day to thwart the oppressive humid heat and into a rust-colored sport dress and low-heeled brogues before retrieving all her gear, including the leather-and-horn thumb ring that her archery instructress had given her as a parting gift. Her target she would have to do without; she had packed that into a crate, and goodness knew where it was at this moment. That was all right; she solved that problem by nipping down to the servants' quarters and grabbing a bag of rags. She slung that over her other shoulder, and after requisitioning some rope from the garage she went off to find a place to shoot.

The house's grounds were actually very nice. The backyard was wide and flat, perfect for croquet or lawn parties, but Fin was more interested in the small wilderness on the western side of the property, beyond the gazebo. It was a well-maintained wood; someone came through here fairly regularly with clippers and axe, given how the old trees still grew tall but between them sunlight fell on the forest floor in golden puddles.

When she found a likely spot Fin rigged a target, tying the ragbag between two oaks with the rope. It wasn't ideal—if she missed, she risked burying a few arrows in the surrounding trees, but she'd make the best of it. Soon enough she'd have her target unpacked and she could really practice.

She twisted her left leg through the bow and strung it. That felt good, as did slipping her shooting ring onto her thumb and clearing her mind as she got into her shooting stance.

Fin's archery instructress had taught her that shooting well wasn't about being a body full of muscles, but rather about being a mind empty of thoughts. She had to learn to be only the feel of the string, the tension of the draw, her breathing, her stance. She'd practiced all that as much as she'd practiced her shooting, and it had served her well—the peace that came to her had been a welcome feeling over the years; a relief from her concerns, whatever they might have been at the time.

Pressing her shoulders down and away from her ears forced those muscles to stretch and lengthen; she hadn't realized just how tense she was. She wriggled a bit to loosen up further before drawing with her thumb, the special Mongolian way her teacher had taught her. She breathed, and released, her shoulder and arm cocking back as if she were tossing a flower behind her.

The arrow sank into the bag with a satisfying thump.

Fin might not know what she'd do with herself here on Long Island, or what was going on with her marriage these days, but she knew her bow and what she could do with it. Feeling good and warm, Fin gave herself over to her archery practice. She even did a little combat archery, practicing the quicker style of holding arrows in her hand instead of drawing them from her quiver, all while dipping in and around the trees.

She worked up a fine sheen of sweat and was glad to have thought to grab a cold bottle of lemonade before heading out—

some sort of locally bottled brand. It had warmed in the sun, but was still delicious.

Only when the shadows were too long for her to see did she pack it in. It was time. Not only was she ravenous, her arms were weary and her shoulders ached—her feet and legs, too.

She'd figured the others would have come back while she trained, but she was surprised to find the house ablaze with light. Beyond the gauzy fabric of the curtains people were milling about. Lots of people. They were having a party!

Fin left the ragbag and the rope outside. Even so, with her bow and her quiver and her sweaty athletic togs it was impossible for her to wander invisibly through the crowd, who were all in a mix of casual and eveningwear. They laughed, ate, and drank together. Fin couldn't remember having bought food or procured spirits or even hiring enough staff to serve them, but somehow they'd managed it.

Snagging a canapé to take the edge off her hunger, Fin scoured the crowd for her husband. When she found him, he was standing side by side with Bobbie, talking to a man and a woman Fin had never seen before. Bobbie had clearly washed and changed and put on fresh makeup after her nautical jaunt; she looked absolutely gorgeous, her dark curls setting off the paleness of her skin. Fin felt ashamed to walk up to them with her damp hair plastered against her sunburned cheeks and half-moons of sweat evident under her armpits; she was just turning away to go make herself presentable when Jimmy noticed her.

"Hey, look who it is!" he cried. "Where've you been, kid?"

Fin's eyes slid to her bow, but she decided to answer the question anyway.

"Exploring the grounds. I did a bit of shooting, too."

"Oh yeah? Great! Well, while you were gone, some of our new neighbors came by to say hi, and they introduced us to some more neighbors, and someone brought over some hors d'oeuvres, and somebody else had some champagne! Pretty swell little get-to-gether, don't you think?"

"Very nice," she said, and turned to smile at the strangers to be introduced to them.

"Oh, oh, right—Fin, this is Frank and Myrtle. They live up the way. Frank's got some business interests he's been telling us about."

"Delphine Coulthead," said Fin, shaking Myrtle's hand, then Frank's, "but you can call me Fin. You know, like at the end of a French film. How do you do?"

"Jimmy didn't say he had a sister," said Frank. "Nice to meet you."

"I'm his wife," said Fin.

This revelation cast an awkward pall over the gathering. Frank and Myrtle looked surprised, Jimmy had the decency to look abashed, and Bobbie . . . Bobbie just looked completely calm, as if nothing strange was going on.

"Get you a drink?" asked Jimmy, after a moment.

"Sounds like just the thing. Here, why don't you show me where the hooch is?" said Fin.

As they made their way through the crush, Fin squeezed Jimmy's hand. Hard. She could accept the boat—she could even accept his inattention to whether she was present or absent—but she could not accept this casual public humiliation.

"I'm amazed at you, James Coulthead."

Jimmy took his hand back from her grasp, shaking it out a little and looking wounded. "What's wrong?"

Fin tried to compose herself, but her mortification had turned to anger.

"That man thought I was your sister."

"Who, Frank? Well, he knows now, doesn't he?"

"I had to tell him," she said. This was amazingly dense behavior, even for Jimmy. "You received our first visitors in this house without me, and then I had to tell them I was your wife."

"Are you kidding?"

Bobbie had appeared behind Jimmy, her affect cool and cheerful and unforced. No outside observer would suspect or detect any malice in here at all, and Fin momentarily doubted herself for ascribing any to her friend.

"I mean, you're being funny, aren't you?" continued Bobbie. What is this, some sort of Jane Austen novel? *You received our first visitors without me.* Surely you can't be serious? Who cares who 'receives' whom? We're all renting this house together, aren't we? And anyway it's just a party."

Again, Jimmy said nothing to this. Fin wondered what he must be thinking, but then she remembered the confused looks on Frank and Myrtle's faces, and decided she didn't care.

"Jane Austen novels are indeed chock-full of scenes where characters are revealed by their manners at a party," said Fin, looking evenly at Bobbie. She didn't appreciate her friend butting into a private conversation, and she didn't like being treated as if her feelings were inconsequential. "She was a keen observer of human nature. After all"—Fin's eyes slid over to the silent Jimmy, who was watching this discussion with a confused furrow upon his manly brow—"it seems she was right, that fair or not fair, there will be 'unbecoming conjunctions, which reason will patronize in vain.'"

"Who's being patronizing?" said Jimmy.

"Enjoy your party," said Fin, and left them to go upstairs. Edgar waved at her as she passed through a room where he was holding court among a lot of smartly dressed, arty-looking young men, but she did not do more than wave back. She didn't want any more conversation; she wanted a bath.

The night was warm, but the hot water felt good as the jasmine-scented breeze plucked at her bare shoulders through the open window, chilling the nape of her neck. She finished her cigarette and listened to the sounds of raucous laughter and snippets of conversation. Someone had brought a banjolele and was strumming some popular ditty.

The longer Fin reflected, the stupider she felt for having gotten so upset. So they'd had a party without her. Was it really that big a deal? And even if it was, snarling at Jimmy in the middle of it wasn't mature or reasonable. She'd made herself ridiculous, and worse than that, she'd seen the look on Bobbie's face as she'd left the room — superior, calculating, and aloof.

She'd pay for storming off. Bobbie always objected to what she called *dramatic gestures;* Fin would have to walk on eggshells around her for a while, as her friend wasn't one for apologies; she never had been, even as a girl at school. One had to demonstrate one's remorse to her, through deed as well as word.

The water had become too cool, so Fin got out and dried off. By then, there were fewer voices outside, but they were louder, grosser. She heard Duke's belly laugh and Edgar's snide snicker as she wrapped herself in a fluffy towel, happier to be upstairs and alone than down there with her friends and husband.

She'd thought to do a bit of reading before turning off the light, but her eyes would not stay open. Nor would her mind settle, so she half listened in the dark as the party finally broke up.

She was just drifting off when a knock at her door woke her.

"Come in," she said, turning on the light and sitting up.

It was Jimmy. He looked sauced as he slouched against the doorjamb.

He'd come to bed. Fin wasn't sure why that surprised her. She hadn't gotten the impression that he and Bobbie had been introducing themselves as a couple — rather, it had seemed they'd forgotten her existence entirely.

"Still up?" he asked, slurring a bit.

"Up enough."

"Hey, kid, about earlier . . . I never meant to offend you. Really."

"Would you like to come in?" She felt ridiculous inviting her husband into their bedroom, but she felt more ridiculous talking to him as he lounged in the doorway.

"That's a swell idea."

Jimmy was in a good mood—so good that he comically looked up and down the hallway and then loosened his tie as he shut the door behind him.

Fin quickly assessed whether she was in any mood for some hanky-panky; she was. If they were both going to be awake in the same room, they might as well enjoy it.

"Jimmy?"

It was Bobbie, outside the door.

"Hey Jimmy-Jims, you in there?" Edgar was, too. "We need you."

Fin had her suspicions about Edgar and Bobbie—they spent an awful lot of time pretending not to notice one another while always somehow being within another's orbit—but she was baffled why they would be after Jimmy to join them, and after everyone had left or gone to bed.

"Hold on just a sec," said Jimmy, and answered the door.

"There you are. We need you. There's a problem—a mistake," said Edgar, nodding at Fin as she pulled the bedsheet up to cover herself. "There's some big old armoire in my bedroom blocking everything. I got Bobbie here to help, but she and I can't shift it—and I can't get past it to get into bed. I hate to ask, but will you help us?"

Jimmy turned to Fin. "I won't be long," he said.

Fin waited on him for a bit, and then a bit more, before turning in for good.

He made it to bed, though she knew not when; he was there beside her when she woke early in the pale light of first dawn. She'd been dreaming of the water—not the calm water of the Great

South Bay, either; an angry sea, with fierce swells and wind that whipped her hair about her face. She'd been on a boat, clinging to the gunwale, but it had been what lay beneath the churning surface that frightened her most.

She turned to where Jimmy slept beside her, but pulled back her hand before touching his shoulder for comfort.

4

THE MEMBERS OF AMITYVILLE'S SUMMER ELITE could not seem to get it through their heads that Fin was not Jimmy's sister or his cousin, but his wife. Their inability to get it right became genuinely unsettling the longer it persisted — Fin couldn't understand why her constant correction didn't help. It made her feel rather like a child insisting an imaginary friend was real to adults who indulged her fantasy with a nod and a smile. Or like the victim of a prank.

It didn't help her state of mind that neither her husband nor her friends could understand why it bothered her so much. They laughed off those awkward moments, but for Fin there was nothing amusing about it. She even confessed to Jimmy how much it was troubling her, but he did nothing to help, not even after the confusion resulted in a hostess not realizing she'd invited six of them to dinner. She'd assumed five.

Fin started declining invitations. It was easier on her nerves to stay at home and read, or practice her archery, or to take the Ford on long drives around the island, to remote and wild locations that soothed her soul.

She used Todd Rockmeteller's *Sea Songs* as inspiration for these little day trips. Though at first she had been wary of Long Island and its pleasures, she came to love the various "moods of the bay." She dusted off Jimmy's binoculars and went birding to see for herself "the indignant look of the kingfisher / at the oystercatcher's cry," risked the awful mosquitoes to listen to the marshlands, and visited various farms to smell the "woodsmoke," "fresh-turn'd earth," and "heavy scent of livestock."

Fin had grown up in Philadelphia, and except for her years

at school in the country she had always lived in the shadow of tall buildings, but she quickly agreed with Rockmeteller that any meadow or country road on Long Island was "as busy as the city, but twice as beautiful." There was something about this place that just felt *right* to her. Every visit to some spit of rocky beach or shadowed forest felt like coming home.

Fin was pleased as well to discover Rockmeteller's other volume, *The Ginger-Eaters,* was every bit as good as *Sea Songs,* though much different. It was not a musing on nature and its virtues. It was, instead, a cautionary tale.

While the style of *The Ginger-Eaters* was about as far from Tennyson's poem as Tennyson's was from Homer's, the thematic overlap was obvious. In the poem, a nameless, troubled girl was lured into joining a coven of demon-worshippers. At first it was wonderful—she ate of the demon's sacrament and found joy in her newfound enlightenment. They were all indeed "like Gods together, careless of mankind," but only for a time.

The longer the girl spent communing with the demon, the more of herself she lost to it. It fulfilled its promises to her, giving her peace through enhancing her experience of her five senses, but it was all a trick. By isolating her from everyone from her former life, the demon was able to change her so slowly, so subtly, but so profoundly that when her former friends and even family saw her, they didn't recognize her. She didn't notice it, either, until she could no longer tell if the meals she ate, the games she played, the clothes she bought, or even the lovers she took were ones she would have selected before her bargain.

Reading it, Fin was reminded of the bargains she'd made that had gotten her where she was. She was also reminded, queerly, of a book she'd loved as a child by the American children's book author "G. Baker."

Georgiana Baker was the author of twenty-seven novels for

children, for the most part sweet little books with titles such as *The Wet Day* or *What They Found in the Tree*. Somewhat surprisingly, Baker had also been a member of the radical Social Democratic Foundation and a proponent of women's sexual freedom, and had authored "Shackled by Love: An Argument for Lesbian Separatism" under the pen name Miss S. A. Pho.

Baker had died in 1915 at the age of 47, one year after the publication of her final and her strangest novel, *The Demon in the Deep*. Usually, Baker's protagonists were children, but *The Demon in the Deep*'s heroine was Susan Fentwick, a young woman of fourteen—which had been exactly Fin's age when the book came out. The oldest of five children, Susan was brave and resourceful, like most of Baker's heroines, but Fin had especially liked Susan's no-nonsense attitude, fearlessness, devotion to her friends and family.

Fin had also liked the villain of *The Demon in the Deep*, even if Miss Depth, with her white hair and white skin and black eyes, had genuinely frightened her. The thing was, she was also more sympathetic than the typical Baker villain. Miss Depth had no sinister designs on an orphaned child's inheritance; no greedy desire to knock down a magical, historic home in order to build a polluting factory. Grief over her sister's death had turned Miss Depth into the most terrifying, ruthless, and dangerous villain of them all.

Fin had no idea why Rockmeteller's poem might share any similarities at all with *The Demon in the Deep*, much less crucial details like demons being real and able to work their will in this world through man, losing one's self being a potential consequence of their influence, and needing to consume something infused with demonic essence in order to communicate with them and share whatever power they possessed. In *The Ginger-Eaters*, that something was, naturally, ginger, and it gave the girl insight into beauty.

In *The Demon in the Deep*, the villain conjured the demon into a regional delicacy called "beach plum jelly," and it granted Miss Depth an understanding of the truth, and the ability to compel people to speak it.

Fin had given her Baker books to charity when she'd put away childish things—but not *The Demon in the Deep*. That one was special; she had taken the train into New York City to get it signed when Baker was appearing at Hinds & Noble. Fin had read what Baker had written to her so many times as a girl, tracing her fingers over the spidery handwriting, that she could still recite it from memory:

> *To my dear Delphine,*
> *I sincerely hope you never have need of the Truth, but if you do, let this book be a lantern to light your way. Everything in it is true.*
> > *Yours,*
> > *G. Baker*

That was another thing Rockmeteller and Baker had in common, come to think of it. The introduction to *The Ginger-Eaters* also claimed it was a work about the truth.

Fin's memory of her meeting with Baker had always unsettled her, as much as she loved the book and its author. Baker had been kind to her, gracious even, but she'd also been a bit, well ... *odd*. Fin had felt like her favorite author's eyes hadn't been on her, but rather on something *inside* her as they spoke. And though Fin had planned to tell a few fibs to her idol—like most girls her age, she had wanted so badly to appear older, more sophisticated, better read—she hadn't been able to. Every time she'd tried to lie Baker's smile had just gotten wider, until it was almost predatory, as Fin stammered out the answer to every question truthfully.

On the train ride home, as she read the inscription to herself, Fin had had a moment of fancy where she supposed Baker might have actually summoned the demon in the book. Susan had not been able to lie to Miss Depth, either.

But of course that was impossible. She'd just been nervous.

Still, the idea of summoning a demon that could extract the truth had always been uniquely appealing to Fin, now more than ever. She could use it on Jimmy, to better understand what he wanted from her and from their marriage, and on Bobbie, too. There was something going on with Bobbie that Fin could not perceive; some angle to her actions that eluded her. It wasn't a bid for Jimmy—that, Fin could understand. It was something more subtle, and more dangerous.

These thoughts rattled around Fin's head as she reread *The Ginger-Eaters* while the rest of her companions chatted on the veranda, drinking pitcher after pitcher of some cool and bubbly drink. She'd lost the thread of their conversation, in part due to the liquor, but mostly because of Rockmeteller's writing.

"Nothing to add, kid?"

Fin looked up, and blushed with embarrassment when she realized everyone was looking to her for some answer. She desperately searched for a clue in Jimmy's tone or expression of what they might have been talking about, but there were none to be found.

"I think it sounds perfectly lovely," she said, hoping her response would disguise her inattention, and excuse her from further contributions to the conversation.

"You think dealing with the mob will be perfectly lovely?" Edgar snickered as Jimmy, confused, said, "Maybe Bobbie's right and it'll be easy, but I can't imagine what could be *lovely* about it."

"See, Fin agrees with me," said Bobbie sweetly, looking from Jimmy to the also-skeptical Duke. But that wasn't the case at all—actually, now that she knew what they were talking about, Fin strongly preferred they *not* get immediately involved with the Mafia so soon after moving to a new town, especially given that it was said Al Capone had many ties to Long Island's sub-rosa booze trade.

Before she could protest, however, Bobbie continued. "It'll be easy—you'll see. Rose says she knows the guy to talk to."

"Oh, well if *Rose* says so," said Edgar, with affected irony. Bobbie shot him a look, which made him simmer down.

"But Oscar—Oscar's the guy who fixed the car," said Jimmy, when Fin looked mystified, "—he knows that local smuggler. The way I see it, a local guy will be cheaper and less likely to . . . you know . . ." Jimmy shrugged uncomfortably. *"Ask for favors later,"* he said, lowering his voice as if someone might hear them.

"A local smuggler," Bobbie said the phrase with distaste, "who can get us what? Bathtub gin?"

"Bobbie's right," said Lily. "Jimmy, there's no way around this if we want the good stuff. A local bootlegger won't have Bacardi and Veuve Cliquot, but we must get some. The Percys had it at their party, and everyone was *so* impressed."

Fin was amazed by the passion with which Lily spoke, especially as she'd never cared about anything less in her whole life than what the Percys might have served at some party she hadn't gone to.

"Oscar says the local stuff isn't bad," said Jimmy, looking to Duke for help, but no help was forthcoming.

"Oh, I'm sure he thinks it's *swell*," said Edgar, with another nasty snicker.

"But Bobbie, the *mob*," protested Jimmy, clearly sensing he was losing this argument.

"Everyone around here deals with them, and last I checked they haven't all had their knees broken or been *tommy-gunned* to death in their own homes," said Bobbie in a bored tone. Her sangfroid was impressive, but Fin couldn't help but wonder how cool her friend would be if something actually did go wrong.

"Yeah, but what about Oscar?" said Jimmy, grasping at straws.

"He'll be offended, maybe, if I don't take him up on his offer, and he did such good work on the Ford."

"He'll probably be more offended that he's not invited to the party," tittered Lily.

"We could always invite him," said Fin. The silence that followed was brief but heavy.

"Invite the mechanic?" Duke chuckled. "That's mighty white of you to suggest."

Fin stared at him. "I'm sure I don't know what you mean," she said icily. "Would you care to explain yourself?"

Duke's face went red. A few weeks ago, they'd had a row over some similar remark and the peace between them was a fragile one, born of agreeing to not discuss the matter further. At the time, Jimmy had begged her not to get into it with him again over what Fin considered to be some extremely objectionable and dismaying attitudes, to say the very least; then as now she felt justified in her response of "I won't if he won't," which Jimmy had called childish.

"Mechanics and moonshine! I thought we wanted to make a *good* impression on our neighbors," said Bobbie, and for once, Fin was grateful to her friend for butting in. Duke was furious; he stood and took his leave of them, muttering under his breath. Lily followed after her husband, cooing at him like a dove. Fin pretended not to notice.

"Maybe we'll make a good impression by supporting the local economy," said Fin. Jimmy, Edgar, and Bobbie all looked at her like she was insane; Fin blushed, embarrassed. "The local non-Mafia economy, I mean," she added, which didn't help.

"I'm sorry, I'm confused," said Bobbie. "I thought you'd agreed to the idea of buying from people who could sell us liquor that was distilled in some reputable way?"

Fin knew she ought to keep quiet, or at least pretend to come around to Bobbie's point of view, but she decided against it. It was a small matter to assert herself over, but if she didn't want to end up a stranger in her own life, like the girl in *The Ginger-Eaters,* she had to start somewhere.

"It just seems safer to work with a trusted local," she said.

Jimmy looked from one woman to the other, clearly unsure what to do. Curiously, it seemed to Fin that her siding with him had made him less fond of the idea of working with the local guy rather than more.

"Well . . ." he said, rubbing the back of his head.

"We'll do what everybody decides is best," said Bobbie, with a toss of her dark hair. She withdrew a cigarette from her silver case on the table, somehow managing to light and smoke it angrily.

"Don't believe *that* for a second," said Edgar, also helping himself to a cigarette. "If she doesn't get her way, she'll pout."

"If I'm the only one who actually cares about it, maybe we just shouldn't have this party," said Bobbie, her tone so chilly Fin shivered even in the heat of the day.

Jimmy looked panicked. "Let's—let's split the difference. We'll get some from Oscar's guy, and some from your friend. How does that sound?"

Bobbie rolled her eyes. "If we have to have moonshine at the party to satisfy some sort of backwards local pride, I'd certainly rather it be *some* rather than *all* of what's available to our guests."

"But I can't see how that solves anything," said Fin. "If we want to avoid Mafia entanglements, buying *less* from them doesn't . . ." She trailed off as everyone stared at her like she had her head on upside down. She had been willing to battle a bit, but resisting a rout was beyond her strength. "So . . . when is this party again?" she asked.

"We hadn't decided," said Bobbie, "But I'm thinking Saturday. It's only Monday; that's plenty of notice for everybody."

"*This* Saturday?" That was the night of Rocky's reading at the library that Fin had been so looking forward to.

"Is that a problem?" Bobbie was looking at Fin keenly, like a terrier who'd heard a rat scrabbling beneath the floorboards.

Fin felt embarrassed, her face hot as she spoke. "It's just, I had plans that night. Could we do Friday or Sunday?"

"What did you want to do?" asked Bobbie. She spoke as if she were genuinely curious, but there was a sharp, hostile look in her eyes that didn't make Fin feel as though her friend was being sincere.

"A local poet is doing a reading. From his next book," said Fin, still red-faced. Even to her own ears, it didn't sound so very important. "The local Literary Society is hosting him."

"A local poet . . . is reading from a book?" said Bobbie, as if she'd never heard of poets, or books, or reading. "And on a Saturday night! Imagine that. Who knew anyone would schedule such a thing, and that people would want to go to it."

"They're expecting a crowd from the city . . . the librarian said to come early to make sure I got a seat," said Fin, not bothering to mention that she was a person who wanted to go, and that's why they were discussing it to begin with. She looked to Jimmy, but he was smiling blithely, as if they were having some other, completely different conversation.

"It takes all kinds, I suppose," opined Edgar.

"Is it so important?" asked Bobbie. "It's only that the Terrys are having a party on Friday we're all going to, and Sundays are never as popular for a big bash. No one wants to commute into the city on Monday morning with a hangover. Enough of our set are still beholden to the workaday world that they'll blow us off, and then where would we be?"

She spoke lightly, but Fin could tell from Bobbie's stiff posture and the way she wouldn't meet her eyes that there was only one correct answer.

Fin decided to go along with it. It was just easier that way. Plus, Bobbie had only just warmed up again after that exchange they'd had at the first party. The truth was, she'd rather miss Rockmeteller's reading than go back into the doghouse.

"I can easily skip it," said Fin, calling on her finishing school charm to sound as sincere as possible.

"Are you sure?" said Bobbie, but as she stood up before Fin nodded, it was obvious her concern was for show. "I suppose I should go call Rose, then. We'll need the liquor soon."

"I'll come in too," said Edgar, standing up as well. "It's getting so damn hot out here."

Jimmy slapped his thigh and rose. "This is gonna be great," he said. "I just know it. Better than that awful funeral the Irvings threw last week." Fin wondered if it had been an actual funeral; she hadn't gone. "Well, I'd better go and hit up Oscar," said Jimmy. "I guess I could just drive over to see him. Be nice to get out of the house. Say, Bobbie . . . you sure you should be calling Rose? On the phone, I mean?"

"Are you worried that the Mafia's had the wires tapped, or the feds?"

Fin sat listening to the bugs and the birds and the breeze now that no human voices interrupted them. It stung a bit, how neither her friend nor her husband had acknowledged her as they left. Bobbie was often one to be swept up in a moment, but Jimmy's rudeness was new—though he was often oblivious, he had never before failed to be gentlemanly toward her. He'd always held doors for her; put a hand on the small of her back as they crossed the street. Little gestures like that had been one of the things she'd first liked about him. Leaving without saying farewell or kissing her goodbye was nothing short of a shocking change.

The thing was, Fin wasn't shocked.

She'd known her marriage was in trouble, but now she began to suspect it was already over. Like a mosquito from the marshlands, the thought buzzed and whined around her skull, soft but impossible to ignore.

In *The Demon in the Deep*, Miss Depth had been so changed by grief and fear that she'd summoned a demon. As a child, Fin had been unable to comprehend that sort of desperation, but now that she was an adult it was easy for her to understand.

To really know the truth . . . For that, it might be worth summoning a demon, if it were possible.

5

ELLIE SAT AT THE KITCHEN TABLE, staring in despair at the stacks of bills and coins. She'd dumped out the wallet containing Lester's college fund, had counted every single penny, and no matter how she'd tried to make it work, there wouldn't be enough to send her brother to school in the fall. Even with as hard as they'd been working, they'd be a full fifty dollars shy of the estimate given to them by New York Medical College.

It didn't help that five of Ellie's clients had cancelled their regular orders over the past week and a half. Sometimes the demand for her product decreased—mostly after some traveling preacher came through town with a message of temperance and redemption—but usually her clients didn't go to such meetings.

They'd all been dodgy about it too. Not a one of them had looked Ellie in the eye as they told her they didn't require her services any longer. Even more bizarre, only two people on her fairly long wait list had been excited to hear she could now accommodate their needs. The rest had also blown her off with mutters and headshakes.

Ellie's spirits were low as she returned the cash to the wallet and set out along the familiar route through town to get to her skiff. She'd been working so hard—and yet apparently, it hadn't been hard enough.

Not that she minded hard work. In fact, staying busy made it easier to forget about Walter Greene and everything that had happened that strange night. But working so hard just to fail . . . That felt like a blow, and she'd had enough of those recently.

Her bruises might have faded a bit, but that night had wounded Ellie in other, deeper ways. Her mind kept wandering off, returning to what she'd seen, what she'd felt, distracting her from everyday concerns and making her miserable.

Gabriel knew something was wrong, but she'd been unable to tell him more than what she already had about the incident. It was strange, keeping something from him, but she couldn't see how to even begin the conversation.

"Hey, Ellie!"

Rope in hand, Ellie looked up from untying her skiff to see Oscar Fenton jogging up to her. His face was so red and he was puffing so hard that Ellie wondered if he'd hustled all the way from his garage over on Ireland. "Glad I caught you," he wheezed. "I got — gotta proposition for you."

"You know I'm an engaged woman," she said, turning her back on him. Experience had taught her not to give Oscar too much of her time or her attention. He always took kindness the wrong way.

"Not that kind of proposition." Oscar took another few steadying inhales.

"Whatever it is, there's no need to give yourself a heart attack," said Ellie.

"It's good. *Really* good." He finally stood up. "I found a new client for you."

Ellie felt the touch of hope like a fresh breeze on a hot day, but decided to play it cool. "A new client, huh? Well, I'll have to talk to my supplier about that."

"This won't be a regular commitment. Just a one-off. Fifteen cases of" — he winked broadly — "by Saturday night."

Ellie gawped at Oscar. "Fifteen cases!" They might as well ask for a hundred.

Then again, she had some extra stock from all her cancellations . . . she'd just have to get SJ to consent to sell her a bit more. *Consent,* of course, meaning agree to charge an exorbitant fee on top of what Ellie usually paid. And of course, Oscar's commission would reduce the figure, so these buyers would have to name a pretty big number for Ellie to even consider the job.

"They gave me half up front," said Oscar.

He looked left and right so obviously that any cop in the area—well, any cop who didn't buy from Ellie—would have sidled up to see just what was going on, but Ellie forgot her irritation when he presented her with a thick stack of bills. Even with SJ's inevitable price gouging and Oscar's commission, taking this job would secure Lester's future. They'd even have some money left over that they could save toward next year's needs.

"All right," she said, swiping the bills off his palm and pocketing them. Oscar didn't protest, meaning he'd already skimmed his bit of cream off the top. Even better. "Where's the handoff?"

"Guy lives on Ocean Avenue," he said, and gave her the address. Ellie was pleased to hear they had their own dock. It would make delivery a lot easier. "Says he wants to make a big splash with the neighbors. Getting a bunch of other liquor elsewhere, too."

"More than fifteen cases? I guess he *does* want to make a splash." Ellie favored Oscar with a rare smile. "Hey—thanks for this. I really appreciate it."

"Oh yeah?" Oscar leaned forward, as if she might reward him with something more than words, and Ellie was reminded of why she was always so wary of him.

"Yeah," she said, and jumped on board her skiff without another look at him.

ELLIE LOVED THE Great South Bay with all her heart, but just the same, she knew it wasn't her friend. The bay was too mercurial for friendship. That stormy night had been a good reminder of its temper.

Now, however, the bay was in a fine mood. The water was

smooth and dark; above it, the pale blue of the late afternoon sky
was flecked here and there with wisps of white cloud. No wind
stirred the little hairs on Ellie's neck or the trees on the bank as
she motored toward SJ's. A few birds cried and soared above; more
floated in the shallows or rested, their legs tucked up under their
fluffy bodies as they sat on the shore. Off in the distance, a dolphin
surfaced, and then another, before they both disappeared.

Ellie killed her motor before she turned into the narrow, over-
grown inlet close to SJ's shack. Quietly she glided up to the rickety dock that was completely hidden by low branches and long
grass—even knowing where it was, Ellie had to sniff around for
it a bit in late summer, when the leaves grew thick. She tied up
carefully, making sure her skiff would not drift into sight, and
darted up the rough path.

A bit of steam puffed out of the structure's chimney. Otherwise,
there was no other sign of human presence—no sound, no footprints, nothing. Ellie quietly knocked a special knock.

The shack wasn't that big, but it took SJ a long time to answer
the door. That wasn't unusual—SJ liked to make sure Ellie knew
who called the shots.

Not that Ellie ever forgot; she'd known SJ a long time. The local one room schoolhouse had been integrated, so they'd grown up
together, in a way. Ellie had always admired SJ's ability with math
and science, two subjects that had never come easily to her. That's
why Ellie had been confused when she'd overheard their teacher
talking to another about SJ. He'd said it was "a shame" that she was
so bright. Ellie hadn't understood what he meant; she'd only been
about ten years old.

But as time wore on and Ellie had watched SJ struggle with her
limited options for further education or employment, Ellie had
come to realize what he'd meant. Finding lucrative, satisfying work
had been difficult enough for Ellie; for SJ, also being black had
meant that moonshining ended up being the most rewarding and

lucrative profession available for someone as scientifically minded as she was, though the job's necessary paranoia had sharpened her already barbed tongue and caution had made her even less inclined to be sociable.

SJ enjoyed the work, too, and the good money she earned at it. All of her distributors, including Ellie, were able to charge a premium for her safe, high-quality liquor. It even tasted pretty good, which was almost unheard-of—but that was "pure chemistry," as SJ liked to say.

When the door to her shed finally swung open SJ didn't say hello—she just nodded at Ellie and turned away. Ellie saw why —there was another woman in the room, to Ellie's surprise, standing by some complex piece of distilling equipment. She was also black, and very pretty, with big dark eyes and a thoughtful expression. Unlike Ellie and SJ she was not in coveralls, but rather a pink calico dress.

"Hey," Ellie said to both of them, feeling awkward, though she didn't know why.

SJ grunted in response, and then nodded at the five crates that were waiting for Ellie. Beside them was SJ's enormous crossbow. Ellie had once remarked that a gun might be a more modern weapon for self-defense only for SJ to scoff at her and ask if she thought a firearm was a good idea around a bunch of high-proof liquor.

The other woman was much friendlier. "How do you do," she said. "I'm Georgia."

"Ellie. It's a pleasure to meet you."

"Likewise."

SJ was of course allowed to have friends over any time she might like, but both of them seemed vaguely embarrassed, as if they'd been caught doing something wrong.

"So, SJ . . . I need to ask you something," said Ellie, jumping right in to cover the awkwardness. "It's a bit of a favor, but the money's good."

"You have my attention." SJ didn't look up, but she was clearly listening.

"So, Oscar—" She paused for SJ to snort. "I know, but he met a guy who's looking to buy fifteen crates of booze for some big party this Saturday night."

"Do you want me to leave?" asked Georgia. SJ shook her head.

"Ellie will be going in a moment. Won't you, Ellie?"

Ellie stared at SJ in genuine confusion. "You aren't interested?"

"I can only provide you with what I always do. I'm not going to let my other customers go thirsty just because some rich fool wants to get liquored up with his friends."

"It's a lot of money." Ellie withdrew the stack of bills. "He paid half up front."

SJ deigned to look up, and at the sight of all that cash she definitely made tracks over to Ellie, adjusting her glasses to see it better.

"No need to pay anyone that much for moonshine," she said, and Ellie agreed. "Is there a catch?"

"I don't think so. Oscar seemed to think the buyer was loaded."

SJ crossed her wiry arms, making a dark slash against the pale blue denim of her coveralls. "Loaded he might be, but not sauced. No deal."

"SJ, please?"

"You can give up those two cases of the good stuff I've put aside for your *impending nuptials,* but that's all I can offer on top of what's sitting right there in the corner."

Ellie winced, but at least she'd already paid for said "good stuff" . . . no way SJ could upcharge her. And Gabriel would understand. At least, she thought he would. He knew she had to do what was right for Lester.

SJ looked surprised at Ellie's hesitation. "You're considering it?"

"You know I've never been the best at math, but two more cases to sell is two more cases to sell."

"I can't see why you'd give anything up for some folks you don't know and never even heard of."

"Because I'm trying to send my brother to college. If I make this sale, I can."

Ellie had never spoken of her family's struggles to SJ. Their casual childhood acquaintance had turned into a business relationship, not a friendship. But given that SJ's brother, Aaron, was Gabriel's bookkeeper, and go-to guy for fine carpentry work, she'd figured SJ knew most of the story. As it turned out, that wasn't the case.

"Smart kid, huh?" This level of interest from SJ was shocking. Ellie nodded.

"Yeah. He got a scholarship—wants to be a doctor." Worried SJ would think Lester idle, Ellie added, "He had the polio, so he has some troubles. He's a hard worker, though, and his mind . . ." She snapped the fingers of her right hand.

"All right, all right. In that case . . . I guess I can spare two extra cases."

Ellie did a quick mental calculation . . . If she shorted her clients just this once she could make up at least some of the difference with the "special reserve," and all the excess she had stashed at Gabriel's house. With the case of liquor she'd gotten from Greene the night of the storm, that was pretty close to fifteen.

That storm . . . The memory of the crazed man, the boat, and how exactly she'd come by that liquor oozed its way into her mind. Ellie closed her eyes, but she only managed to see the scene more clearly that way.

"Don't think I'm not gonna charge you extra, though. Maybe your kid brother needs to get to college, but I got needs too."

Bless SJ's sharp tongue. Ellie forced a smile and waggled the wad of bills at her, her spirits somewhat higher now. "I can pay, no problem."

"Put that away; no one wants to see that."

"Not even you?"

"What the fuck do you mean by that?" SJ had been slowly thawing, but all the ice melted at once to reveal a volcano beneath.

Ellie took a step back, unsure what she'd done. Her eyes flicked to where Georgia stood, but the other woman's expression was just as tough to read. "I just . . . you said you'd charge me a tidy bundle . . . ?"

"I know what I said." SJ turned on her heel—literally, since she was barefoot—and went back to her equipment. "Come by Friday. I'll have it all for you then."

"How much for the extra?"

"Whatever I decide. Now get the hell out of my sight."

Ellie offered an unanswered farewell to SJ and Georgia before grabbing a crate of clinking bottles and heading through the door. She set it down instead of taking it down to her skiff, electing to shift all the stock outside in one go so she was out of SJ's hair as quickly as possible.

Aaron ambled up just as she was hauling the final crate down the slight hill. He had his shirt slung over his arm, and Ellie blushed to see his bare chest.

"Pardon me," he said, shrugging back into his shirt.

"It's a warm day for woodworking."

"A warm day for anything. I was sweating like a pig looking over your lover-boy's finances."

"I bet."

"Don't know why he can calculate how to build a house but needs me to balance his checkbook. Maybe he just likes my company."

Ellie grinned. "I know for a fact he likes it, but ledgers do make him nervous."

"How about you?" He eyed the final crate of booze. "You need any help?"

"Thanks, but this is the last of it. I better get going ... SJ ran me off like a dog."

"Nah, she likes dogs."

Usually Ellie was fine with teasing, especially from Aaron. But today, after SJ's inexplicable surliness, his jibe made her unhappy. It must have shown on her face.

"SJ likes you fine, Ellie. She wouldn't sell to you, otherwise."

"Yeah?"

"Yeah." Aaron sighed and shook his head. "My little Sally Jane. It's hard for her. I just try to stay out of her way."

"Me too, but ..." Aaron was peering at her, and Ellie decided to come clean. "I said something, I don't even know what, and ..." She trailed off, realizing how childish she sounded.

"SJ whet her tongue on you? That doesn't mean she doesn't like you." Aaron punched Ellie in the arm. "I thought you were supposed to be some kind of tough girl."

Ellie snorted derisively, but when Aaron gave her a meaningful look she shrugged and looked away. Talking about her troubles wouldn't help. It would only waste everyone's time.

Aaron shook his head. "Boy. I don't know why I ever even try to say anything nice to either of you."

Ellie finally relented. "I hope you'll both come over for dinner once the house has a finished kitchen, and I'm not running around like a chicken with its head cut off."

"Maybe so," he said.

Ellie didn't comment on his obvious skepticism; she'd show him later that she meant it.

AIDED BY THE FINE WEATHER, Ellie sped through her deliveries that evening. She really wanted to get home and add all that money to the wallet in her mother's desk. It felt strange, casually carrying around the solution to all her problems in her pocket.

She made it home just as the last of the daylight was fading. Her family would have had their supper, but hopefully there would be something in the icebox. Usually, her mother kept back a morsel or two, just in case.

"Ma!" Ellie bounded into the house. "Ma! Guess what—I . . . Ma?"

The scent of dinner lingered in the air, but Ellie's mother was not in the kitchen finishing the dishes, nor did she answer Ellie's summons.

"Ma?"

Ellie poked her head into the living room, but there was no one there either. It was her father who appeared, startling her when he emerged from the parlor.

"Ellie. You will keep your voice down in this house."

The annoyance Ellie felt must have shown on her face, for her father's frown deepened as he stared her down.

"Unless it is a matter of life and death there's no need for you to holler like a wild Indian."

"But—"

"No buts! Go upstairs and make yourself presentable. We have company."

"Who—"

"Do as I say!"

Ellie was confused enough to obey. After shoving all that money into her mother's desk with none of the fanfare she'd hoped for, she washed herself as best she could in her room with some cold water from the jug and yanked a comb through her hair. After drying herself off, she reached for her newer cotton dress . . . and then paused before selecting a clean pair of slacks and a button-down shirt.

They were perfectly respectable clothes, and looked well on

her—at least she thought so. Ellie rolled up the cuffs of the shirt above her elbows. She was an engaged woman. She did her part for the family, and she was who she was.

Both she and her father could stand to remember that.

She checked herself out in the mirror. Her hair was dark from being damp, but at least it was combed nicely. The bob had grown a bit shaggy—she ought to have it trimmed. She was flushed under her tan from her hustle; it made the remains of her black eye and the other bruising from that night a bit more noticeable, but there was nothing she could do about that.

As she approached the parlor Ellie heard a strange man's voice. Deep and soothing, it had an almost mesmeric quality to it. She paused to listen.

"It's just common sense to acknowledge that people who aren't from here won't be interested in preserving what those of us who have deep roots in the community have built with our own hands—what our fathers built with their hands. They'll naturally be more interested in what they're owed, rather than what they've earned; they'll be more likely to commit crimes, having no reason not to."

"I agree with you." That was her father. To Ellie's dismay, he sounded more enthusiastic about this speech than he had about anything in years. "But if, as you say, the police aren't interested in common sense, what do we—"

Not inclined to listen more, Ellie strolled into the parlor. The look on her father's face told her immediately that he was furious with her. He started in his chair, but then his eyes slid to their visitor, who had stood up respectfully when she entered, and he recovered himself enough to rise with some dignity.

"Elizabeth," he said through clenched teeth. "Meet Reverend Joseph Hunter. Reverend Hunter, this is my daughter, Elizabeth West."

"It's a pleasure to meet you, Miss West."

Reverend Hunter was a tall man, lean of face and figure, with short white hair but dark eyebrows. He eagerly shook Ellie's hand; his grip was firm and dry.

It was warm, too. *Very* warm, hot almost. Ellie felt the air around her contract and thicken. It felt charged, like that night on the boat, and the memory of what had happened again swelled like the ocean inside her. Certain he would be able to hear the sound of her heart beating too quickly, too hard, she looked up into Hunter's eyes. They were like lamps, brighter than they ought to be in the dim parlor, and Ellie felt cold rain on her skin; a hand closing around her neck.

She tried to push away the memory, but she could not; wanted him to release her, but he held on. She knew it had only been moments, but it felt like hours. The air in the room was so thick Ellie couldn't breathe it. It wouldn't go into her lungs. She gasped as he smiled; when he exhaled, small motes of something like dust came out of his nose and mouth, rainbow-bright and swirling on the eddies of his breath. She watched them, mesmerized.

When she woke up, she was on the floor, looking up at her mother, her father, and Hunter, who were all peering down at her. Hunter's eyes still shone, but then again her mother's and her father's did, too, and she wondered if the light was playing tricks. She was very dizzy.

"Ellie?"

"I'm okay," she said, though she wasn't. Her shoulder hurt; she must have come down on it when she fell. *Fainted.*

"When did you last eat, Ellie?" asked her mother. Her fussing brought Ellie's attention to her current situation.

"Oh . . . I don't know," said Ellie. It was true; she was hungry and exhausted. That must be why she'd gone down so hard, and so unexpectedly. That made a lot more sense than Hunter reminding her of the man she'd killed. She'd been hallucinating, just like the night when Greene had tried to kill her . . . which had absolutely nothing to do with this man in the room with her now.

Real worry took root then, in the pit of her stomach. The possibility that she was going insane loomed larger in her mind than ever.

"Let me get you something," said her mother.

"She can eat after our guests have left," said her father.

"Don't stand on ceremony on my account," said Hunter, "but no need to rush right out of the room, Ellie, if you're unsteady on your feet. Have a seat, and rest for a moment, chat with us."

"Yes, that does make sense," said Ellie's mother. Ellie peered at her—Harriet West was not one to put aside an opportunity to care for people by feeding them.

That wasn't the only strange thing about her. She looked pretty as always, but her hair was coming out of its bun and she was wearing a dress Ellie knew she'd never usually receive company in. Usually, her mother was so attuned to those little touches of respectability that kept her connected to better times, when her father had been working and they had never felt the pinch of needing more money than they had . . . Something very strange was going on. And where was Lester?

Ellie gingerly sat down, rubbing at her shoulder, and an awkward silence descended. Hunter was looking at her keenly, as if searching for something. Ellie felt almost grateful to her father when he spoke.

"You were saying, Reverend Hunter?" he said.

"Oh, the moment's passed." In spite of his earlier fiery tone, Hunter was all kindly smiles now. This didn't make Ellie feel any better; to her, he looked like a shark who'd just eaten his lunch. "I'll just conclude by saying that if we cannot make the police listen, it will be up to us to defend our island from those who would seek to destroy it."

Ellie was plenty curious how they'd like to "defend" Long Island. Sounded like Klan talk to her. Anger pushed her fears aside and she opened her mouth to speak, but then shut it again . . . She got the impression her questions would not be particularly welcome, either by the cloyingly avuncular Hunter or by her father, who currently seemed torn between his desire to act like a stormy, domineering patriarch and the need to use his Sunday manners.

He opted for Sunday manners, and sighed heavily. "I wanted to defend more than just this island, but that didn't work out so well. I know there aren't many ways I can help these days"—he laughed bitterly—"but I'm still a man."

"I've no doubt of it," said Hunter, with a solemnity that was almost comically sincere. "There is still a place in the pack for a wounded wolf."

Ellie found this pronouncement more ominous than comforting; in fact, it was bizarre that Hunter was here at all, in her mother's parlor, preaching something that didn't sound like the gospel. Maybe he was thinking of getting into politics.

Though it gave Ellie quite a fright, it broke the tension in the room when a young woman she hadn't noticed spoke up. It was one of Hunter's daughters; she'd been sitting beside him on the couch this whole time.

"Your father said you were working this evening, Miss West, and that we ought not to expect you. I'm glad you could make it. What exactly do you do that keeps you out at such unusual hours?"

She looked just like the girls who had come to their door with that pot roast. In fact, she might have been one of the same. She shared their oddly luminous quality, and their dark hair and eyes. Strange, that Elle couldn't tell for sure—and strange, too, that the girl hadn't spoken before that moment . . . or been introduced.

Ellie felt unsure what to say. She didn't like to admit what she had been doing, not in front of this man. Hunter struck her as someone who would very much disapprove of rum-running.

"I was at my fiancé's house," she said; when Hunter looked surprised, she realized that had probably also been the wrong thing to say. "He's, ah, restoring it right now for us, for when we're married. It was in quite a state when he first bought it. Maybe you've noticed it, if you've been out that way? It's that old saltbox over on Clinton, with the roses out front, on the creek side, right where it starts to narrow ... Has a dock out back ..." Neither Hunter nor his daughter seemed to have any idea what Ellie was talking about. "Well, sometimes four hands are better than two — even if two of them are mine."

"You were alone with him?"

Before Ellie had a chance to reply, her mother stepped in. "Ellie and Gabriel will be married when he finishes it, so all the more reason to get it done quickly," she said. Her hypocrisy annoyed Ellie — the first time she had stayed over with Gabriel her mother had voiced a token protest about Ellie being "sure" about her choices, but she'd said nothing further.

"I'm sure your daughter's fiancé is a perfectly upstanding young man," said Hunter. "But it's my understanding that you also work, don't you, Miss West?"

"I do my best to help support my family. We're lucky that the bay provides for us so well."

"You don't go out on your boat alone, do you?" The nameless girl was astonished.

"About every chance I get," said Ellie.

"Isn't that dangerous?"

"When you've been out on the water all your life, it's safe enough."

She felt the reverend's eyes on her bruises as he looked evenly at her. "Of course," he said, his politeness obviously rooted in disapproval.

"It is a bit unusual," offered her father, to Ellie's dismay and outrage. Why, he was the one who'd taught her everything she knew! He'd never thought it unusual before—he'd always said it was good for a woman to know the bay. Why had he changed his mind now, when what he'd taught her was keeping them all afloat?

"These are unusual times, just as we were saying," said Hunter gently. "The world is changing. The idle profit while the weary starve. The sapling thrives while good oaks with deep roots wither. People mock the idea of what it is to truly be a woman, or a man. It is sad to see. Those who built this world seem to have less and less place in it." More speech-making, though even a politician ought to be shy about such claptrap. And yet her father seemed incredibly moved—he looked stern, defiant, and proud. Her mother just looked at her hands. "Ah well," said Hunter, "maybe I'm just old-fashioned, but I like to think that with a little work, we could bring back those good ways. Does not a pruned bush put forth strong new growth?"

The parlor clock chimed, bonging nine times. "Ah, but we've imposed on your time long enough," said Hunter. He still had not introduced his daughter. "Thank you for the delicious dinner, Mrs. West. Now, let us pray."

"Yes, let's," said Ellie's mother, who didn't normally bother saying grace before dinner, except on Sundays.

Some words were said, though Ellie didn't listen. She could never focus on preaching—it tended to slip out of her mind like a fish from a net. Frankly, the only thing that would inspire her right now was some food in her stomach. She'd been hungry before her fall, but now she was ravenous. She was relieved when at last the reverend finished up and stood, his daughter with him.

Ellie's mother rose as well, like a woman in a trance, as her husband lurched to his feet. They both looked extraordinarily well, like they'd eaten a feast and then slept for ten hours. The girl, too, looked illuminated from within, like an angel in a stained glass window.

"Thank you for honoring us with a visit, Reverend, and you too, Mercy," she said. Ellie perked up at the mention of the girl's name.

"Thank you, Mrs. West—and Robert . . . and Ellie, you too," said Hunter. "I appreciate you letting me get to know you a bit better."

Ellie didn't know what to say, as "likewise," or "the pleasure was mine" would be lies. Thankfully, Hunter just pressed on.

"I invited your mother and father to come and hear me speak sometime—I hope you will, too," he said. One of those strange motes, the orange-red of a candle flame, escaped his mouth and swirled away. Ellie followed it with her eyes until he said, "I need no answer now. Just think it over; that's all I ask."

She blushed, embarrassed to have been caught staring, but he was peering at her again, as if looking for something. It made Ellie uncomfortable, like she was some sort of specimen in a jar, so she nodded just to get away from him. She was certain she would never, ever willingly listen to Hunter speak, whether she was in a group or they were alone.

Ellie slipped away while the final goodbyes were being said— she couldn't remember being so hungry, not ever. Horrifyingly, there was nothing in the icebox. Ellie was about to make herself some toast when her mother came in, carrying a tureen with the remains of a fish stew. Ellie tore a hunk of bread off the loaf rather than cutting it and dipped it in the flavorful sea-salty broth the moment her mother set it down.

"This is good, Ma. Thank you." Ellie chewed, the feel of bread in her mouth sweet relief. "I didn't know you were having anyone over for dinner."

"It wasn't planned," said her mother serenely. "I saw the reverend out the window as I was dusting, but before I had time to ask your father why he might be calling, and with his daughter, there was a knock at the door." Ellie was relieved to see a ripple across the surface of her mother's strange tranquility when she added, "If

I'd known they were coming, you don't think I'd have made fish stew, do you?"

"Everything you cook is good enough to serve the president," said Ellie. Her mother was so pleased by that she didn't say anything as Ellie scooped up a piece of flaky flounder with more bread and jammed that into her face, though Mrs. West didn't usually allow poor manners at her table.

Lester came into the kitchen, rubbing his eyes. "Let me get a bit of that," he said.

His dark hair was standing up in the back. Ellie watched him for a moment, concerned — it was odd that he would sleep through dinner and a social call, unless he was feeling ill, but he seemed all right. He even made a grumpy protest when their mother swatted his hand away from a platter of biscuits.

"Those will keep until tomorrow. Eat the bread."

"You fall asleep or what?" asked Ellie, as her brother tucked in. He disliked her fussing over his health, so she made it sound like she was annoyed rather than concerned.

"I guess I did," he said vaguely. "I was studying, Pop came in, and then . . ." He shook his head. "I have been reading a lot. My eyes must have been tired."

This sounded strange to Ellie. She thought with regret about how she'd been gone a lot of late. If Lester was tired too much it might be time to convince him to make an appointment with more than just his veterinarian mentor. Anyway, the bigger question was why hadn't their mother or father awakened him for the visit, if they were going to eat in the dining room and then have small talk in the parlor?

Ellie let Lester have the last bit of bread, hoping it would give him some strength, but she was still hungry.

"You might give me at least one biscuit, Ma. After all, in a few days, our money troubles will be over because of me."

"I beg your pardon?"

"Got a big job," said Ellie, pleased to have this in reserve to wake both of them up a bit. "Look in the desk—that's just half."

"Thank God." Ellie's mother did not usually swear. Nor did she usually sit down at the kitchen table when there were dishes in the sink. "Ellie . . . oh, and of course you can have a biscuit! Lester, you too."

Ellie had only been half-joking, but she didn't turn down that biscuit, either. As she bit in, savoring the buttery taste, she heard the front door shut. After a moment Ellie's father entered the kitchen. He did something he hadn't done in a very long time— he sat down at the table with them.

Robert motioned for Ellie's mother to keep her seat when she got up to do the dishes. For her part, Ellie continued to eat. Being out on the bay always gave her an appetite.

"Reverend Hunter is a good man," said her father. "I was pleased to welcome him into my home for the first time, having spent many a pleasant afternoon in his."

Ellie was surprised to hear that her father had spent "many" pleasant afternoons with Hunter; as far as she knew, they'd barely spoken before a few weeks ago.

"It's important to repay hospitality, but you might have told us all he was coming, Robert." Ellie was pleased to see her mother get a bit of her energy back.

"I told him to come any night he liked."

"Well, I might have cooked a better supper, is all. And tided up a bit more."

"Joseph is a discerning fellow, but not judgmental. I value his opinions greatly."

"What's so great about them?" said Ellie.

She looked down at her stew at her father's murderous glare. "He has thought long about the problems facing our community, and come up with good answers to hard questions. And I've asked his thoughts on the problems facing our family, too."

Ellie paused, a bite of stew halfway to her mouth. Problems, as in financial problems? Surely her father wouldn't speak to a near-stranger about that . . .

"We are in disarray. I blame myself. I cannot control what happened to me," he said, "but I can control how I act from here on out. I lost my way, after my injury—I see that now. I came home, but I didn't return. I apologize for that. I've been the wind, when I ought to have been the bedrock of this family. But it's not too late for me—for us."

Uncomfortable, Ellie shifted in her seat. Her father had never been one for rhetoric; she felt as if Hunter was still in the room with them. She caught herself looking to see if her father's eyes were glowing unnaturally; of course they did not seem to be, and she was furious at herself for checking.

"Some things I cannot fix," her father continued, his eyes on Lester. Ellie bristled. He held up his hand. "Some I can. Ellie, I want you to promise me you will stop bootlegging. I do not think it is right for me, as your father, to tolerate lawbreaking, especially lawbreaking that enables the consumption of spirituous liquors, encouraging wantonness in women and shiftlessness in men." Ellie was starting to regret coming home—if only she hadn't, she might be engaging in some wantonness instead of eating cold fish stew and getting a lecture. "Better to reduce our standard of living than lower ourselves." Ellie's mother did not look convinced, but her father continued, "Were you not ashamed when Joseph asked where Ellie was, and we *lied* about it?"

"Does the reverend disapprove more of lying, or drinking, I wonder?" Ellie's archness was not appreciated. Her father's face darkened.

"I will no longer allow criminal activity to take place in this house. You will stop at once."

"I won't!"

"You will."

"Like hell!" Ellie snorted. "What church does this *reverend* even preach at? Because an Episcopal priest is one of my best customers, and he doesn't have any problem at all with pulling a cork."

"Hunter is currently raising funds to build a church," said her father, not actually answering her question.

Ellie's reason triumphed over her defiance. "Pop, I was just telling Ma, and Lester . . . I'll have all the money we need soon, to send Lester to school." Ellie kept talking, even if her father's frown deepened. "Some bigshot over on Ocean Avenue's offered me so much, and for just one job . . . I've agreed to it. He gave me half up front." She appealed to his sense of honor. "I can't go back on my word, not now that I've taken his money."

Her father glanced to where Lester sat, silently and so very still.

"Well . . . it must be the last time, then," he said at last.

Ellie nodded in agreement. She could do what she liked soon enough. Once she'd moved out, he wouldn't know what she was up to, or where, or when, or with whom—and even if he found out, he'd have no say in the matter.

"Good," he said. "This is only a first step, but it is a good one. The reverend was right—control is necessary for order. Rules and limitations help men thrive, just like the healthiest fields are the tended ones."

Ellie wondered if Hunter had farmed a day in his life. She knew her father hadn't—back before the war he'd worked on a trawler and before that he'd crewed a whaling ship, just like Ellie's grandfather.

"Well, I suppose I'd better get started on these dishes if I'm to get to bed tonight at a decent hour," said Ellie's mother.

"I can help," said Lester.

Ellie handed over the plates and stayed to put away the dry ones. Soon enough, the work was done, and they were all off to bed. Presumably her father was already there; she didn't check. She had nothing to say to him. She was appalled by his behavior, especially discussing private matters with a stranger.

Their family wasn't so bad. They minded their own business, at least.

Exhausted, Ellie sat down on her bed in the small room that had been hers since she was a girl. The little pink flowers on the wallpaper seemed at odds with the coveralls that lay in a lump where she'd hastily tossed them, damp and crusted with salt. She'd outgrown this room, but she also couldn't seem to leave it.

She sighed, and went to pick up her coveralls, hanging them up so they'd have a better chance of actually drying by the morning. But that was her only concession to responsibility. Though she knew she ought to take a proper bath, go check on Lester, or barring any of that, go to sleep and get some rest, instead she slithered between her cool sheets and grabbed *A Few Figs from Thistles* from her nightstand. She'd be tired tomorrow, but the humor of Edna St. Vincent Millay would be a well-deserved bit of escape tonight.

6

THE AFTERNOON'S SHADOWS WERE LENGTHENING, but the heavy air was still very hot and very humid as Fin and Jimmy made their way over their damp green lawn to the dock, where they would meet this bootlegger that Oscar had recruited on their behalf. He looked strange as he slouched on the docks, hands shoved in the pockets of his coveralls; as Fin approached, she realized it was because the person was not a man at all but a woman of about her own age, with bobbed hair tucked behind her ears, and the sleeves of her men's button-up cambric shirt rolled up above her tanned forearms.

That wasn't so very shocking ... The women on Long Island often did men's work, especially Polish or German women. What was shocking was her fading black eye, and the shadow of a bad bruise on her neck, too.

"Mr. and Mrs. Coulthead?" Fin didn't think she'd ever get used to the way Long Islanders abused their vowels. "I have your package."

"Excellent." Jimmy was like a kid at Christmas. He was rubbing his hands together and smiling broadly. "Oscar says your stuff is pretty damn good."

"It *is* good. But I have to tell you, I only could get thirteen cases together. Thirteen and a half." The woman nodded back to her little boat. "But, some of it's actually been, you know. Aged in wood."

"Delightful," Fin said. She was fascinated by this woman, with her brusque, direct speech. "Thirteen cases will do just fine."

"Thirteen and a half."

Jimmy was peering at the woman. "Didn't expect a *girl* to drop it off."

"Drop it off? I'm Oscar's contact."

"Gee whiz!"

"Didn't he tell you to expect me?"

"He told us to expect the delivery."

"Well, here it is."

The woman's expression was unreadable; she still slouched as if this was all nothing to her, but Fin got a sense she was actually holding herself very still out of nerves.

"Hell of a lot of liquor," said the woman conversationally. "Oscar told me you were having some kind of big party?"

"Just getting acquainted with our neighbors," said Jimmy. "We're new to the area."

"It's a nice one," she said. "Lived here my whole life, and I wouldn't leave it for a fortune."

"High praise indeed," said Fin. "But not undeserved. I've done enough exploring to know there's so much here to appreciate."

The woman nodded, and her loose hair fell all in her face. She wasn't bad-looking, just tanned and boyish. There was something wild about her, feral and delicious and intriguing and *real*—something governesses and finishing school hadn't buffed away.

At the thought of finishing school, Fin remembered her manners. "How silly of me," she said. "I haven't introduced myself. I'm Delphine Coulthead, but you can just call me Fin. All my friends do."

The girl's eyebrows went up at the word *friends,* but she replied, "I'm . . . Ellie."

She offered no last name, so Fin replied, "Very nice to meet you, Ellie."

"I'm Jimmy." He turned, and Fin winced as he hollered up at a servant who had been hovering in a doorway, "Hey! Go get someone to help us here!"

"I can get it all," offered Ellie.

"No need, no need. We'll have some guys down here in a jiffy."

"Would you like an iced tea? Or something stronger?" Ellie hesitated, but Fin urged her again. "It's so hot. Why not sit down and cool off a bit before you run home?"

Two men had appeared behind Jimmy. Ellie wouldn't let them onto her boat, but after she'd handed over the crates she agreed to relax for a bit.

"Just tea for me," she said. "Thanks."

"Jimmy, will you be a dear and let the servants know we'll be in the gazebo?" said Fin. Jimmy looked surprised to be dismissed, but he shrugged it off.

"You girls have fun," he said.

"I'll be in for dinner," said Fin.

"Sure." Jimmy hesitated just long enough to make matters awkward before taking out his wallet and handing some money to Ellie.

"This is too much," she said, after counting it right there in front of them. "I didn't deliver what you asked for." She peeled off a few bills and held them out in an attempt to give them back.

"The age on some of the bottles more than makes up for the decrease in volume," said Fin quickly, as she saw Jimmy's hand twitch uncertainly.

"No," said Ellie, shaking her head. "It's not fair. We had an agreement."

"Consider it a tip, then," said Fin. It was an inconsequential amount of money to them, but who knew what use someone like Ellie might find for it. "You got us so much on such short notice. I'm sure you had to hustle."

"Yeah," said Jimmy. "Keep it."

Ellie was blushing furiously, her expression a mixture of anger and embarrassment as she shoved it all in her pocket. Fin wasn't sure why the woman would be upset, so she tried to smooth things over by pretending she didn't notice.

"Jimmy, do have someone send down that pitcher? We're parched."

"Right," he said, and took off.

"I thought he'd *never* leave," said Fin conspiratorially, but this did not cheer Ellie up. The girl still looked sullen and resentful as they walked, so to break the tension Fin said, "So, you're the shadowy entrepreneur Oscar was so excited about! I must admit you're not what I expected."

"No?"

"I don't mean to be rude, but I've met Oscar, and while he seems like a decent mechanic, I hadn't any real desire to meet his friends. Turns out I was wrong."

"You throw that word around a lot."

"What word?"

"'Friend.' He's not my friend." Fin heard *and neither are you* as clearly as if Ellie had said it aloud.

"Oh!"

"He's not so bad, but he's also not so great." They'd reached the gazebo. Fin selected a lounge; Ellie a teak chair with a white cushion that glowed lavender in the early twilight. "So there it is."

Fin was grateful when the pitcher of tea arrived; it was something to talk about, at least. The ice was already melting in the glasses from the heat. Fin poured for both of them.

"So," Ellie said, after taking a polite sip, "what are these parties like?"

Fin felt exhausted just thinking about it. "About what you would expect. People will drink, and talk about the news, and about each other. Someone will kiss someone they're not married to; someone else will get thrown in a pool, and be a good or a poor sport about it, depending. People will wander off into the woods, likely, for obvious but clandestine purposes." Fin sighed. "Honestly, these sorts of parties are really about everyone acting like they're having a good time whether or not they really are."

"You don't sound too excited about it."

Sometimes Fin forgot that some people spoke plainly and directly. She tried to return the favor. "It wasn't my idea."

"Whose was it?"

Actually, plain speech was a drag. "Let's say it was my husband's."

"He didn't ask your opinion?"

"I don't mind him throwing a party, if that's what you're asking," she replied, a statement that was both untrue and absolutely not an answer to Ellie's question.

"Do you have to go?"

"To the party? Well, it's here, isn't it? In my house. It would look pretty strange if I didn't at least put in an appearance." It occurred to Fin that wasn't really the case, given that people were more confused when she *did* show up at parties. Probably she could go to Rocky's reading—slip away from the party and not be missed . . .

"How dressed up do people get?"

"There's always a range. Some people come in sportswear; others, as fancied up as you'd get for dinner in the city." Fin shrugged. "Depends on who you're trying to impress."

"So what will *you* wear?"

"You know, the party's tomorrow and I hadn't even given it a moment's thought. What does that say about me, I wonder?"

Ellie sipped her tea silently, her eyes on her boat in the distance.

"Maybe," said Fin, "I should just appear mid-party, naked, and run through the house like Lady Godiva."

"I can't imagine anyone would object."

Fin chuckled. "That's kind of you to say. Perhaps I should consider it . . . I suppose a party like this would be the place for it. I could scarcely have disrobed at one of our charity balls."

Ellie glanced back at Fin. "A charity . . . ball?"

"Oh, yes!" Fin got a bit excited about this change of topic. "Back at home in Philadelphia I used to put on several balls during the year. People would have to buy tickets, and a portion of it would go to some cause or other. Often we'd also have a donation bowl, or an auction or raffle to raise additional funds. The recent one for unwed mothers was a particular success, and last spring we managed to raise enough to replace the orphanage's roof after they had a fire, and the Christmas before that we had a grand gala to benefit the Families of Crippled Veterans."

Ellie didn't sound impressed—in fact, she sounded annoyed when she said, "You put on fancy parties as a way to help people in need?"

"Well . . . yes," said Fin uncertainly.

"How do those mothers and orphans and veterans feel about being treated as an excuse for people to eat caviar and drink champagne?" She snorted derisively. "So at those sorts of parties do you people still kiss and ruin your fancy clothes in the pool, or do you have some sort of speaker to tell you how terrible it is to be the family of a crippled veteran?"

Fin was silent, too shocked to speak. She'd never thought about it that way; she'd always just assumed that to the beneficiaries of her efforts, money was money. She hadn't thought pride would come into it. In fact, she'd told herself exactly that when Jimmy's interest in her became apparent, after he'd spied her across the courtroom when she'd been brought before the venerable Judge Glasser, along with several other women, on charges of "disseminating information on contraception unrelated to disease." The judge had let them all go after they'd promised to stop, a mandate Fin had planned to disobey. But after Jimmy began to pursue her in earnest, and the more she had thought on it, the more Fin had liked the idea of trying some new way of making a difference. She'd been angered to find that the birth control movement had many of the same problems as suffrage—racial prejudice being the most offensive to her mind—and she'd naively hoped that Jimmy's world of politicians and lawyers would be an ideal place

to make a fresh start; do some real good. It genuinely hadn't occurred to her that someone like Ellie would find her desire to do
so repugnant.

"Usually we do book a speaker or two," she said, recovering her
wits a bit, "but there's a fair bit of nonsense that goes on, too, to
be honest. You can't put those people together without tempting
fate."

"*Those people.* You're not one of them, huh?"

Fin had indeed always considered herself a high society outsider,
but under Ellie's angry glare she realized that on every meaningful level she'd been as much a part of Philadelphia's elite as anyone
else. "I mean, I . . ."

"You seem exactly like them." Ellie was on her feet. Fin cow-
ered before her anger. "You embarrassed me by insisting I take
money I didn't earn, like I'm one of your charity cases," she said,
her cheeks pink. "Well, I'm not one of your families of crippled
veterans, okay?"

"No!" Fin shook her head. "I didn't think you were; I mean, I
wasn't thinking about you in that way, I just . . ." She realized she
had assumed Ellie would be needy, which was incredibly, unac-
countably rude.

"Just what?"

It seemed manipulative to say the truth, which was she'd just
wanted to be kind. She hesitated too long, so Ellie finished her
sentence for her.

"Just a big snob, maybe?" Ellie set her glass of tea down carefully. "Thank you ever so much for your hospitality, Mrs. Coulthead," she said. "I had a delightful time. We simply *must* do this
again, don't you agree?" And then she stalked off back toward her
boat before Fin could think of a thing to say to stop her.

Fin couldn't believe she'd goofed like that, but as she thought
over what she'd said, she also felt some annoyance at Ellie's atti-

tude. That woman had been hostile from the start—and why? It wasn't fair at all to say she'd treated Ellie like a "charity case."

For someone who'd assumed Fin was judging her, she had been extremely judgmental in turn about Fin's motivations. She didn't know anything about Fin's life or her troubles.

Feeling wounded and indignant, Fin marched back up to the house, determined to have a pleasant night. It was possible. She knew the rules of having a good time with Jimmy and his friends —and when she played by them, she usually did enjoy herself. The reason she was in this situation to begin with was that they could all be a lot of fun. It's just that to keep things fun she had to dedicate herself to saying the right things at the right time, laughing when she was supposed to instead of when she wasn't, and agreeing with what was being agreed upon.

So, she did that, and hours later she went to bed sleepy and happy, pulling Jimmy in after her. They made love for the first time in weeks, and she fell asleep wondering why she didn't always just behave as she was supposed to.

AT BREAKFAST THE NEXT DAY Fin was pleased when Bobbie and Lily invited her to get ready for the party with them. It was fun—they got into the champagne while putting on makeup and helping to arrange one another's hair. Bobbie was especially pleasant, cheerful and excited about the evening to come; everything seemed to have come together nicely; the evening would be a triumph for her.

A lot of deliveries—food and drink packed in ice, blocks of ice packed in sawdust, and a lot of sawdust-covered crates large and small—had arrived during the day Friday, so Saturday had a rather festive air about it as people came to hang decorations, mark off a spot away from the pool but close to the house for the musicians, and dig a pit so they could begin to barbecue a whole pig kālua style, for the event was to be a luau. Bobbie had heard that a troupe of Hawaiian ukulele players were in the city as some sort of exhibit. God knew how she'd managed it, but she'd hired them to play, and based the party around their act.

The musicians arrived in a beat-up station wagon an hour or so before the party officially began, dressed only in brightly colored but manly skirts. They were really quite wonderful when they began to tune up; Fin wandered down to watch them. Afterward, one of them produced a marijuana cigarette. They seemed surprised when she was pleased to share it with them, but she'd smoked loco weed before and enjoyed it. As she inhaled, Fin was keenly aware of the eyes a young man named Koa was making at her, but by then people from all over the neighborhood were arriving to *ooh* and *ahh* at the tropical paradise Bobbie had engineered for them right here in Amityville, so Fin had to go and socialize.

Fin had finally settled on a yellow Empire waist dress with a hem that just skimmed her knees in layers that looked like petals. As she'd fumbled with the clasp of her jade bead necklace, she'd thought about Ellie's question about dressing to impress. Who among her acquaintance would notice her ensemble tonight?

Not Jimmy, who had been distant that morning, telling her she looked "nice" when he'd found her in her dressing gown before he ran off to do something for the party at Bobbie's behest. Fin got the sense he regretted what had happened between them. She didn't. It had been nice to make love, even if love seemed to have had little to do with the act on either side.

Well . . . if not Jimmy, then perhaps Koa. He had tucked a yellow plumeria blossom behind her ear before going to play while whispering that he'd find her later, maybe, if she liked.

Fin was surprised how high she was. She and the other women

had frequently passed "jazz cigarettes" around the office while printing up birth control pamphlets, but that had been a long time ago. That's why she'd limited herself to two puffs — even so, there was a veil between her and the party as Fin moved through it, sipping a drink made of rum and crushed ice and lemon and pomegranate syrup. It really was quite good, and she doubted it would have been so tasty with moonshine.

She ought to tell Bobbie that; she'd surely appreciate hearing it. Perhaps with a little work they could find a way to live happily together, as they once had . . . Anything seemed possible in the cheerful twilight, with the bending notes of the ukuleles drifting through the warm air and the lights twinkling like fireflies and the delicious smell of roasting pork and sweet potatoes all around her.

The groups of people shifted like clouds, billowing and thinning. The distance Fin had gained from the marijuana seemed to be two-way; Fin moved among them invisibly, but for once it felt fun — a masquerade in plain sight. Since she was just another person at the fancy party, rather than its hostess, women felt free to discuss with her the service and the house's decorations, and the men were universally eager to preen before her, and sometimes to flirt.

Fin approached the swimming pool just as a man in a cowboy hat lassoed a passing reveler on the opposite side, pulling him into the water. The splash was tremendous, but not as loud as the cheer that went up from the onlookers. Fin squinted — why, that was the actor Fred Stone! And the man beside him, slapping his thigh as he laughed at the man in the water, that was Will Rogers! Fin had no idea how Bobbie knew them, but it was certainly quite glamorous to have them there.

Watching the soaked and sputtering man swim to shore, Fin finally spied her friend. Bobbie was sitting at the edge of the pool, her bare feet dangling in the water, laughing along with a smartly dressed and somewhat damp crowd. Jimmy stood above her, a drink in his hand. He looked relaxed, at his ease—happier than he'd looked in a long time. Duke and Lily were there, too. Her dress had been splashed; Duke was dabbing at it with a handkerchief, but they were both laughing as well. They all looked so natural together; they didn't seem to be wanting for anything . . . or anyone.

Fin felt a pang. Her absence did not trouble them; it was her presence that did. They enjoyed themselves more without her. Even—no, especially Jimmy. It was obvious, watching him like this, invisible and obscure.

She wondered why he didn't tell her. It wasn't money; Jimmy didn't need her dough—he had his own now. Perhaps it was pride, or misplaced chivalry . . . but it wasn't chivalrous to leave it up to her to discover. Perhaps he hadn't realized it himself.

She smelled cigarette smoke, and sensed a presence behind her.

"She's the star of the show, isn't she?"

In the light of the tiki torches Edgar's face was a pink smear. His lips were contorted into an ugly smile.

"I was going to be Dogberry in *Much Ado about Nothing*," he said after she didn't answer. "She convinced me that I oughtn't stay behind, that we'd have such a *nice* time this summer that I wouldn't miss the stage. Too late I found out she just wanted to be the prima donna of a different production."

"Edgar, you're drunk."

He looked down at her. "Maybe," he said. "Or maybe I've just realized I traded a standout role to slouch in the lead's shadow. Oh well . . . Better than being an extra," he said, giving her a significant look before melting into the crowd.

Fin wandered away from the pool. It wasn't that she was angry at Bobbie over what Edgar had said—he had been intoxicated and jealous and looking to start a quarrel. It was the gossipy, petty meanness of what he'd said that dismayed her. They had come here to be happy, and yet she was not happy—neither, apparently, was Edgar, and Duke and Lily were always quarreling. Jimmy too seemed anxious, though less so when she wasn't haunting him like some ghost from his past.

She had little desire to mingle further with anyone, but she wasn't sure what to do with herself. She didn't want to go to bed. She checked her watch. It was too late to skip out and attend the poetry reading; that had ended hours ago.

"Hey, you okay?"

It was Koa, the ukulele player. Just behind him, his fellows were crowded around the bar, and partygoers crowded around them. They must be taking a break.

"I'm fine," she said.

"You sure?"

"Let's say I'm better now."

"Me too, as it turns out."

"Oh?" He really was very handsome, especially when he was grinning like that.

"Would you like to get a drink?" she asked.

"You bet!" said Koa.

The bartender was very busy. Once they reached him he told them he'd run out of rum. There was a little champagne left, and "local stuff." After a brief deliberation, Fin and Koa decided on the local stuff. Fin asked for one of the "nice bottles," remembering Ellie had said some had age on them. When the bartender balked at handing over the whole thing, she finally revealed that she was Mrs. Coulthead. Then he was only too happy to release it to her, but Koa seemed a bit more reserved.

"Hey—you okay?" said Fin as they wandered over the lawn. His smile came back a bit at that, but he still seemed uncomfortable. "What's wrong?"

"I didn't know you were the lady of the house," he said.

"What difference does that make?" asked Fin. He raised his

eyebrows at her, and she realized what he was actually concerned about. "Don't worry about it. If my husband and I can't be described as *estranged* yet, we're well on our way to getting there."

"Oh! I mean . . . I'm sorry to hear it."

"Not the first time it's happened in the history of the world," said Fin. "The important thing is that if I want to have a drink with a nice ukulele player, or do whatever else with him, I feel perfectly at my leisure to do so."

"And you do want to have a drink? Or . . . whatever else?"

"The drink sounds nice, but *definitely* the whatever else."

They wandered far from the party. Fin showed Koa the archery range she'd set up for herself, tucked away at the edge of the wood; he was more impressed by it than she'd expected him to be and actually asked a few questions about her hobby, further surprising her. She wasn't used to people being interested in this part of her life. She felt silly showing off her technique at his request, bowless and in a party dress, but he really seemed to take it seriously.

After that, they ventured into the more private darkness of the forest proper. Fin couldn't remember the last time she'd felt so happy. She was about to say so when she stepped in something that squelched under her shoe.

"Ugh," she said, inspecting the mess. While it wasn't a dog turd, as she'd feared, it wasn't much more pleasant than that—she'd stepped in some sort of gooey plant or growth that had apparently burst, coating the sole of her shoe with its juices.

"What *is* that?" said Koa, his nose wrinkled in distaste.

"I don't know," said Fin, handing him the bottle so she could scrape the worst of it off with a handful of leaves. The liquid was viscous and oily, and had a complex but not wholly unpleasant aroma redolent of gasoline and decomposing earth. In the faint starlight that filtered through the wood, the ichor had a shimmery purple sheen to it like motor oil.

"They're all over the place," said Koa, pointing out a few more of the bubble-like plants, if indeed they were plants.

"I'll have the gardener take a look," said Fin. "But later." She wasn't about to let a dirty shoe ruin her night.

They both paid more attention to where they were stepping after that, and as they picked their way over the forest floor, they saw other couples sneaking off into little groves or copses, or sometimes out of them looking disheveled and happy. Eventually, she and Koa found a nice bit of loamy earth at the edge of the forest, free of those disgusting whatever-they-weres. Though secluded from view by a few well-placed shrubs, they could see the bay, and the gentle breeze off the water cooled their bower.

Koa set aside the unopened bottle in the roots of a tree, more interested in kissing her than having a drink. Fin responded eagerly.

He was an ardent and tender lover. His hands, though large, were surprisingly delicate; he got her dress off quickly, without tearing it, and even hung it on a pine branch so it would not wrinkle or get stained.

His own garment made a wonderful blanket after she helped him unwind it from around his waist, surprised by how much cloth there was. He knelt on it, burying his face between her thighs as she leaned back against a tree. She felt a hell of a lot better about not getting to that reading now . . . It surely would not have ended like this.

"How will you take it?" she asked, reaching for her handbag. She didn't have her Vimule Cap, but it was her habit to always carry a tube of spermicidal jelly with her.

"How about missionary?" he said with a wink.

"Convert me," she said, "but please do pull out, just to be safe."

Fin had been cautiously adventurous during her school years, and therefore had enough experience to know that Koa's technique was a cut above. He was neither too fast nor too slow, and held off withdrawing to finish until she'd kicked the beam herself.

"Thank you," she said as he rolled down beside her. "That was lovely."

"My pleasure."

"I'm very glad of that."

Koa turned over onto his side and looked at her, chin propped up on his elbow. "Say. Want to run away with me?"

"Run away with you!" She laughed, but when she saw his serious expression, she paused to consider it. "Run away where?"

"Come along on the road with us. I could teach you the hula, and you could dance in a grass skirt while we played."

"You don't know how tempting that is," said Fin. "But I really shouldn't make any decisions that big while clear-headed." She grabbed the neglected bottle of booze, flipped open the swing-top, and took a long pull.

It tasted not as she expected, of fire and corn-sweetness and a bit of oak. Instead it was smoky, bitter, greasy on the tongue, with a tang that was both metallic and earthen, like the underside of a rock.

"Gosh," she spluttered.

"Sounds like good stuff," said Koa, and took a swig for himself. "Oh!" He coughed. "I see what you mean. Damn."

"It's not bad, not exactly . . ." Fin took the bottle back and tipped a bit more down her throat.

"Koa?" Someone was calling from closer to the house. "Hey, Koa! You out there? We need to play another set!"

"Shit." Koa got quickly to his feet—as did Fin, to free up his garment. As he tucked and folded it around himself, she brushed herself off and shimmied back into her gown. "Sorry, I gotta—"

"Go!" She kissed him on the cheek. "I'll think about your offer."

"Let me know!" He disappeared back into the wood. "Hi, Kamalani! I'm here!"

Fin didn't feel like hurrying back. Instead she took another sip of booze and stared out at the water. Out of sight of her house she felt at peace, here with the owls and the insects and the small creatures that scurried through the forest on their various obscure errands.

Long Island was a wonderful place, wild and civilized, cosmopolitan yet provincial. She had been telling Ellie the truth when she praised it; she'd come to really love it—and in spite of her current situation at home.

A sharp scream cut through her reverie. It wasn't the shriek of a debutante being pushed into the pool, or the shout of a man challenged to wrestle. It was the genuine scream of someone in distress. Fin hesitated for a moment, but then another wail ripped open the night like lightning across a darkened sky. Fin took a step towards the party—

—And the world turned upside down.

At first, she thought she'd just put her shoe in another of those nasty plants, but no, the earth itself was wetter, soggier. It was hot, too—boiling even, breaking apart under her feet in wet bursts of steam. She tried to avoid the rumbling patches of unstable ground as she jumped from solid patch to solid patch, but soon there was not enough ground to do even that. She wondered if she was dreaming, only to realize she couldn't be—such a thought would cause her to wake up, if she were.

It occurred to her that given how long she'd been walking, she should have gotten back to the party. She looked up, wobbling as her feet sank into the wet earth, and saw she was no longer in the thick of a forest, but in a clearing she was certain was not on their property. Not only was it an unfamiliar shape, but in the center was *something*—she wasn't sure what.

Looking at the thing hurt her eyes. It seemed unnatural in some way. She couldn't quite tell if she was looking at a glistening hole in the earth or something that puffed up above it. Lit by a massive bonfire behind it, it shone purplish black in the firelight. It was repulsive, but that's not what frightened her most—no, what really terrified her was that she could feel its will. It was so strong, it emanated from the horrible object like an odor, powerful but invisible. It desired, and what it desired was to destroy and remake the world into something different than what it was and always had been.

She glanced back down at her feet; the smaller versions of the thing were all around her on her patch of land, some the size of a marble, others larger than a baseball, all with that impenetrable quality of being neither presence nor absence. On that scale, she recognized what lurked in the clearing—it was a larger version of that revolting plant she'd stepped in.

She ducked behind a tree when a figure emerged from the darkness beyond the bonfire, holding a copper vessel in its hands. It chanted some words, and the massive oily entity began to undulate and pulse. When the bottom unfolded upward like an umbrella into flabby petals whose gills glowed faintly, as if lit by distant stars, the figure in the robe poured whatever black and viscous fluid he had in his bowl onto the thing. It dripped and then swirled over the surface in chaotic whorls of light and color, pooling into eye-blindingly bright rainbow blotches as the cap began to swell and swell.

Fin glanced down—the little ones at her feet had also opened to glow like fireflies around her feet. As the larger one drank, they expanded so quickly the spongy earth around them began to crumble and then to dissolve in a wave. Fin stumbled as the patch she stood on gave way beneath her, then slipped, landing in a puddle of fluid that was greasy like oil but warm like blood. She tried to swim for the remains of the patch of land, but the wave of destruction grew and grew, and any ground she could reach was no longer ground, but something else. The grass upon it had turned to feathers and fur and scales; the dirt to streams and snaking stripes of impossibly black solids and bright liquids in more colors than her eyes could drink in. The trunks of trees bent down, probing and searching the carnage for some unknown purpose, like the tentacles of some sightless seeking creature.

Something from beneath the surface of the pink puddle wrapped itself around Fin's ankle. She uttered one long but pointless scream before she was tugged under. The fluid filled her eyes and lungs, and she knew no more.

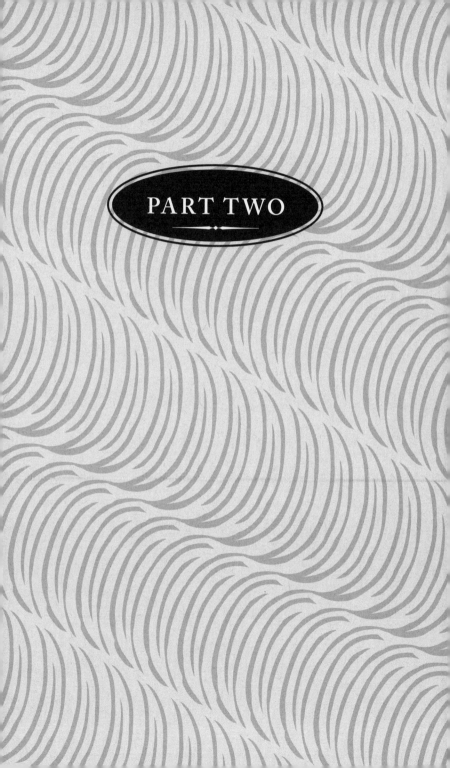

PART TWO

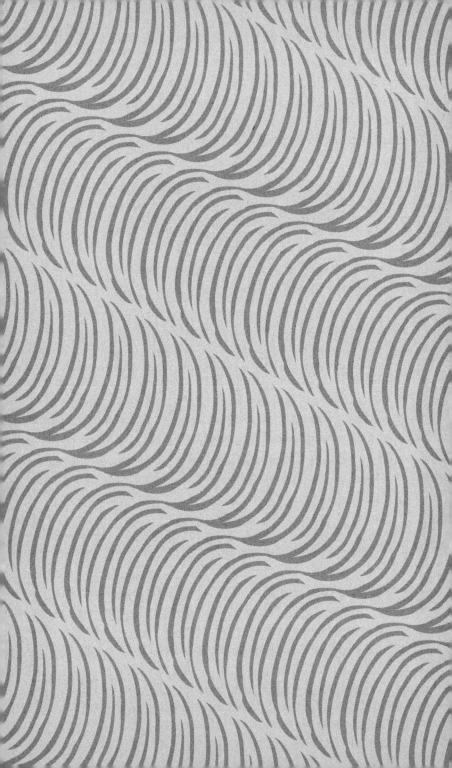

The Demon in the Deep
by G. Baker

S USAN'S BROTHER TURNED AWAY. He could not bear to look at Miss Depth, not now that their friend's eyes had gone black and her hair had gone white and she spoke with a different voice with a black tongue inside her mouth. Susan was frightened too, but she would speak her mind to this thing that claimed to be a demon.

"You have been causing too much trouble," she said. "The seagulls are silent, the fish can't swim, and the oysters' pearls have all turned to dust. They are all afraid of you, because you have stolen our friend's body and they think you'll steal theirs, too. So you must go away—go away, and never come back!"

Miss Depth's hair waved in the wind, her bare feet stood on the freezing sand, but it was not Miss Depth to whom Susan spoke. Something else now wore her skin, and when she laughed, it was not her laugh.

"I will *not* go," said the demon. "Miss Depth invited me; it is not for you to turn me out."

"Why would she do that?"

"Because your friend could not understand the ways of the world after her sister's death, and she knew I could show her the truth of it all. It was a fair price I named, to grant her such understanding, and we struck a deal, she and I—and make no mistake, girl, she paid me gladly."

Susan knew well how Miss Depth had suffered through her sister's illness and after her death. Tears started in her eyes, freezing there before they could drop and sink into the sand.

"You dare speak of truth? Miss Depth loved her sister, and her sister loved the seagulls, and the fish, and the oysters. She would not have wanted you to frighten everybody and everything so badly!"

"I do dare speak of truth, and the truth is that Miss Depth could no longer see the usefulness of seagulls, or fish, or oysters after her sister's death . . . but she did see the usefulness of *me*."

Susan knew the demon wasn't lying—its words cut through her like a knife, straight through her oilskin and what she wore beneath it, through her flesh, into her very bones, into her heart. Nothing but the truth could do that.

"Ah—I see at last you believe me," it said. "So, will you believe me when I say that when the seagulls and the fish and the rest flee before me, it is because they are wise?" The demon smiled at Susan with her friend's lips. "Are you that wise, Susan? Will *you* flee?"

1

I T HAD LOOKED LIKE RAIN that morning, but by the afternoon the clouds had broken apart and burned away in the summer sunshine, and Ellie had herself a nice haul of weakfish and fluke, as well as a bucket of crabs. Her mother was delighted, and declared her intention to make crab stuffing for the fish, so Ellie spent a pleasant hour picking crabmeat out of claw and leg after her mother boiled them. She was happy to help; it was one of the family's favorite dishes, but Gabriel loved it especially, and he was coming over for dinner.

Lester, too, did his part; he was picking raspberries from the thick bushes that grew in a tangled clump at the edge of the back yard. For dessert, her mother would make them into a sauce for some ice cream that Ellie and Gabriel would fetch from Lombardi's, and Lester would come too, if he was up for it.

It was lovely and quiet on the back porch. The bees buzzed, dipping in and out of the wild climbing roses and the shocks of black-eyed Susans that her mother loved so much. Ellie had looked out on this yard almost every day of her life, in every weather, but the view hadn't afforded her much pleasure of late. It was nice to just sit and appreciate it, for a change.

"What do you have for me so far?"

Ellie's mother emerged from the kitchen to sit down beside Ellie, where she began to look over the generous pile of crabmeat and the yet larger pile of picked-over shells. Ellie didn't mind her mother double-checking her work; she always managed to find a few more shreds than Ellie ever could.

"When the weakfish started biting I had hoped we could have stuffed fish for dinner," said Ellie, cracking her knuckles noisily.

"It's a nice little celebration."

"I'm ready for one. It weighed on me, not knowing if he could go."

"I know it did. The last two days, you've seemed much more yourself."

Ellie frowned. She had tried to not let it show how much she'd feared failing her brother.

"All I meant is that you deserve leisure time, too . . . especially as you having leisure time means we have so much lovely fresh fish for dinner."

That finally brought a smile to Ellie's face — a smile that brightened further when she heard Gabriel's footfalls on the grass. He'd come around to the back to say hello, the evening paper tucked under his arm. The look on his face when he saw Mrs. West and that pile of crabmeat side by side was everything she'd hoped it would be.

"Stuffed fish!" he exclaimed. "I hope you didn't go to all that trouble on my behalf, Mrs. West."

"And so what if I did?" She accepted a kiss on the cheek from Gabriel. "I do wish you'd call me Harriet, though."

"I'll be calling you Ma soon," replied Gabriel, scooping Ellie up into his arms and planting one on her mouth that left her blushing. "Not soon enough, though."

"Speaking of," said Ellie's mother, "when will I meet your folks?"

"My parents? Leave the farm? To pay a social call?" Gabriel pantomimed horror. "I'll be amazed if they show up to the wedding."

"Hello, Gabriel," said Lester.

"Picking raspberries, eh?" said Gabriel, stroking his chin thoughtfully as he looked at Lester's basket. "Wait, does that mean . . . Are we paying Lombardi's a visit tonight, too?"

"That's the plan," said Lester. "The weather's so nice, I'll come along with you, I think . . . If that's all right?"

"Why wouldn't it be?" said Ellie. "Right, Gabe?"

"Of course." Gabriel's smile was big and wide, but Ellie detected a slight drop in his enthusiasm — so slight Lester didn't notice. It was true she had spent the past few nights at home . . . She wondered if Gabriel was feeling neglected.

"I think we're down to the briny jawbone, here," said Ellie's mother, looking over her work. "There's no more crabmeat hiding in *these* shells."

"I did my best," said Ellie. "I look and look, but I never find as much as you do."

"Your eyes are good for catching them."

"I think I've picked over the raspberry bushes, too," said Lester.

"Robert will be home soon. I suppose I'd better start cooking," said Ellie's mother. "I ought to have had the potatoes in the oven by now."

"Push me on the swing for a bit?" said Ellie to Gabriel as Lester followed their mother inside.

"It would be my pleasure," said Gabriel.

Ellie's father had hung the ancient rope swing in the boughs of the old oak tree as a treat for her eighth birthday, but the hemp was still sound and the board solid. Ellie's rear end was a bit of a tight fit these days, and she had to hold her legs out straight so they didn't drag, but it was still fun, especially when she had Gabriel behind her.

He tossed the evening paper into the grass and gave her a gentle push. When she swung back, he caught her and bit her neck, gently.

"*Finally,*" she murmured. "But not too hard; they'll see the mark. Save it for later."

"Are you coming home with me tonight?"

"Tomorrow," she said. "I'll rush through my run and be in your arms as soon as possible."

"Run!" Gabriel seemed surprised. "I thought you were done with that now."

"Oh, no. Why would I?" She turned around to grin at him. "After all, now I need to start saving for a trousseau."

"In that case, I won't object."

Ellie still hadn't told him about selling their wedding liquor . . . or about the man she'd killed. As to the former, she was hopeful she could afford to replace what she'd sold with something equally nice, therefore avoiding any wounded feelings on Gabriel's part. As to the latter . . . she was hopeful she could just avoid telling him about that at all.

"Will you stop by Rocky's on your way home tomorrow?"

Gabriel's voice was studiously neutral, but she could feel eagerness radiating from him.

"Sure." She too kept her voice even, but in truth, the idea excited her. *Really* excited her. She wondered if they had time for a quick one now . . . They could slip away from the house, out of view down the road a bit, or—

"Are you kids reading my paper, or may I have it?"

Ellie's father stood on the back porch. The sun had sunk a bit; he was partly shadowed by the roof, a sharp slanted slash across his face that left only his right cheek and chin illuminated. Without seeing his expression, that hard and severe look he'd worn even in moments of relaxation since he'd come home, it was almost like seeing her father as he had been. There was even a touch of humor to his tone.

"You don't have time for the paper now," Ellie heard her mother say. "Dinner's almost on the table."

"You heard your mother. Come in and eat." Over his shoulder, her father added, "And don't forget my paper," before disappearing.

Ellie hopped off the swing. "I'm glad you're here," she said. "It's been so tense, recently."

"Oh no," said Gabriel.

"What's wrong?"

Gabriel was staring at the edge of the newspaper—it was

coated in some sort of dark juice or slime. Ellie touched it with her fingertips. It was oily to the touch, but thin enough to get into the creases of her fingerprint, like ink.

"Yuck," she said. "What is it?"

"I guess it's from one of these . . ." Gabriel nudged something with his toe, a dark and grotesque protuberance that looked out of place in the lush green yard, and at the same time seemed oddly familiar. Ellie squatted down, and upon closer inspection the golden rays of the late afternoon sunlight revealed an oddly cold and repellent greasy rainbow sheen playing across its surface.

That was why she'd recognized it. Walter Greene had had a sack of them in his hold, along with that booze. Ellie's throat closed up at the thought of that night, too tightly for her to gasp.

"I've seen them around our place, too."

She inhaled delicious air, once again able to breathe. "Oh?" she said.

Gabriel nodded. "My mother makes this stuff for her potatoes when they get blight. I've been using it on them. Works okay. They go away, but they keep coming back in other places. Odd for summer . . ." He shrugged unhappily, returning his attention to the paper. "It's soaked in; what a mess."

"Only just here," said Ellie. "It was an accident; he'll understand." The fear that he wouldn't pushed everything else out of Ellie's mind, but thankfully her father told them not to worry about it.

The fish was flaky and good, and the potatoes crisp from the hot oven. There were also new peas from the garden, and sliced ripe tomatoes. It was simple food, simply prepared, but it tasted delicious—it tasted like home. And even more than that, while they were eating it *felt* like home, with everyone seeming to enjoy one another's company.

"I don't know when I've ever had such a good meal, Mrs. West," said Gabriel as Ellie cleared the table.

"You're always welcome," she said, "and after you're married, too, if you ever need a break from Ellie's cooking . . ."

"Hey!" said Ellie, but she was smiling, as was her mother.

"Oh, I'm a modern man," said Gabriel, winking at Ellie as she cleared the plates. "As long as my bride does the dishes, I don't mind cooking." Ellie rolled her eyes, but as she left the room she heard him say, "Anyway, I'm sure my mother will be sending me home with more pierogi and kielbasa than we can eat, given how she spoils me already."

"And once you give her a grandchild or two, I'm sure she'll be bringing them over herself," said Ellie's mother, to her dismay.

"Gabriel, Lester . . . let's go for a walk," she said, glowering at everyone from the doorway.

Ellie's humor was quickly restored by the feel of Gabriel's fingers twined with hers as they strolled down the lane into town with Lester. Lombardi's carried more esoteric flavors like stracciatella and pistachio, but everyone in the West family liked their vanilla custard, flecked with luxurious bits of the bean itself. What with saving every penny they could, they hadn't had ice cream in a long time — now that they had a bit of surplus they could splurge on a treat, which was nice.

They took their time getting there and then sat down for a bit to let Lester rest; Gabriel bought them a Coca-Cola to share in the shade of the Triangle Building.

They made good time home so that the ice cream would not melt too much, but as soon as she walked in the back door Ellie knew something was wrong. She and Lester instantly recognized the urgency in her father's voice as it drifted in from the other room; they exchanged a significant look. Her brother put the ice cream in the icebox to help it stay firm, but Ellie had a sinking feeling that it would be quite a while before they ate it.

"Should we . . ." said Gabriel, but then Ellie's mother appeared in the doorway.

There was a look that Ellie and her mother had often shared when Robert West was out of sorts. Tonight, however, Mrs. West wouldn't meet her daughter's eye. She stood there for a moment in the doorway, looking pale but resigned, staring at her hands.

"Ellie . . . your father would like to speak to you."

"Alone?" Ellie's stomach sank yet further. She had genuinely no idea what would be so serious as to require a private audience.

"I'm coming too."

"It's all right," said Ellie, and was surprised to see a flash of annoyance flit across Gabriel's handsome face. She couldn't understand why on earth he would feel put out. "I'll come right back."

"All right. Lester and I can finish the dishes," said Gabriel. "Mrs. West, go on and sit down."

Ellie's father was sitting in his chair in the dim parlor under the bright puddle of light from his reading lamp—but he wasn't reading. The paper lay folded across his knees. He looked up at her as she approached.

"Ellie, I need to speak with you about something very serious," he said.

"What is it?" she asked. "What's happened? Ma wouldn't say—"

"Your delivery—the one you said would be your last—it was to some people who lived over on Ocean Avenue?"

"Yes . . ."

"What was the family's name?"

Ellie glanced down at the paper, feeling nervous now for different, unexpected reasons. "I can't tell you," she said.

"Was it Coulthead?"

Ellie tried to keep her face impassive, but her father saw what he needed to see in her expression. He stood, and handed her the paper. Ellie sat down in the other chair, so that the puddle of light from the lamp fell over the page. It was the trash gossip column written by an anonymous reporter who simply went by "The Prying Eye." Ellie privately felt that column ought to be called "The

Flapping Lip," but this evening it contained something more than descriptions of people she didn't know wearing dresses by designers she'd never heard of and jewelry she'd never be able to afford:

SCREAMS ON OCEAN AVENUE
LATE-NIGHT PARTY ANTICS SHOCK
GUESTS AND NEIGHBORHOOD ALIKE

Readers will know that the Eye can be counted on to report on parties, but the truth is that parties do not always go according to plan. As Saturday night became Sunday morning, screams were heard on Ocean Avenue, when a light and lively luau-themed party at Mr. and Mrs. James Coulthead's residence became much more serious. Eyewitnesses report that several guests, both men and women, began to exhibit symptoms of disorientation and babble about horrors no one else could see. Anyone who tried to comfort or soothe these people received only abuse for their trouble—one woman pushed her would-be savior into a rosebush; a man socked his best friend, perhaps former best friend, on the jaw. Police were called, and The Prying Eye (who was of course on the scene) saw the distinctive truck of Officer Hector Jones pulling up, meaning it is not unreasonable to suspect that liquor was involved in the disturbance. Whether too much, or perhaps some rotten stuff, was the cause of the scene remains to be seen; but we do know that whatever the cause of the outburst it was indiscriminate; even the sister of Mr. Coulthead, Miss

Diane Coulthead, was spotted among the affected parties. No arrests were made, but it is possible further inquiries should—or at least, *ought to*—be made into this matter.

Part of Ellie wanted to dismiss the entire report as trash. Between its sensational style and the fact this "prying eye" had misreported Delphine Coulthead as being Jimmy's sister "Diane," there wasn't much reason to believe anything it said.

And yet, it did disturb her. The crate of unidentified moonshine loomed large in her mind—usually, she wouldn't sell booze like that. She always bought from SJ because she knew how careful SJ was about hygiene; how she did her best to produce a product of the same proof each time. Not all moonshiners did—in fact, not only did they run unsanitary operations, making mash out of who knew what, people added all sorts of things to their batches to give the finished drink more "kick," including bleach, embalming fluid, and other unimaginably awful substances. The consequences of drinking that stuff were terrible, too—blindness, even death.

Ellie had tried the mystery booze, but it's true she hadn't sampled every bottle. She should have, but Amityville wasn't exactly a hotbed of tainted moonshine.

And yet, it seemed she'd found some.

"Is this the big sale you made?" said her father, drawing her away from these jumbled thoughts. "Is this how you paid for Lester's college? Selling tainted liquor to the unwary?"

"No!" Ellie shook her head. "I mean, yes, it is the family who hired me, but I didn't... or I didn't mean to sell them tainted liquor. I didn't think I had. *If* that's even what happened—this could all be a bunch of drunks scaring one another. Everybody knows 'The Prying Eye' is nothing but gossip, and—"

"It is in the paper just the same. You've exposed us."

"Exposed...?"

"You think that lowlife Oscar won't tell everyone it was you?"

This was an unfortunately good point, and Ellie cringed as she considered just how far this story might spread. Her father saw, and an odd light came into his eyes. Ellie was well acquainted with her father's various angry moods, but this was a cold, righteous mania the likes of which she had never seen before.

"All Amityville will know this family's shame," he said, his voice still soft, low, and terrifying. "I told you I wanted you to stop, Ellie. I told you it was time for you to give this up, to leave that life behind you. But you would not listen."

He got a bit louder toward the end of his speech, so Ellie got louder too when she replied, "It's honest enough work, or at least, there's nothing *wrong* with it."

"Nothing wrong with selling illegal spirits to thirsty drunks?" Her father snorted. "I'm not sure either the law or the"—he sniffed —"*Italian* operations in town would agree with you."

Ellie wasn't worried about the police for obvious reasons, but the mention of the Mafia gave her pause. She hadn't spent too much time worrying about the big-time importers coming to shut her down or ask for a cut of her profits—that usually happened when people got greedy.

But she *had* gotten greedy. After a public incident like this, some opportunists might well take the opportunity to move in on her. That was more upsetting to Ellie than what people might say.

"What matters is that now Lester can go to school," she said firmly. "The plan was for me to stop anyway, wasn't it?" She had dismissed the idea before, but retirement was looking a lot more attractive after this, that was for sure. "People may talk about this, but so what if they do? People will talk about anything. Lester will still be making us proud long after they've forgotten all about it."

Ellie's father made a disgusted sound. "If he wanted to go to school, he ought to have earned his own way like a real man and left you to live like a proper woman!"

"He earned that scholarship like a man would—like *anyone* would—and I'm sure there's nothing improper about a woman supporting her family. Or at least, helping to do so."

That was the wrong thing to say—Ellie saw it instantly. The thunder in her father's voice coalesced in his face as it went purple as a storm cloud and his brows crashed together like two angry swells. She'd only meant to defend herself against this bizarre accusation of not being a proper woman. After all, her father had taught her everything she knew about the bay, from boating to fishing to digging for bait clams with her pants hiked up above her knees . . . And when her mother was nervous about the idea of her learning to swim, fearing she would drown, it was her father who'd insisted she'd be less likely to if she knew how to save herself.

Ellie had been heartbroken when he went to war; she had always loved her mother, but her father had *understood* her. She'd been so grateful that he'd shared his bayman's wisdom with her, even though she was a girl and could never get a job on a trawler. Because of him, she'd been able to pick up the slack when he left—that had made her proud, and she had thought her father would be proud of her, too. That he had quietly resented her for it had always stung, but even that did not prepare her for his open criticism.

"Supporting your family," he said, chewing the words, with an expression as if they tasted bad to him. "Is *that* what you think you're doing? You're not supporting this family, Elizabeth West. You're breaking it into pieces."

"How is that?" It was an outrageous accusation, and Ellie did not bother to check her tone, nor did she repent when he glared at her.

"Your self-serving actions, which you consider 'support,' have done more to undermine the structure of this family than my injury. Everything you do, Ellie, you do for your sake, not ours. You take pride in it when you should feel shame. It's time you accepted that you're no man of the house, no matter how much you affect being one."

"I've never affected anything! I've only ever done what needed to be done," insisted Ellie. Though she wanted to, she did not add *and who else would have done it?*

"A woman your age shouldn't be out on a boat, fishing. She ought to be keeping house for her husband, giving him children, and being quiet about it."

"Who *are* you?" Ellie exclaimed, shocked. "Don't you remember taking me out on the bay? I am who I am because of what you taught me!"

"I don't remember teaching you to sass your own father."

"Do you remember teaching me to stand up for what's right? Because that's what I'm doing for Lester. If this family is too fragile to withstand me doing right by him, then it wasn't strong to begin with."

"Stop it. Stop quarreling."

Lester had come into the room, pale and spare and fragile-looking in the dark parlor full of solid wooden furniture. Ellie wanted to take him away by the hand, as she'd led him away from the edge of the dock or other dangerous situations when he'd been small. But she saw it, for the first time perhaps in that moment: Lester was becoming a man. She couldn't protect him anymore—and he didn't need her to.

"Don't you *dare* speak to me that way," said Ellie's father, far louder now than he had been with her. Any restraint he showed toward his daughter was gone as he addressed his son. "There's no cause for you to become a part of this conversation."

"I am a part of this conversation, as I'm one of the causes of it," countered Lester. "My name has been mentioned, and I have a right to be in the room when I'm being talked about." Ellie blushed. She knew she'd been defending him, but it had probably been awful to listen to.

"You have no right to tell me how to behave in my own home," her father said. "I have a right to be heard."

"Oh, we've heard you," said Lester, again impressing Ellie—she wouldn't have dared to speak to their father like that, not in a million years. "We've heard you again, and again. All you do is sit around and complain about how dissatisfied you are. And ever since you've been spending time with Hunter you've been *more* unhappy, not less." Ellie was surprised to hear this. She hadn't really noticed a difference, but Lester was home more than she was. "If anyone ought to feel badly about speaking rudely, it ought to be you, the way you talk to Ellie."

"It's all right," she said hastily. "I don't mind, I—"

"*I* mind," said Lester, over her. "It's not right."

"What's not right is two children attacking their father, especially when one is an embarrassing cripple and the other a—"

Ellie never found out what she was, as their father's insult to Lester was too much for her to endure. The look on Lester's face was heartbreaking. Their father had said plenty that was awful over the years, expressing disappointment in his son, but this was the first time he'd ever just come out and said it.

"That's it," said Ellie, interrupting him. "I've had enough." She spoke softly, rather than yelling more. "Lester, go pack. I will too. We're leaving. Neither of us needs to put up with this anymore. We're clearly not welcome in this house."

"I agree," said Lester quietly. It killed Ellie a little to see him so upset. "I'm sorry you find me embarrassing, Pop. There are moments I've felt the same way about you—but not because of your injury."

"Let's go tell Gabriel we'll be coming with him," said Ellie, as her father's mouth moved without making sounds. Likely, her fiancé already knew they were, but it was a good excuse to have Lester leave the room.

"Gabriel!" Apparently, it hadn't occurred to Mr. West where

they'd go if they left. "You'd leave this house to go and live with that—that *foreigner*?"

"Foreigner!" Ellie actually laughed, though not from any particular humorousness to her father's remarks. "He was born in a farmhouse in Center Moriches."

"His parents weren't."

"So what? Mother's great-grandparents were French!"

"That's different." Her father made a disgusted sound. "And the company he keeps!"

"What company would that be?" Ellie was no longer laughing. She was fairly certain her father meant Aaron, but she wanted him to say it, to own it. He did not.

"I'm talking about how Long Island really isn't what it used to be," said Robert, sidestepping the question.

Ellie couldn't believe she was hearing this. Her father had always liked Gabriel—or at least, liked him as much as he liked anything. He hadn't even had a problem with Gabriel being a few years younger than her, and inclined to talk about ghosts, and monsters, and colonies on Mars at the dinner table.

"Long Island used to be a safe place, free from the corruption of the city. Men here worked for a living; women kept their homes for them. Now, it's a teeming cesspool of outsiders and vacationers. You should come Sunday morning, Ellie—even if you leave tonight, you should come to hear Hunter speak. We're gathering in Paul Edwards' field, and my friend will speak to right-thinking Long Islanders on how we can stop further social deterioration."

"Social deterioration, huh?" Gabriel was in the room now, too, standing in the doorway, his big arms crossed over his solid chest. "You mean like farmers who prefer their potatoes in pancake form, rather than mashed or roasted? The horror of it all."

Ellie went to him, took his hands in hers and squeezed. He

looked down at her fondly, but there was a hardness to his eyes and to the set of his mouth.

"Let's get out of here," she said.

"If you leave you won't be invited back," said her father, without deigning to reply to Gabriel.

"What a shame," said Ellie, and ushered Gabriel and Lester into the hall.

Gabriel had walked, so Ellie decided it would be easier to come back for what she couldn't carry. As she packed up a few days' worth of clothes she heard the front door slam and her father's distinctive tread on the front walkway. Her mother, however, remained in the kitchen, alone with the forgotten ice cream melting in the icebox and the smell of raspberry sauce hanging in the air, just sitting, looking at nothing, her hands folded in her lap.

Lester wouldn't say goodbye to her, shocking Ellie. Their mother's failure to stand up for him had hurt him badly, it seemed. Ellie, on the other hand, couldn't leave without saying farewell.

"Ma," said Ellie, "you could come too . . ."

"My place is here."

"Ma." Ellie sat down at the table. "Even with everything he said, you—"

"They're just words. There are things that are more important."

"Like your children being driven out of their own home?"

"You're choosing to leave." Her mother looked back down at her hands. "He's always been a man of strong opinions. And some of the points he made are fair."

"The points about your son being an embarrassing cripple, or . . . ?"

"No, about Long Island, and our way of life changing—being lost."

"If it is being lost, I don't see how what he's doing is helping get it back."

Ellie stood and grabbed the wallet of Lester's college money out of her mother's desk.

"I'm taking this," she said. She chose not to elaborate on why. Ellie's mother just nodded her head, serene if sorrowful.

Ellie joined her fiancé and her brother on the lawn, where they stood in the gloaming for a long moment, silent, all turning over what had happened in their own way. Then Ellie shrugged once and started off down the road, toward her new home. Gabriel and Lester followed without a word.

2

ELLIE MADE PANCAKES AND BACON and coffee for everyone the next morning. She burned all of it, including the coffee. Neither her fiancé nor her brother complained about the unfortunate meal; they just put more butter and syrup all over everything that had a bit of char on it and thanked her with compliments she knew she didn't deserve.

She was grateful for their forbearance. It wasn't that either of them was the sort of man to get upset over a badly prepared meal; it was just that she was frustrated to have ruined an attempted nice gesture. She didn't want them all walking on eggshells around one another—she'd had enough of that for a lifetime.

Honestly, it wasn't such a big deal, moving out, moving on. She'd been planning to do so anyway after Lester went to school. That there was a rift between her and her parents just meant she'd be saved the trouble of heading into Amityville as often as she usually did.

She had to go in to town that night, however. Her remaining clients were expecting her, and she wanted to talk to Officer Jones.

When she got to the police station he was just packing up for the day, which he had clearly spent in this awful hot office. His tie was loose around his neck, his shirtsleeves damp around his forearms. Even though she came bearing gifts he did not seem pleased to see her; neither did Cleo, for that matter. The dog barely raised her head when Ellie entered.

"Come on outside with me, Miss West," he said grimly, grabbing his bag.

"And a good evening to you, too," she said, trotting to keep up with him as he headed for the door.

"Is it? You're here, which means yet another problem for me. But, lucky for you I'm too hot to handcuff you and throw you in jail like you deserve."

"Jail!"

"Yes, jail. It's not like I don't know who sold that liquor to the Coultheads." He waved away her protest. "I don't want to hear it. That column . . ." He shook his head as Ellie winced. "Everybody's talking about it. That reporter's a damn nuisance, if you ask me. This entire incident, weird as it is, could have easily been hushed up if it hadn't gotten into the paper, but since it did it'll rile up everyone, including the preachers, the Klan, other temperance kooks . . . We'll have no end of troubles." Jones glanced at Ellie, and seeing her dismay, changed his tone. "Hopefully none of it will touch you. As always, I'll do what I can to keep people off your back if I hear of anyone sniffing around with an eye toward, ah, shutting down local operations."

"As always?"

He cocked that eyebrow of his at her. "Yes, *as always.* With the exception of Klansmen, I'm pretty friendly with most everyone who might make trouble for you, and have made it clear I would prefer they leave you be."

Ellie was startled to hear this, but it made sense. She'd operated for years without a problem, whereas many others in her trade had come and gone over the years — or paid hefty bribes for the privilege of remaining in business.

"Thank you," she said awkwardly. His sardonic smile told her he had intuited exactly the mix of mortification and gratitude she was feeling about this new information. Not for the first time, Ellie wondered if he might be interested in a form of payment other than a bottle or two of liquor for his services rendered — something some other cop, in some other county, would have demanded of her a long time ago, regardless of her interest.

"Look—you know bad booze is just about the only booze I won't allow in Amityville. So if your distributor is selling you junk—"

"That's not what happened," interrupted Ellie. Jones raised that one bushy eyebrow at her, but Ellie didn't back down. "I sold those people a case of stuff that I . . ." She paused. "Let's say I acquired it somewhere along the line."

"You *acquired* it, huh?"

"Yeah. I should have known better, but . . ."

"But?"

"I was desperate."

"Desperate." Jones looked at her appraisingly. "And now?"

"Now I'm not desperate anymore."

"All right," said Jones. "But if it happens again . . ."

"It won't."

"Good. I don't want to get nervous when I drink up your profits. Speaking of . . ."

"I know for sure this one's fine," said Ellie, handing over a bottle. They'd reached his truck and were now standing in the shade cast by its cab, Cleo panting by Jones's feet. Jones tucked his take behind his back seat.

"Glad to see you're healing up," he said after turning back to her. "No fresh bruises?"

"Nah."

"So things are all right at home?"

"I wouldn't say that." She noted his increased interest, and specified, "Between me and Gabriel, sure . . . but as for my ma and my pop . . ." She sighed.

"Go on then. Tell me what happened."

"We had a fight. And . . ." She swallowed her pride. "I need your help."

"Oh?"

"More specifically, I need your truck."

"Typical."

"I'm moving out. Lester and I both are, actually, so there'll be a few boxes."

"When?"

"Sunday: I thought that would be the best time for it. My old man will be out of the house."

"Doesn't that Polack of yours have a pickup?"

"Don't call him a Polack," snapped Ellie.

Jones grinned at her. "Is that a way to talk to a man when you're asking to borrow his truck?"

Ellie wouldn't back down. "There's enough of that sort of talk going around without you joining in. My pop called Gabriel a 'foreigner' yesterday. Said I should break off the engagement and start living right."

Jones looked taken aback. "I'm sorry," he said. "I didn't know, obviously, or I wouldn't have teased you."

Ellie nodded. "I know. It's just a lot. His new pal Hunter has him saying some pretty appalling stuff, I think. And Hunter's not stopping with him—he's speaking to a crowd on Sunday. That's why I know my old man will be out of the house."

"Hunter?"

"The Reverend Joseph Hunter. Don't ask me where he preaches; I don't think he does." She frowned. "I don't like that man. That scene last night . . . I think he had something to do with it. Pop was cross at me over the bootlegging fiasco, but then he said some really horrible and insulting things about immigrants like Gabriel not being Americans and . . ." She saw the look on Jones's face. "What?"

"I'm more of an immigrant than your fiancé! I was born in Cuba, you know." Ellie was amazed—Jones sounded like any other Long Islander. "It's true. My father served in the war, and he married a Cuban woman. She died when I was little, and we moved back here."

"Oh, well, I . . ." Ellie didn't know what to say. The knowledge didn't bother her; it just surprised her. Jones had never talked about his parents to her; then again, he'd had no reason to.

"It's no problem. Sounds like it got very personal last night, and I'm . . . not personal."

She wasn't quite sure what to say to that, beyond "Thank you for understanding."

"I do. And I'll do you this favor . . . on one condition."

Ellie smiled in spite of herself. "Oh? What's the condition?"

He leaned in close to her, his lips almost brushing her earlobe. She shivered, and wondered if she'd been right—if he was interested in her, and the strange tension between them hadn't been just her imagination.

"I want you . . ."

"Yes?"

". . . to tell me everything you know about Hunter making speeches in some field."

Ellie tried not to register either surprise or disappointment. "Sure, but I don't know much. Why?"

"Because I want to go."

"Oh!" Ellie frowned. "But I'd hoped you'd help me move while he was out of the house for it . . ."

"How long could that possibly take? A few crates—you need crates?" Ellie nodded. "Fine, we've got plenty around here. How much furniture are you taking?"

"Next to none. Lester has plenty of books, though."

"That's no problem. We'll get it all and then head to the event. I just want to see what it's all about, given the climate around here of late."

Recalling what he'd said about the attacks on immigrants, Ellie felt her stomach tighten. "You don't think Hunter is involved with any of that, do you?"

Jones shrugged. "I know you want to hear me say 'of course not,' but I don't know. That's why I want to hear what he has to say."

Ellie nodded, seeing the wisdom of this—though she did wish he'd said "of course not." The idea that her father might be mixed up with a group that attacked and killed people, that attacked and terrorized *children* . . .

"All right," she said. "We'll go."

"What time?"

Ellie thought back. "He only said morning."

"Probably between ten and eleven. Why don't you meet me here at half past nine? We can head over to your folks' place and wait until they're gone."

"Won't they see us?"

Again, that eyebrow. "I'm a cop," he said patiently. "I can watch your house without being seen."

"Oh . . . right."

Jones climbed into the cab of his truck, and Cleo jumped in after him. "All right. See you then."

The engine roared to life, and Jones rattled away. It was only after Ellie had walked halfway across town, slapping at the mosquitoes that were taking advantage of the still evening air, that she realized he might have given her a lift.

GABRIEL HAD COOKED DINNER while she was out—some sort of tasty fish soup with cabbage and carrots. She and Lester did the dishes. As she washed and he wiped, her brother noticed her humming, and remarked that she seemed happy.

"Relieved maybe. Are *you* happy? I mean . . . I know you didn't want to come here . . ."

"It's all right. It was time to go." He kept wiping a dish that was already quite dry, and Ellie felt he wasn't saying what was really on his mind. Rather than press him, she waited. "I suppose I'll be leaving for good before too long anyhow."

"Not *for good*. You'll come home to visit, of course."

"Home."

Ellie wiped her hands on a towel and embraced her brother. "Wherever that is, whatever it means to you. I just want to be there."

"Of course you'll be there!"

The sounds of Gabriel's wireless drifted into the kitchen. Lester enjoyed listening to it, but when Gabriel came in to see if they might like to hear a jazz program, her brother elected to go upstairs.

"Are you sure?" said Ellie. She was worried he was leaving them alone because that's what he thought they wanted; really, she would have enjoyed his company—treasured it, knowing she'd have so much less of it in the near future.

"Come on; you'll have plenty of time to study once you get there," urged Gabriel, but Lester would not relent. He excused himself and shut the door to the second bedroom behind him.

"Proud creature," said Ellie with a sigh. "I wonder where he gets it?"

"Hmm," said Gabriel, drawing her into the living room.

Unhappy as Ellie was about her new estrangement from her family, snuggling with Gabriel on the sofa in their living room—the living room where they would live together as husband and wife—was really very nice. The space, though half-finished, already felt homey. This really would be such a nice house, with its strong walls, small private dock, well water, and garden plot. They would live happily here.

The ever-burning embers of desire for Gabriel flared up within Ellie, fierce and hot. She was just thinking of snaking her hand across his flat belly to unbutton his fly when the program playing on the wireless ended.

"The next one is pretty good, too," said Gabriel, surprising her. "Want to stay up and listen? We can sleep in tomorrow."

"That's true . . ."

"And Saturday morning," he said warmly, "and Sunday . . ."

"Oh, not Sunday," said Ellie. "I'll need to head in to town pretty early."

"For what?"

"I'm meeting Jones. He's going to help me move while Pop's at that stupid speech Hunter's giving." Ellie was just about to add that they'd peek at the speech afterward, given Jones's worries about Hunter, when she noticed Gabriel's face. "What's wrong?"

"That cop is helping you move?"

"That cop?"

Gabriel was really annoyed. "Why did you ask *him* for help?"

"He has a pickup," she said, a half-truth to save his feelings.

"I have a pickup, too, and I doubt Aaron will need it on Sunday. I could have helped you."

"I know you could have, but there's no reason for you to," she said.

"No reason!"

Confused, Ellie sat up to meet her fiancé's eyes. "What's going on?" she said. "Why are you angry?"

"I'm not angry, I'm just . . ." Gabriel resettled his thick glasses on the bridge of his nose. "Ellie, we're going to be married. We're supposed to be a team. You could let me support you."

"You *do* support me." Ellie was amazed. "Why would you think otherwise? Here I am, living in your house—"

"*Our* house!"

"Okay, *our* house. All I meant to say was that I was living here a bit ahead of schedule, and *with my brother*," she whispered this so Lester would not hear and think she meant something other than what she did, "and you have been nothing but kind about it."

"Why wouldn't I be?"

Ellie felt a flash of annoyance. "I never thought you wouldn't, but not everyone would be so generous or so accepting. I'm complimenting you."

He relaxed at this, but only a little, and he still looked troubled. "I still would have liked to know you were planning this," he said.

"All right, that's fair," said Ellie. "I'm sorry, Gabe. I just didn't in a million years think it would upset you. All I was thinking about was sparing you from more abuse if something goes wrong and Pop happens to be home."

Gabriel relaxed further. "I appreciate that, but I'd rather you'd have talked to me about it than just decided on your own."

"I understand. So, in the interest of total transparency, Jones and I were planning to load up his pickup and then go take a gander at whatever Hunter's up to. After, you can help me and Lester move in—into *our* home."

Gabriel wasn't as mollified by this as she would have liked, but he accepted it with reasonable grace. By then, the radio drama he'd wanted to listen to was starting. Ellie proposed that instead, they go to bed, hoping she could still tempt him to do something there other than sleep.

"You go on, if you're tired," he said. "I'd like to listen to this."

"Of course," she said lightly, though in truth she felt disquieted. She'd not yet gone to bed on her own in this house—*their* house—and this didn't seem like the best first time to do that. Indeed, the room seemed too empty without him; the bed, too large.

She wondered if she'd have trouble nodding off without him there, but she was so exhausted she fell asleep quickly between the cool sheets.

BECAUSE OF THE FUNNY PLACEMENT of the little saltbox, it was actually more efficient for Ellie to take her skiff to the boatyard and walk from there to the police station. As she tied up, she noticed the usual gang of regulars were clustered by the lee side of the boathouse, staring at something. One of them, Ephraim, had a hose and was spraying down the hands of a man named Matthew. Curious, Ellie wandered over.

"Ever seen anything like it?" asked Fred as she approached.

Ellie was less than pleased to see more of the oily-looking dark fungal growths clustered in the shade of the boathouse. An effort had been made to dislodge them; a trowel lay abandoned, off to the side, covered in the same foul residue that had coated Ellie's father's paper the other night, and a huge smear soiled the side of the boathouse. It looked like the fungus had exploded, and the smell of kerosene lingered in the air.

"Yeah," said Ellie, as her stomach turned over. "Nasty stuff."

"I heard one of 'em pop," said Fred. "Matthew said it felt like the juice was *burning* him, almost."

"Still does," said Matthew as water splashed over his hands. His trousers, too, bore the stains. A shame — it looked like he was already dressed for church.

"Maybe I should piss on you? Might help," said Ephraim.

"Maybe you shouldn't! Vinegar might not be a bad idea, though," said Matthew. "Damn. It's on my pants. I'll have to go back home to change, and it's a drive to Paul's farm."

"For that meeting?" asked Fred. "Why are you going to that?"

"Why aren't *you?*" countered Matthew.

"Sunday is for church," said Fred stoutly. "I'm a Methodist."

"Methodists are welcome," said Matthew.

"You said you've seen these things before? Where was that?" Ephraim asked Ellie as the two men began to bicker.

"At my folks' place, in the back yard. Gabriel's seen them too, in his — *our* — yard. He says fungicide works okay on them."

"Good to know."

With that, Ellie took her leave of them. Her business in town couldn't wait any longer.

Jones was waiting for her at the police station, leaning back against his pickup. Instead of his uniform, he was wearing plain clothes. Ellie couldn't help but let her gaze linger on how he looked in them, especially the crease of his trousers as it pulled across his thigh.

He noticed her staring, and grinned. "Considering raiding my wardrobe?" he asked, glancing at her coveralls, with the loose button-down beneath. "Just be aware, if you're thinking of stealing anything, I still write my name in the waistbands and collars."

"You walk around all day with OFFICER JONES printed on your underwear, huh? More than I needed to know." Ellie walked around the side of his truck and clambered in as he stammered a few abortive replies.

"You coming?" she called out the window as she scratched Cleo behind her pointy brown ears, much to the dog's delight.

Jones looked vaguely annoyed as he climbed in beside them, but as they drew nearer Ellie's home — or, rather, *former* home — the officer's spirits seemed to lift as her own sank. It felt wrong to abscond like a thief with what was rightfully hers.

"I'm going to park a bit up the street, and go knock on the door," said Jones, making Ellie jump in her seat — she'd been mentally far away from her present situation, even if she'd been thinking hard about it. "If no one's home, we're clear. If someone answers, I'll just say I was looking for you."

"Good plan," said Ellie.

No one answered his summons, so Ellie let them in, and in surprisingly few trips they had everything down the stairs and on the front lawn.

Jones took over when it was time to load up his pickup. "My father was a longshoreman after he got out of the navy," he said. "I was watching him pack things securely before I could walk."

"I can't believe there isn't more," she said softly, watching as Jones tied it all up with a few efficient knots. Cleo watched too; her eyes never left her master. "Our whole life, Lester and me . . . Here it is, and it all fits in your truck." She looked it over. "But probably not in my skiff. Damn."

"I can always drop you off."

"No . . . I think I'd rather go home alone tonight," she said.

Jones looked amused, but didn't argue. "How about I bring what you can't take Monday or Tuesday?"

"You're very kind, thank you," said Ellie, her face going red as tears she wouldn't let fall gathered behind her eyes. She was embarrassed by this display of emotion, but Jones didn't tease her; he put his hand on her shoulder and squeezed gently. Surprised, Ellie stiffened at his touch, and he pulled his hand away immediately, breaking their brief connection.

"It's after ten," he said gruffly. "Better get going to this what-have-you in the field."

She didn't know how to tell him that she'd been taken aback by his affection, not disgusted by it, so she just said, "Good idea."

They didn't speak much as they rattled their way to the outskirts of town, both lost in their own thoughts. Cleo sat between them, her tongue lolling, just enjoying the ride.

At least *someone* was happy.

They turned down the lane that would take them to Paul Edwards' place. There were a surprising number of automobiles parked already, and an even larger gathering of people beyond that. The crowd spilled out from under the edges of a large canvas tent; there were hundreds of people in attendance, all staring at a sort of stage in the distance, and the air, already thick with humidity and loud with insects and birdsong, seemed to tremble or hum with an angry energy, like a beehive before a swarm.

"Jesus Christ." Ellie was shocked, but the sudden drop in her clientele actually made some sense now. Clearly, Hunter's ideas were resonating with the residents of Amityville—and beyond, given the breadth of the crowd. "Look at them all."

"I wish I was surprised."

Ellie was intrigued by the bitterness in his voice. It had never occurred to her that Jones might have had a different experience of living in Amityville than she did, but clearly he had.

"Do you think it's safe?" she asked, and then felt like a coward. Thankfully, Jones didn't make any arch remarks.

"We'll keep to the back. A few other people are ambling up late, see? We won't be noticed."

Ellie wasn't sure about all that, especially since they had a dog with them. Jones plunked his hat down on her head. The band was sweaty, and it was too large for her. She peered at him from under the brim.

"Wear that," he said, "and no one will think you're anyone's daughter. As for me, well, I just have to show my face and hope everyone feels I've a right to be here. As usual."

Ellie scanned the crowd for her father as they wandered up, but the throng was so big and so overwhelmingly male that she soon gave up. Instead, she focused on the man at the front of the crowd—it wasn't Hunter, but someone in a Sunday suit who looked less like a preacher and more like a wealthy farmer. He was speaking vehemently about the need to find ways to "protect" Long Island, just as a man protects his family with locked doors and a loaded shotgun. Ellie shuddered to think about what that meant, but she was seemingly alone in that sentiment. Most of the heads in the crowd were nodding.

Eventually the man wound himself down and left the stage to thunderous applause. Ellie was feeling hot and annoyed. She wanted to get away from here—to get home to Gabriel and unpack. She didn't need to hear anything further to know all she needed to about this set.

It certainly made sense of her father's recent rhetoric. This was a volatile place, simmering from the summer sun and other, more dangerous sources of heat.

When Hunter finally took the stage the crowd went quiet except for a baby wailing desperately and incessantly in spite of the efforts of its mother to quiet it. Fans and hats waved, but people were otherwise still. Hunter stood with his eyes closed, lips pressed together into a thin, inexpressive line as he waited for a group of five men in dark suits to file up on stage behind him. One of them was his eldest son. He was unmistakable, as he looked almost uncannily like a younger version of Hunter.

As the tension reached a breaking point, Ellie saw her father. He was one of the five men standing behind the reverend. Ellie nudged Jones, jutted her chin stageward, her heart pounding. Jones saw and frowned even more deeply.

Ellie was fairly certain her father couldn't see her—from that distance she would be just another face in the crowd—but when he looked her way she was consumed by a desire to hide. She pulled her hat down low to avoid any chance of him catching a glimpse of her.

"Take it easy, Ellie," Jones muttered, and Ellie blushed, not from the heat.

"Thank you all for coming, you sons and daughters of the island." Hunter was as good a speaker to a crowd as he was in a parlor; Ellie had struggled to hear the other man who had kicked off the proceedings, but the reverend's voice came through loud and clear. "It is good to see you all today—so many of you, and from all over Suffolk County, too! I had not let myself even dream that my call would reach so far. And yet, you have heard, and what's more, you have heeded." He paused, and even from such a distance, Ellie could see his smile, could feel his gaze. "That you have come to hear me gives me courage. It gives me hope."

It did the exact opposite for Ellie, but the crowd was on Hunter's side. They hung on his every word, too enthralled to even smile.

"I am glad so many of you came out on this hot day for another reason, too. You can look around here, see the face of your neighbor—the sons and daughters, the mothers and fathers who are willing to take off the masks we are forced to wear and let our real face shine through. I am pleased to see there are so many . . . aren't you? It's hard to get the sense of the size, the strength of a movement when all of one's conversations are one-on-one or in small groups. Why, I see many of you whom I know have more family at home—that means that there are even more of us out there than it appears."

Ellie hadn't realized that her father had joined some sort of social movement; she'd thought this would be much smaller, much less informal. Preaching of the Billy Sunday sort, but more prejudiced.

"Next time, for there *will* be a next time, bring your families. Let them hear what I have to say—what people like Mr. Raleigh had to say, and any others among you who feel compelled to speak out. A young mind is supple, eager. It is fertile earth where good seeds can take hold and sprout when they are watered and nourished." Ellie rolled her eyes. Hunter had missed his true calling when he turned preacher instead of being a carnival barker. "The truth is, it is their fight too—or rather, it will be, if we do not act."

Ellie glanced over at Jones. She couldn't read his expression. He seemed highly interested in what Hunter was saying, and wasn't frowning.

"The truth is, we are sorely in need of *community* these days . . . of knowing who stands beside us, even if they don't live next door to us. Long Island's population may be growing—we may have a train to get us to the city more easily, and new roads to get us to the ends of the island more quickly than ever before . . . and yet, people are lonely. They feel isolated; they feel alone. The Great War made the world smaller, brought it closer, and yet, all that has done is made man feel insignificant, while adding to our growing sense of disconnect from the news. The word from Washington is that we live in prosperous times. And yet, most of you seem to feel as if that prosperity is not yours to share in—that you are still sweating every day working on farms or in factories or out on your boats. You feel shame that your wives work part-time, or that you have had to ask for a loan to repair your home. Your fathers and grandfathers would not have had to endure either. But do not despair, my friends. We can go back to those times, those ways—at least, I believe we can. And I also believe that if we believe together for a better future, we can change our course—be reborn in glory instead of dying, doomed and despairing. We will cleanse this island and heal it of its wounds."

Ellie's mind wandered after this—the heat of the day and her dislike of the subject leading her to daydream. But claps and cheers brought her back to the present, and she listened as Hunter declared he'd be "demonstrating" the power of belief in what was right and good.

Ellie nudged Jones. "Let's get out of here," she muttered. "I've seen enough."

"Hmm?"

"He's going to do some sort of trick. I don't need to see it."

Jones looked confused. "A trick?"

"Haven't you been listening?"

Hunter's voice boomed out over them, even louder than before. "Corrosion eats away at our community from without, and we must act to keep that from weakening us further. But there is something else that nibbles at us from within, like a cancer. Yes, I am talking about liquor. I have already spoken about its dangers, though I know that most of you don't believe me. But I will prove to you that liquor is not part of God's plan and it has no business in our homes, in our society, or in our faith. I will need a volunteer, and I see that someone perfect is in the audience today."

"I could have sworn . . ." Jones seemed queerly disoriented.

"Swear later; let's go!"

"Ellie West!"

She and Jones both stopped like Hunter had just grabbed them by their collars. She felt a cold stab of fear in her gut at the idea of answering the reverend's call; she really did not want to turn around and go up there. How had he known she was in the crowd? Or was he only calling her name on the off chance she'd showed up? Ellie glanced up at Jones, but his expression was unreadable.

"Ellie West, in the back!"

Ellie swore under her breath—he *had* seen her. Heads and eyes swiveled in her direction; mutters were exchanged. With so many eyes upon her, going up to the stage seemed safer than trying to escape.

"What do you want to do?" asked Jones, under his breath. Ellie got the sense he'd be willing to cheese it or stand their ground, but they wouldn't get far if things really got ugly—not with the pickup loaded down with all her and her brother's worldly possessions.

The hairs on the back of her neck were up, and so were her balled fists. She was poised to fight any one of them, *all* of them if necessary . . . but *would* that be necessary? Would they really grab her if she ran; drag her kicking and screaming to the stage?

Probably not . . . though Ellie couldn't say *definitely* not. Cleo wasn't pleased either; the dog was tense, her back bristling as everyone stared. Ellie had a momentary vision of how badly this could go, and decided it would be best to obey.

"Ellie, come up here. Please!" said Hunter. His tone was kindly —not that Ellie for one minute felt he had good intentions toward her.

"All right, I'm coming," she said, loudly enough that the folks around her could hear. Actually, they did back off. Perhaps they might really have gone for her, had she refused.

"I'll be right here," said Jones. He put his hand on Cleo's collar when the dog whined. Smart dog.

Getting to the stage where Hunter and his companions awaited her felt like a longer walk than it really was. She didn't look at her father as she passed him by.

"Ellie, thank you for being here today," said Hunter. He looked luminous, like the baby Jesus in a nativity scene. She did not, however, spy any of the strange specks or motes that had appeared to come forth from his mouth the last time she'd seen him, and chalked up his appearance to the glow one might get from working a crowd. "Your father did not think you would come." Ellie felt her face flush but stood up very straight. She would not slouch or cower in front of this puffed-up con man. "I asked you to join me because you are . . . *skeptical,* are you not? Of what we talked about in your parlor . . . and about temperance?"

Ellie didn't answer. Answering meant participating in his little sideshow. Hunter surprised her with a grin, though not a kindly, avuncular smile—a wolfish leer of a man challenged. Ellie crossed her arms. She wasn't having a good time, so why should he?

"Silent as Miss West may be, she will help me prove that when I say God has shown me the way to heal this island, from within and without, He has not done so without giving me the attendant ability." From beneath his pulpit, Hunter pulled an unmistakable bottle, the slosh of which was very familiar to Ellie. She just didn't usually see it out in the open among hundreds of people.

"Moonshine. White dog, hooch … Whatever you call it, this bottle contains ardent spirits." Hunter flipped the top open and held it out to Ellie. She let him hang there for a moment, but then took it grudgingly. "You agree?"

Ellie sniffed the bottle—it definitely smelled like moonshine whiskey. Not breaking eye contact with him, she took a swig and then a second, longer one, eliciting a few satisfying gasps in the audience. As she swallowed, she nodded. Hunter looked so enormously pleased by this she wondered momentarily if it had been poisoned.

He took the bottle back, and the air thickened around Ellie. Her stomach lurched to feel that too-familiar but inexplicable sensation that she'd felt on her boat, and again in her parents' parlor. As Hunter took the bottle from her, she also saw an odd flash of rainbow-hued light that was gone so quickly she couldn't be sure it had even happened.

The memory of the night she'd fainted made her shiver, though the day was hot enough that her shirt was clinging to her sweaty skin—clinging to her skin just like it had clung to her that night on the boat, when the rain had poured down on her. Ellie wanted a glass of water, wanted to sit down. She swayed on her feet as she tried to remind herself that none of these incidents had anything to do with one another, that her mind was addled and confused, but what ended up steadying her was thinking about how awful it would be to faint in front of these people.

Fortunately, when Hunter spoke again, the feeling of pressure in the air dissipated, and so did Ellie's memories. She felt more solid, more reasonable. The odd colors she'd seen must have been just the sun reflecting on the greasy liquor within.

"Miss West has no reason to lie in my favor," said Hunter. "You have only to look at her to see how little she wishes to be up here with me." Ellie stood her ground, though she felt embarrassed to be called out like this. "Never fear, I need only a few more moments of your time, Miss West. But before you go, I'd like us all to pray."

An audible sigh escaped Ellie, again bringing an amused expression to Hunter's face.

"Not for too long, Miss West," he said apologetically, setting the bottle down on the stage. "I want you all to pray with me now—silently, in your own way. Pray as I do that the scourge of liquor shall be lifted from the back of Amityville—of Suffolk County—of Long Island, and the world. Pray for deliverance from wanton ways, drunkenness, and all its attendant plagues. Pray for those who drink who would do better to be sober. Pray for the victims of crimes committed by the intoxicated."

Ellie watched him as he went on for a bit longer, and also watched the bottle. She'd seen stage magicians use misdirection to fool a crowd; perhaps sleight of hand was among Hunter's tactics. But he'd have to touch the bottle to pull some sort of switch—wouldn't he? And after setting it down on the ground he hadn't touched it again.

"Miss West," he said at last, after calling for attention. "Will you see if our prayers have had any effect?"

"You're encouraging me to drink *more?*" she asked.

No one laughed. Hunter wordlessly indicated with his hand that she ought to pick it up and take a sip.

Ellie grabbed the bottle. Sniffing it, the liquid had no nose at all, unlike before when it had the expected aroma of raw alcohol. She took an experimental sip, and spat it out in shock.

It was full of musty-tasting water—not moonshine.

The crowd gasped as one at her reaction, and started to talk among themselves.

How had he done it? Ellie would have seen it had he switched the bottle—and anyway, where would he have kept the other? It wasn't something he could secrete away easily, like a rabbit in a top hat. The pressure in the air . . . no. He had made a fool of her, somehow.

"What is it, Miss West?"

She couldn't play it off, not after that reaction. "It's . . . water," she said.

"What's that?"

Ellie took a deep breath. "It's water," she said, louder this time.

"So why did you spit it out?" asked Hunter.

"Well, it's not very *fresh* water," said Ellie.

This time, her defiance did not make him smile; it was clear he'd hoped she'd be more impressed by his display. And while in truth Ellie was more than impressed—she was disturbed, astonished, and barely keeping herself together—she still wasn't interested in being a part of his act. He took the bottle back from her and crouched down, passing it to a man in the front row.

"It *is* water. Praise the Lord!" cried the man, and passed the bottle to his neighbor, a woman in a Sunday hat.

"As you see, Ellie . . . there is power in goodness."

This, Hunter said softly, just to her. She met his eyes; they were a light golden brown and glittered like amber.

"You must have changed it out," she said.

"I changed nothing. *Faith* did." He smiled at her. "It is not too late, Ellie. Your father is here. Apologize to him; I'm sure he would allow you to move back home . . ."

"Allow! *He* ought to be begging *me* to come back." Ellie tucked her loose hair behind her ears. "Look, I gotta scram. Hope your other party tricks go as well as this one."

Ellie didn't look back at Hunter as she climbed down off the stage, but she did spare a glance for her father. He wasn't looking at her; his eyes were on Hunter. Ellie was pretty certain he'd never looked at her—or at his son, or even at his wife for that matter—with that much love in his expression.

She felt exposed and strangely ashamed as she walked along the edge of the crowd to get back to where Jones and Cleo anxiously awaited her. As soon as she reached them he nodded wordlessly at his pickup and headed in that direction. The mutt trotted ahead, seemingly even more eager to be gone from that awful field.

Only after they were bumping along toward the boatyard, and Cleo's head was in her lap, could Ellie finally speak.

"Well, that was strange."

"Yeah." He cast a look her way. "You okay?"

"In what regard?" She shook her head, the ends of her increasingly shaggy bob brushing her chin. "It *changed*, Hector. He turned booze into water. He really did it—I watched him the whole time, expecting tricks."

"I did too. Either he's the greatest stage magician in the world, or . . ."

"Or what?"

Jones shrugged. "Or he really changed it."

Ellie briefly considered telling him about her various experiences over the past few weeks, but decided against it. She'd sound insane if she reported feeling the air "tighten" or having seen rainbow spores pour from a man's mouth.

It would also mean telling him about the man she'd killed.

"Come on," she said, playing it off. "You don't really think we just saw *magic*, do you?"

"Could be" was Jones's reply, which set Ellie sweating again. "You saw what you saw, as did I. And I don't like the way I lost track of things . . . That felt odd." He shook his head as he turned onto Ketcham Avenue. "Regardless, I didn't like the sound of what Hunter had to say before my mind wandered. Your father's friend has decided he knows who ought to live here, and who ought to go somewhere else. I've heard it all before, though his language was more esoteric, I guess. The idea of making Long Island into an oasis in the scorching desert, or an island in a stormy sea where people can feel safe . . . a moon hanging above the poisoned earth . . ."

"Poisoned earth!"

"Yes, seems as if that's my fault. My service in the Great War and my service to the town don't make up for being a corrupting foreigner," said Jones wryly as the boatyard came into sight.

No wonder Ellie's father was so steamed up, if this was what he was listening to. She shook her head.

"I'm sorry you had to hear that. It's not true."

"I don't need you to tell me that. I fought for this country, and now I serve it every day—even, obviously, on Sunday."

They'd arrived. Ellie sat for a moment, not sure what to say. There was a flintiness behind Jones's words she'd not heard before; she didn't quite believe that the policeman was as unaffected as he claimed, and she couldn't blame him.

"He mentioned masks, too," said Jones.

"Masks?"

"He said at the start that it was good to take off masks to let your face be seen. Remember? Those attacks, that kid who survived . . . The nurses said he'd had nightmares about masked men." Ellie opened her mouth, anxious to believe there wasn't any connection, but Jones held up his hand. "I'm just considering possibilities. That's enough for me to get interested, and if I get more interested . . . well then, we'll see what needs to be done."

They started unloading his pickup into her skiff in uncomfortable silence, sifting through it all to make sure she had everything she and Lester might need immediately.

"I'll bring the rest by soon," he said as they repacked the remainder.

"I'll just come by and—"

"It's no trouble," he said. "I was planning to drop by anyway. I have something of yours — the booze I salvaged from that party. I ought not to give it to you, given that some of it's tainted . . ."

"I know which bottles they'd be."

"I figured you would. Well, it's yours. I'll bring it by sometime later this week . . . and see how you're settling in."

"Why, Officer Jones, are you finding excuses to check up on me?" Ellie jumped aboard. Cleo barked at her, and she waved at the dog. "You might as well eat if you're stopping by — name a day and I'll tell Gabriel to make pierogi."

"If it's all the same to you, I'll just drop everything off some evening after work." The coolness of his tone surprised her, until he winked at her from the shore. "Don't worry; it'll be soon. If the feds get a wild hair to conduct a raid, I'd rather it all be in your basement than mine."

Ellie's skiff sat low in the water and her heart low in her chest as she made her way home. Then the bungalow came into view, and Gabriel came out as she tied up, and she leaped onto the dock to embrace him.

"I'm moving in, if that's all right with you," she said, and kissed him. He kissed her back, and in that moment, everything felt like it would be all right. His touch was so familiar, so understandable and human and urgent and normal, that Ellie was quite certain that nothing strange or uncanny could ever trouble them while they were together.

3

THE ARROW HIT INSIDE the gold circle at the center of the target, but the moment it sank into the straw Fin felt the vision lapping at the edges of her mind like an oily sea on some incomprehensible shore. She practiced the breathing she'd learned in school, tried to clear her mind as she nocked another out of the handful she held as she ran, focusing on her body, on her target, but she could not fully push away the memory of what she'd seen. Even so, she kept at it; the familiar feel of her shoulders sliding down away from her ears, the tension across her chest as she drew, the feel of the string against her thumb, the twang of the release were all that she could count on since that night.

A few more arrows in her hand, Fin hopped up onto a bale of hay, trying to stay light on her feet. The breeze kicked up, making the grass of the lawn rustle like crinoline; she corrected her angle and let go. This time she hit even closer to the center of the gold, but she didn't pause to admire it. She had more arrows in her hand, and far too many thoughts to keep from her mind.

Fin had moved her archery range right into the center of the back lawn, and set it up with hay bales and other obstacles in order to do dynamic, combat-focused target practice. The light was better there anyway, and the space broad enough that she could work up a sweat running between targets. Simple archery practice had not been enough to keep her mind empty; she needed the extra bulwarks of where to put her feet, how to maneuver around obstacles, the changing angle of the sun.

Plus, she had set it all up while the rest of her entourage were away somewhere, and it had been hilarious when they'd returned. She'd actually laughed at the confusion on Jimmy's face, the annoyance and exasperation on Bobbie's . . . Edgar's amusement had been surprising, but she'd drunk it all in, thirsty for it. It wasn't that she wanted to inconvenience them. She just wanted to be seen.

Bobbie hadn't spoken to her since the night of the party. She blamed Fin for its chaotic, premature, and embarrassing ending—and also for being the cause of the problem to begin with. After all, Fin had been the one who'd bought the moonshine, who had insisted they should have it at the party at all. That made it all her fault, to Bobbie's mind, and of course Lily and Duke had agreed. While it was true that neither of them had ever had much to say to Fin, the silent treatment was exhausting even from people she'd rather not talk to.

Fin, for her part, had apologized—*profusely*—for inadvertently procuring the liquor that had induced the hallucinations, but she would not agree that the liquor itself had been tainted. At least not with methanol or some other poison.

What she'd seen hadn't been a hallucination.

It had been a vision.

Fin's companions wouldn't even consider the idea that something other than bad booze could have caused the fits experienced by a handful of their guests and one very unhappy ukulele player. They were more worried about what the neighbors were saying now that it was known that they were the sorts of cheapskates who would bring in a live musical act, but wouldn't spring for quality hooch.

Not Fin. She could tell the difference between dreams and reality—and what she'd seen had been *real*. She was sure of that—more sure than she was about the viability of her marriage to Jimmy, or why on earth she was staying in a house where her presence was barely tolerated by people who disliked her.

It bothered her that they didn't believe her. None of them had seen what she had, true, but their doubt was nevertheless an insult. Even if the other partygoers subscribed to the theory that poor-quality liquor had been the source of their troubles, there was no reason for Fin to lie about what had happened to her; at least, not as regards to it feeling—no, *being*—real.

She ducked behind a lawn chair she'd set up as an obstacle, crouching low and angling carefully, but her concentration had slipped. The bow twanged as she fumbled her shot; the arrow hit next to her foot. Fin sucked her teeth in annoyance.

Ever since that night she'd felt like a cracked vase that someone had turned to the wall to hide the damage; like a tree chopped nearly through and then abandoned, alone and in danger from every gust of wind. In the absence of support she'd had to turn inward.

Archery helped, but she could only do it so much. Reading, which had always been her other retreat, was of no use. Now that she'd drowned, at least in her mind, her collection of books about the sea were anathema to her, and none of the rest of what she'd brought with her could hold her attention for long. The words blurred together, forming roiling mounds of fur, waves of dull scales, and pools of liquid iridescent light that flowed like lava.

That wasn't even the worst part. The worst part was the terrible desire she'd felt emanating from that thing in the woods, the determination to destroy—no, to remake the world into something else entirely, something fecund and feral, more alien than the moon.

The man in the robe hadn't been dropping a bomb.

He'd been serving a master.

It had been a mistake to tell Jimmy about the vision, but she'd been frightened, and had wanted to feel like someone was on her side as she sat, shivering, wrapped in a blanket, disoriented by the trails bright lights left in her vision as she waited to be questioned by the rather mercurial local police officer who had shown up on the scene. She should have known Jimmy couldn't offer her any such solace.

Her next arrow hit well outside the blue border of the target. Two arrows left, she headed back across the range toward the stand to grab some more.

Chatting with Officer Jones had been more comforting than speaking with her husband, though Jones's dog had played a large part in that. The prick-eared mongrel with a fox's face had sniffed her hands before submitting to being petted, but eventually the dog had settled in, and so had Fin.

It wasn't such a bad conversation, either, even if Jones had laughed in her face when she claimed she hadn't been drinking alcohol and had no idea where any booze at the party might have come from. Eventually he revealed Bobbie had already given him Ellie's name, but when Fin went pale and started to stammer, all he'd done was commend her for protecting a friend. "Shows a good deal of loyalty," he'd said, while scribbling in a little book.

Her next arrow, though she fired while jumping down off the seat of a lawn chair, hit dead center within the gold circle.

"Kid?"

Fin fired her final arrow, hitting the gold again. Only then did she look at her husband. He was standing off to the side of the range, his hands behind his back. He didn't look particularly at his ease, but his tone when he spoke was horribly jovial.

"Hey," he said. "What'cha doing out here?"

If it hadn't been Jimmy Fin would have suspected him of asking her some sort of trick question. She stared at him, unsure what to say. She was sweating; she could feel it trickling down her body from under her arms and breasts, and she was still holding her bow, if not her arrows.

"I mean, I can see what you're doing, but . . ." He produced from behind him a cocktail shaker, its metal exterior frosted and dewy in the heat, and a small picnic basket with a blindingly white cloth peeking out invitingly. "Wanna take a break for a minute? I've got gin in the shaker with some ice, and a bottle of tonic . . . some caviar and dill cream and some sandwiches, and I think maybe a piece of cake?"

In *The Ginger-Eaters,* the girl made her pact with the demon willingly, and having been advised of the consequences of her choice. Even so, she failed to predict all the ways it would change her—one being a massive and overwhelming sense of alienation. Her secret knowledge made her view the world differently. What secrets did other people keep? What else was not as it seemed?

Fin understood that better now that she'd experienced something that had changed her relationship to the world. It seemed impossible that her husband could come out with a picnic basket and invite her to eat caviar and cake and drink cold gin as she struggled to keep a vision of the nightmare apocalypse from her mind.

Caviar did sound nice, though. Fin's stomach rumbled.

She retrieved her arrows before joining Jimmy at the edge of the lawn, where he'd spread out a blanket. It was undeniably sweet of him to bring out a picnic so they could eat a meal together, alone. She couldn't remember the last time they'd done anything so pleasant, just the two of them.

He didn't say much at first, just poured her a drink to sip as they tucked into the light meal. The cool, salty caviar and sweet white cake were both delicious, but Fin was hungry for more than food. The unforced, quiet companionship was nourishing her soul.

"Fin—kid—I've been worried about you." Jimmy took a pull on his second gin and tonic as Fin continued to nibble at her cake. "I think you're really taking it a little hard, what happened at the party."

His words spoiled the illusion. She looked at him coolly but just kept chewing. She had seen a vision of Long Island destroyed incomprehensibly at the behest of some unknowable monstrosity, and he felt she was taking that *a little hard?*

"I know it's embarrassing, and that article in the paper didn't help." He had the decency to blush as he made reference to that trash reporter who had not just exposed them, but described Fin as Jimmy's sister, not his wife. "But clinging to this wild story about some kind of volcano, and—"

"Not a volcano."

"Well, whatever it was, you have to see how sticking to your guns is just making it worse for you, right?"

It *was* making it worse for her; that was true. More than once Fin had wondered if she should apologize, say it had all been a big story . . . but she couldn't bring herself to do that.

"The only thing I'm clinging to is the truth," she said evenly.

Jimmy looked really worried. "Fin, people think you've cracked up." He rubbed the back of his neck. "I dunno. Do you wanna talk to a psychoanalyst, maybe? One of our neighbors sees some Jew in the city, says it does him a lot of good ever since his wife, uh . . ." Jimmy trailed off.

"His wife . . . ?"

"Oh, she left him."

The silence after he said this was louder than the buzzing cicadas.

"What does him being a Jew have to do with it?" she asked.

"Oh, come off it," said Jimmy, finally snapping. "You know what I mean."

"I'm not sure I do. All I know is that this doctor is a Jew, but that doesn't seem to be your point. Are you trying to say you're thinking of leaving me?"

"Leaving you?" Jimmy stared at her. He looked confused, but also guilty. "Why would you think that?"

Fin refrained from saying anything sarcastic, a herculean effort with the gin in her system. Instead, she said, "Regardless, I don't think I need to see a psychoanalyst."

"But—"

"But nothing. Unless they put me in shock therapy to zap out my brains, no amount of talking is going to convince me you're right and I'm wrong. I know what I saw."

"Jesus Christ, what a thing to say," said Jimmy. "Is that really the way you feel?"

She nodded, and Jimmy stood up, suddenly agitated.

"Everybody's been saying we should move. I wasn't sure at first, with you being so . . . so . . . *disturbed* and all, but I'm starting to see their point," said Jimmy. "A change of scenery might be good for us all."

This brought Fin up short. "Move?"

"Yeah." Jimmy's eyes darted to the hay bales and then back to Fin. "We were already talking about going to Lisbon in the fall. Why not beat the crowd and go now?"

Fin had spent the last few days doing her best to avoid thinking about what she'd seen—what it meant. For whatever reason, the idea of moving made it clear to her that she couldn't just sit around, avoiding the problem.

She had to *do* something about it.

"No," she said. "I want to stay."

He stared at her. "But why?" He seemed astonished. "There's nothing for us here anymore, not after . . . well . . ." He looked embarrassed again. "After the party. We haven't been invited anywhere since, and there's no reason for anyone to come visit us. We're pariahs, and none of us came to Long Island to sit at home all the damn time."

"There's plenty to do here. It's not all parties . . . We could go camping on Shelter Island, or—"

"You want us to stay here to go *camping?* Have you ever even been camping?"

"Not since I was a girl, no . . ."

"You know, Fin, ever since we moved out here, you've been different. And not in a good way." Jimmy's voice was low, intense.

"What do you mean by that?"

"I mean that you used to be a pretty fun girl, but out here you've been ... distant, withdrawn. Either you've got your nose stuck in some stupid book of poetry by a guy nobody ever heard of, or you're sneaking out to take the Ford to places nobody would ever want to go. I was wondering if you had a lover there for a while, but when the chauffeur mentioned that the car's undercarriage was muddy all the time, I just got real confused. You don't seem the type to carry on with some Irish hunter-trapper."

Fin thought about poor Koa. "I wasn't having an affair when I took the car," she said truthfully. "This place, this island—it's just so beautiful. Not the people or the houses, though I do mean them too, after a fashion, but what I mean is more the shoreline and the woods and the fields, the different birds, and the insects and the ..."

"When did you become such a naturalist?" demanded Jimmy. "You've never in your life cared about birds and the shoreline and all that crap. Is this some new cause of yours, since this isn't really the place to host charity events?"

"No—there's just something about this place," she murmured, all the fight going out of her as the memory of the vision loomed large in her mind. She had seen a lot of Long Island in a relatively short time, it was true, but she felt she could spend years here and never truly appreciate the magnitude of its beauty. It was all going to go away, too, unless somebody did something. Unless *she* did something.

"There'll be some kind of something about other places, too."

"But this one's in danger, and I have to try to do something about it."

Jimmy scoffed at her, and Fin felt it like a slap. "Come on, Fin! We were finally getting somewhere in this conversation, and you had to go and bring up that *nonsense* again."

"It's not nonsense, Jimmy. Look, ask yourself this: What purpose would it serve to tell you that I'd had a vision if I hadn't? You think I should be locked up in a loony bin because of it, so why would I keep saying I saw a vision unless I really and truly believed it?"

Jimmy apparently didn't have an answer to that, so he shrugged irritably, as if there must be some sort of explanation they simply weren't considering.

"I have to stay because I have to try to figure out what I saw," she said. "Ignoring this won't make it go away." She realized the same could be said about their marriage, but before she could say that, he sighed.

"I don't know, kid."

"You don't know *what?*"

"I don't know . . . Jesus! You always did like to make things difficult, didn't you?" He said it bitterly, and stalked up to the house without another word. Fin watched him go, but didn't call to him.

She began to clean up her archery gear. More practice didn't excite her now that she'd realized that distraction wasn't enough. She needed to act—to look at this enormous, impossible problem head-on.

The problem was, she had no real understanding of what had happened to her, much less how to stop what she'd seen from coming true. No one even believed her.

At least, no one she'd told . . . *yet.* There might be someone who would.

Fin thought over who she might possibly confide in. She didn't like the idea of going straight to the police. She might end up institutionalized if she went to a cop, even that cop with the dog who'd interrogated her. No, she needed to talk to someone local . . . and the more she thought about it, the more she realized the person she should talk to about it all was the last person in the world who'd want to have another conversation with her.

Fin would appeal to Ellie's sense of honor—the same pride

that had led her to be furious about being given a tip. She'd sold Fin the weird booze that had caused all of this; she had some responsibility here. If she put it that way to her, Fin was sure Ellie would talk. But in order to talk, Fin had to find her.

Well, she had to start somewhere. Hunting down Ellie seemed as good a place as any.

4

ELLIE'S FATHER HAD LIED about his age in order to fight for his country, but unlike most who'd done so, Robert West had claimed to be a younger man. It had worked; he had been a big strong fellow in his prime, and the recruiter over in Nassau County knew just how early most baymen's faces became weathered from all the sun and salt.

Many men would have been relieved to be too old to go to war, but Robert West couldn't stomach the idea of sitting down when others were standing up. Unfortunately, soon after joining the 152nd at Camp Upton, a training accident sent him home a cripple before he even left the state of New York. Though discharged honorably, he left without the distinction of having been wounded in the line of duty.

Ellie remembered the day her father had enlisted—and the day, not long after, when he'd returned home. Her mother had cried on both occasions, but Ellie had not. She'd been unable to speak, to move, to even dare to feel. She remembered thinking that if she kept very still, didn't blink or breathe, time would not move forward—that things would remain as they were in that moment, forever; that no further change could happen. But of course, just like the tides her breath had come back, and her mother had moved or her father had spoken, and all Ellie could do was carry on, wondering how on earth anything could be normal again. The first time, it had been the idea of living without her father that had paralyzed her; the second, living with a man who looked and sounded like Robert West, but was missing some crucial part of his spirit.

What she'd eventually come to understand was that normal was flexible—if you performed it, you lived it. Ellie, her mother, and her brother had quickly settled into a routine without Pop in the house, and another when he came back. Soon, it was hard to remember they'd ever had a different way of living together.

Moving in with Gabriel was similar. Sure, she'd spent the night with Gabriel before, sometimes two or even three nights in a row, but always there had been the expectation she'd be leaving—that she'd "go home," and that home was somewhere else. Now that wasn't the case, which was strange to begin with, but also because Lester was there with them.

But once Ellie got her clothes into the closet, her books on the shelves, her skiff tied up at the dock—once they started all acting like this was normal—well, it *was* normal. Better than normal, in fact. She and Gabriel became easier with one another than they had been in a good long while; Ellie being settled in the house seemed to make him feel like they were finally partners. It was nice to see Lester studying at the kitchen table, instead of in his room as he had back at home. They all ate together most evenings, and afterward they listened to Gabriel's wireless, or played Parcheesi or cards.

Gabriel had installed a porch swing so they could enjoy what breeze they could catch through the mosquito bar. It was awfully romantic, and one fine hot night, after Lester went to bed, Ellie blew out the hurricane lantern and began to kiss her way down Gabriel's chest.

"What are you up to, I wonder," he said softly, though the gentle pressure of his hand on the back of her head to go lower showed her that they were of one mind. Matters were progressing nicely when the sharp snap of a twig off to her left made her stop short.

"Hey," he said plaintively, when she did more than pause for a breath. "I was just—"

"*Shh,*" she said softy as she heard another crack from the wood at the edges of their property. Gabriel heard that one, too.

It wasn't a deer or a bear out there; neither would pause breathlessly after making a sound. It might be a panther, but Ellie had heard enough big cats stalking around over the years that she didn't hold out much hope the sound had come from a predator on the hunt. At least, not an animal one.

The night had gone quiet. Something was definitely out there.

A riotous explosion of every color in the world lit the night, quickly resolving into the pure orange light of flickering flame. The sweat that broke out under Ellie's arms, across her shoulders, and under her nose turned clammy quickly in the evening breeze. She knew she couldn't afford to be afraid, couldn't afford to give in to the touch of madness that had not faded like the bruises she'd acquired that night on Greene's boat, so she leaped off Gabriel and was out of the screened-in area of the porch before a second dazzling blaze appeared just off to her left. This time, beforehand, she felt that telltale thickening of the air.

Gabriel trotted up beside her still buttoning up his fly, and that made for such a bizarre contrast with the danger that Ellie wrested back some precious control just by holding back a giggle. She sobered when a third fire erupted in the middle of the driveway directly in front of her, without anyone around to light it. A fourth flared to life, but worst was the fifth; the flames burst into existence behind them at the base of the front porch steps. Whoever was out there in the night must have set it all up beforehand for effect; there was no way anyone could have gotten behind them so quickly, and Ellie knew for a fact that she hadn't stumbled over some pile of wood and kindling when she rushed out here.

She turned and saw she was right. There was no wood, no tinder. The bare earth was burning—impossibly, but she could not deny the geyser of flame spouting out of the earth.

However it was happening—however it had been done, rational explanation or otherwise—Ellie and Gabriel were surrounded, and by more than just fire. She still couldn't see anyone in the darkness, couldn't hear over the cracking and popping of the fires. Gabriel grabbed her hand and squeezed it, and she looked up at him—his eyes were wide and darting from gout to gout. He was frightened. She squeezed back, trying to reassure him—of what, though, she did not know, as they were outside, away from their house, without so much as a pocketknife to defend themselves against whatever might be out there in the night.

She startled when at last something moved in the impossible darkness behind the fires, and then another something, in a different location. They moved like men, but when one darted through a puddle of uncanny firelight she saw they did not look like men. The shape of their heads was very wrong.

"Why won't they come out?" Gabriel pushed his glasses up his nose with his finger.

As if they had heard him, one of their number stepped forward. He didn't come into the ring of firelight, but stood just outside of it, illuminated by it. It was just a man, after all—a man in a long brown cloak and a round, flat mask that looked like the sun. No, not like the sun—as Ellie studied it, it shifted and looked more like the moon, then like a wheel, and then a coin. It didn't change shape or color or size, and yet the changes were real; Ellie couldn't *see* them, not exactly; it was more like she could *feel* them. The nature of the mask was changing before her. Her mind rebelled from the idea that she was witnessing something supernatural, but at the same time, she knew there could be no rational explanation for what she was seeing.

"Hail!" The masked man was solemn, deadly serious, with a deep and powerful voice more like the sea's rumble than a man's speech. He raised his hand, one finger extended, pointing at Gabriel. "We would parley with you."

"Oh?" Gabriel sounded almost amused. "Well, go on. Parley away."

"You dare mock us, parasite?"

Ellie was furious. She started toward the man, but Gabriel would not let go of her hand.

"Who are you to call someone a parasite when you're out here just like a mosquito, bothering decent people late at night?"

"Our business is with the man who stands behind you, child." Toward her, he sounded somewhat more benevolent, but it was still the voice of a disapproving god.

"Is this some kind of royal 'we'?" asked Gabriel. Incredibly, his voice was steadier than hers.

"There are no kings here, only men, but we are in agreement, speaking with one voice," said the man sternly.

"Great, but how many others do you have out there who agree with you? It's hard to tell," said Ellie.

"Oh, who can say? The number changes daily, and not all whom we speak for could attend this meeting."

"Meeting? That's what you're calling this?" Gabriel was one hell of a stoic. He was so self-assured, so cool in the face of absolute madness.

"What else would it be?"

"I don't really associate intimidation and chicanery with *meetings*, but here we all are."

"We are here because you are here."

"No, we're here because it's late into the evening, and you've snuck up on me and my bride-to-be, and set a bunch of fires on my property."

"Your property," said the man in the mask thoughtfully. "Is a flea's roost on a dog's back its property? I suppose it would depend whether you asked the flea or the dog . . ."

"Who *are* you people?" snapped Ellie. She knew this man wouldn't provide a list of names and home addresses, but she was tired of this palaver. With his mask and his rhetoric this man sounded dismayingly similar to Hunter . . . or her father.

"We are Long Islanders," said the man. His mask now looked

like a plate before switching to a drum. "We love this island, and we love its history. We love its people, and we want to ensure its unique civilization is allowed to continue—no, more than that. That it is allowed, *encouraged* to thrive."

"Sure," said Gabriel, squeezing Ellie's hand again when she opened her mouth. "Sounds like we're not so different, you and I."

"Oh, but we are," said the man.

Arms closed around Ellie, pulling her away from Gabriel. She cried out as she and her fiancé were ripped apart, and struggled out of her attacker's strangely warm grasp for only a moment before a second man grabbed her. With two of them restraining her she could not break free.

For his part, Gabriel had been detained at the center of the ring, but not so gently—he was now on the ground. Another man in a cloak, his mask a triangle, held Gabriel's arms above his head; the other, in a square mask, sat on his chest, keeping Gabriel on his back with intermittent punches, first to his ribs, then to his jaw.

"Stop!" cried Ellie, thrashing but to no avail. "Let us go!"

The air around her tightened again, and she looked to the man in the round mask. The skin of his hands and the face of his mask seemed to glow a bit, and Ellie could have sworn she saw a little puff of those bright motes in the firelight, sparks of blue and gold and pink against the orange.

Either she was going insane, or Hunter, Greene, and these men were all tied together somehow. She didn't like either notion.

"Peace, child," said the man in the round mask.

"*You're* calling for peace?"

She couldn't see his face, but his body language told her he was surprised. Hunter had seemed surprised by her sass, too. What, she wondered, was so shocking? She knew she wasn't the only woman in the world who back-talked men.

"Gag her," he said to her captors. One hand of four let go of her, and then a leather wallet was jammed into her mouth.

"Finally, we can speak in peace." The man turned back to her fiancé. "Gabriel Waldemar Lobasz," he said, as Gabriel gasped on the ground, "it is said that you, a Pole, think you belong here, in America — and have gone so far as to buy land, and own a business here. You've already admitted the former — you have claimed part of this island as your own. As to the latter, do you deny that you are a thief who robs this island of her white oaks and her pines just to sell them to real Long Islanders — at a profit to yourself and a Negro in your employ?"

"I'm a carpenter," said Gabriel.

"And you have seduced a woman whose roots go deep into this island's soil and dared to claim her as your own, too," said the leader of the mob as one of his assistants punched Gabriel in the stomach.

"She — asked *me* out," he gasped.

"She did?" The man in the round mask seemed annoyed by this. "I don't know why I'm so surprised. We are, after all, speaking of a woman who murdered a man in the night and stole his property. Her association with you has led to degeneracy."

Ellie went still. The man in the round mask knew about Greene. And now Gabriel did, too. She saw her fiancé staring at her in the firelight, begging her with his eyes to deny what the man had said. She looked away, ashamed.

If they knew about Greene, he must have been part of this strange group. And if they were sore about her stealing the moonshine, that must have been theirs, too.

She thought back to that night on the boat, in the storm — remembered what she had seen, Greene's bright eyes, his steaming skin, his spit that dripped red, gold, and pink . . . She wasn't mad. She hadn't been seeing what wasn't there. She'd been seeing too clearly what was.

There was a strange sense of relief that came with the horror of finally accepting the truth. These men — Greene, the ones here tonight, and Hunter, too — they did have some strange and supernatural power. She wondered if they would kill her to avenge their lost comrade, or just interrogate her.

"Ah, little wayward one," sighed the leader, shaking his head as his mask took on the appearance of a button. "Will you not go home? You could still atone for your sins, live righteously . . ."

"Mmph," said Ellie.

"Ungag her," said the man in the round mask.

The wallet was pulled unceremoniously from between her teeth.

"It's no business of yours where I go, or how I live," she said, after spitting. "You're not —" She paused before saying *my father;* she did not think he was, but she hated that she couldn't say for sure that he wasn't one of the others. Saying his name felt like summoning him, and she didn't want him to be here, so she settled on "You're not the boss of me."

"It is the business of all justice-minded citizens when someone in their community steals and kills," said the man in the mask. Then with delicious irony he added, "Murder and theft are illegal."

"So's making and distributing moonshine — and that moonshine was yours, wasn't it? That's why you care."

"Whatever you took, or from whom, the point is it didn't belong to you," said the man waspishly. "That you murdered a man for it and then sold it for a profit is monstrous." She had nothing smart to say back to that; even if it wasn't the truth, it was close to it.

The man in the round mask produced an unlit torch, seemingly from nowhere, then lit it on the jet of flame closest to the house.

"We are an organization dedicated to bringing order back to this island," said the man. "We do what we can to right wrongs, to balance the scales, to see good laws bolstered and bad laws struck down . . . or circumvented. Long Island need not suffer while outsiders decide to change who we are and what we value."

"Nobody put you in charge!" Ellie twisted in her captors' grasp, but they would not let go. "What makes you the person who gets to decide what Long Island is or isn't?"

"Daughter of the island, you and I are kin by virtue of our connection to this place. This man with whom you sully yourself is not. He is an expression of corruption, like a canker or a pustule."

That phrase, "daughter of the island"—she'd heard it before . . . at Hunter's tent revival. That's what he'd called them all: mothers and fathers, sons and daughters of the island.

For some reason, that phrase solidified for her what she'd so far failed—or been unwilling—to accept. Her father was mixed up with a group of people who not only had an axe to grind with society, but who had the power to perform strange miracles.

But that wasn't right either—he wasn't just mixed up with them. He hadn't merely been in the audience that day; he'd been on the stage, right behind Hunter. Perhaps he was one of their masked assailants tonight. She hadn't noticed any of them limping, but night was good for playing tricks on the eyes.

"I'm no kin of yours," growled Ellie, almost hoping her father was there to hear her. "So do what you're going to do to me, and get out of my face."

"Do to you! We'll do nothing to *you*. We're not savages. We want you to go home." Ellie stared at him in disbelief. "If that seems a lenient sentence, you are correct. Our goal is to strengthen our community, not to tear it apart. You could be a valuable asset to us and our cause, and frankly, your victim was a traitor to us. He turned on us, *stole* from us . . . You did us a favor by dispatching him before he could do more damage." Ellie's eyes flickered to Gabriel, who still looked horrified by all of this. "Oh, didn't she tell you? No matter. She'll be leaving you soon anyway, if she knows what's good for her . . . and for you."

The threat needed no further explanation. Ellie shivered in the grip of the two men who held her, finally feeling defeated. Her father, in league with these bullies—her crime, announced callously to the one from whom she'd most longed to keep it—inexplicable masks and rainbow fires bleeding into her life as the man she'd killed had bled out into the rainwater collecting in his boat.

"It is time to make you understand that we are serious." The man in the round mask turned to the men restraining Gabriel. "Work him over," he said dispassionately. "I'm going to torch the house."

"No!" screamed Ellie as the man atop Gabriel punched him in the nose, breaking his glasses—the expensive ones they'd gone into New York City to get so he could read his pulp magazines more easily. But as the man wound up for a second strike, the front door banged open.

All eyes swiveled toward the house, and Ellie cried out again at the sight of her brother. He was holding Gabriel's old shotgun in his trembling hands.

5

G O AWAY," SAID LESTER, in his slight tenor. "Leave them be, or I shoot."

The man in the mask lowered his torch. "Put down that—"

"Go away. Get off this property and go."

"Lester, go back inside!" Ellie was proud of her brother, but he didn't know who they were dealing with.

"Listen to your sister, young man," said the man in the mask.

Lester kept the gun trained on him. "Tell them to let Gabriel and my sister go, or I'll shoot."

Ellie's breath caught in her throat. Her brother had once asked her if fish felt pain when she caught them. He was a gentle soul who wanted to save lives, not take them. Seeing him like this broke her heart.

"You won't shoot me," said the man in the mask. He did not call off his cohorts.

A terrible stalemate descended. Ellie was trying to figure out what to do next when a pickup suddenly roared up the driveway, headlights blindingly bright against the raging orange of the flames.

"Don't be seen!" cried the leader, and Ellie was dropped unceremoniously to the earth by her jailers, who then ran for it into the woods along with the others. Officer Jones was out of his truck the moment it came to a stop, but he was too late—the masked men were gone, and their otherworldly flames with them. In the sudden blinding dark, no one seemed to think it was a good idea to follow them.

No one except Cleo, who bounded out of the cab of Jones's truck and raced off into the woods.

"Cleo! Get back here!" shouted Jones, his service pistol still in his hand. *"Cleo!"*

A long moment spent listening to rustling in the underbrush ended with the sound of a bark, followed by the report of a handgun, very loud in the darkness, and a sickening yelp.

"Cleo!" Officer Jones rushed off into the woods in the direction of that awful sound.

Ellie's foremost concern was for Gabriel, who was fumbling with his glasses, trying to settle them on his face though the nosepiece was snapped and one lens was cracked.

"Are you all right?" she asked, gently touching his side where they'd punched his ribs.

"I'll live," he said, but he didn't look at her. Ellie, nervous, started to talk to cover the awkwardness.

"Me too. I'll have some bruises. I was trying to get loose, but—"

"I saw." Gabriel seemed so distant, so hostile.

"Ellie," Lester called out.

Her brother was standing over them now, still holding the shotgun. She followed his gaze and saw Jones returning, a small, limp body in his arms.

The dog was dead; that was clear enough. Regardless, Ellie got to her feet and rushed over.

"Bastards," said Jones, his voice thick. The cab door of his truck was still open where he'd neglected to close it—he put Cleo inside, on the seat where she would have ridden had she still been alive, and then shut it gently, as if she might run away again.

"How did you know?" asked Ellie, after a moment. "I mean, how did you know we were being . . . bothered?" she finished lamely.

"I didn't." Jones pointed his thumb at the bed of his pickup. He had a tarp over it all, but she could tell her belongings and a few cases of liquor were hidden beneath it. "I was in the neighborhood, so I thought I'd drop these off."

"Well ..." It seemed wrong, for some reason, to say she was grateful he'd showed up, given his loss, but she had to acknowledge his help. "Thank you. They were going to burn the house, and ... and other things."

"Happy to help."

Ellie flinched. "Do you ... I don't know ... want to come in? Have a coffee, or a drink? I don't know what to say, honestly."

"No. Wait—yes." He looked at her, and then looked to where Gabriel and Lester were standing. "Maybe. You sure?"

Ellie wasn't ready for Jones to depart for a number of reasons, including that she figured no matter how upset Gabriel was about ... well, *everything,* he'd be loath to bring up the fact that his fiancée had murdered a man in front of a cop. Another few minutes when she wouldn't have to talk about that with him seemed like grace.

"It's no problem," she said, with more certainty than she felt. "But first we'd better get all the booze inside, at the very least, just in case ... you know ..."

"What, afraid of an unexpected visit by the police?"

Ellie was amazed at him, making jokes at a time like this. She was more than a little impressed by his toughness, and looked away, blushing, when he raised his eyebrow at her. She must have had a strange look on her face.

"Let me just go tell Lester and Gabriel." Ellie turned, and saw Lester trying to dab at Gabriel's bruised and bloodied face with one hand as he held a lantern with the other. Why those fools didn't just go inside she couldn't guess, until she saw Gabriel glance over at where she was standing with Jones. His expression was not welcoming, and Ellie wasn't the only one who noticed.

Jones cleared his throat. With a start, Ellie realized she and Jones were the same height, or just about—standing face-to-face she looked him in the eye, not up at him, like she did with Gabriel. She'd never noticed it before, but that sudden spark of physical connection ignited a psychic one—she knew what he was going to say before he said it.

"On second thought, maybe I should hit the road. I'd really rather just mix myself a strong one once I'm home. And speaking of . . ." He walked around the side of the truck and handed Ellie a crate full of Lester's books. She set it down, receiving several more of these as well as a few other few items from her home, and then the moonshine.

"Thanks," she said.

"Just don't resell any of the bad stuff, all right?"

Normally Ellie would have said something smart back at him, but she just replied, "Okay."

"Thanks."

"Hey . . . Hector . . ."

He'd been eyeing the door to his truck. "Hmm?"

"The men here tonight . . . they called me 'daughter of the is-land.'" She wanted to tell him what she had experienced in regards to their ability to change reality, but she couldn't muster the nerve—really, she couldn't take being doubted, not right now.

Jones rubbed his stubbly chin. "Huh."

"Anyway, let's . . . let's talk about it. Later, all right? They're gone, you need to go home, and I need to go . . ." She glanced at Gabriel.

"Right. Yes. We'll talk about it . . . later."

Jones had kept it together so well through it all, but his voice broke on that last word. Ellie gave him a quick hug and then turned away, guessing as well that he would rather be alone than see her pitying him for his loss.

Lester shook his head as she walked up to them, a case of booze cradled in her arms. "Poor man, why didn't you invite him in for a drink?"

"I did; he wouldn't come. And speaking of, what are you two still doing out here?" She heard Jones's pickup fire up. "Come along inside with me so I can set this down and you can tend to Gabriel in the light."

"Yes ma'am!"

Ellie guessed Lester hadn't heard what the man in the mask had disclosed—he was too light, too easy with her. As to whether he'd noticed the odd masks, the strange way the fires had all gone out at once . . . She didn't even know how to ask that question.

The molasses-like silence between herself and Gabriel was much different.

"Go on in, Lester," said Gabriel. "I'm all right."

"I want to see if you need stitches, and take a look at that side of yours tonight, so just don't be too long."

"So . . . want to help me with the booze and the stuff?" asked Ellie, after Lester shut the door.

"Ellie."

"Yes?"

"What they said . . . Was it true?"

He already knew, but she confirmed it. "I should have told you."

"Was it the night you came back all bloody?" He waited for a moment, but when she kept silent he sighed. "I knew it. I didn't want to say anything, but I knew it."

"You knew I'd killed someone?"

"Of course not. I knew you were lying to me, but I couldn't figure out why you would . . . and I wanted to believe you."

"I tried to *help* him," said Ellie desperately. "It was Walter Greene—"

"Walter! Oh God."

"Did you know him?"

"Not really. But I didn't realize he'd been *killed*. They said he'd stolen his cousin's boat and cracked his head open, drunk. He'd been dead a few days when they found him."

"'They'? You mean the police?"

Gabriel nodded.

"When I found him he was still alive, but in bad shape. His craft was adrift, and it seemed like he'd hurt himself somehow. I wanted to get him to shore. He thought I was attacking him, I guess, and we tussled. He tried to choke me, I pushed him off, he slipped and cracked his head hard enough to . . ." She trailed off, pushing away the memories of the details she wasn't sharing. "As for the stealing, yes I did. I'm not proud, but I was sore at him for attacking me when I only meant to help, and I figured I could use the profit to help get Lester to school."

Gabriel relaxed somewhat as she spoke, which made her wonder what he'd thought the story had been—had he really imagined some scenario where she'd killed Greene in cold blood?

"Why didn't you tell me?"

Ellie's words sounded feeble even to her own ears. "I didn't want you to worry—"

"Ellie West!"

She raised her voice to match his. "Fine!" she snapped. "The truth is, I didn't want you to look at me as you are right now." She bit her lip after shouting this last, embarrassed to have lost her temper. "I was already upset, and terrified and hurt and confused and, and I . . . I didn't want things to change between us, and I was worried you'd see me differently knowing what I'd done. And since nothing came of it . . . at least, nothing *seemed* to, until tonight, I just . . . tried to forget it ever happened. I should have known it wouldn't be that easy."

There was so much she hadn't said, so much she couldn't explain, but that was enough for now.

"Oh, Ellie," he said. "I'm so sorry. And I'm sorry you had to bear it alone."

"That was my choice," she said sheepishly, feeling the weight of her fears—at least those related to Gabriel—lifted from her shoulders. "I should have known I could have just told you about it."

"I wish you had." He hesitated. "I have to ask . . . Is there anything else I should know?"

Ellie considered and then rejected the idea of mentioning her belief that some sort of supernatural *something* was at work, and instead just said, "I sold our wedding booze to those people, the rich ones . . . SJ's 'private reserve.' To help make sure Lester could get to school."

Ellie was surprised to see how hurt Gabriel looked, but all he said was "Well . . . all right. Maybe some of it's left in what Jones brought us? Let's shift it inside and see, and maybe have a drink while Lester looks me over."

They did just that, and though none of it was the good stuff, the booze did its job. After he was done with Gabriel, Lester had a stiff one too, though he did not usually partake.

After her brother went to bed Ellie and Gabriel finished what they'd started on the porch in the darkness of their bedroom. He was banged up and she wasn't in the best way either, but he came to her with an urgency she understood. She'd felt it after she'd killed Greene.

It was such a relief to let her body think for her, and yet at the same time the familiar act also made all the strange goings-on that night, like the masks and the fires, seem highly implausible—no, more than that: impossible. Gabriel read all those books and stories about wizards, or cult leaders who served uncaring gods . . . If even *he* hadn't noticed anything otherworldly, surely she had been imagining it.

But the thing was, she knew she hadn't imagined it.

Restless and wakeful even with Gabriel's comfortable bulk beside her, Ellie got out of bed to let her fiancé dream of whatever he would. She went downstairs in the silk nightdress he had gotten her at Macy's, poured another slug of SJ's white dog into her mug, and stepped out onto the porch.

It was cooler out there, and humid. She loved the quiet seclusion of this place, loved the way the bones of the colonial saltbox still showed beneath the new shingles and siding, the way the fresh beams were mellowing alongside the ancient ones. She wanted so badly to live here with Gabriel—to settle here, maybe even start a family one day, once life settled down.

But *would* life settle down? As the night deepened and Ellie's eyes grew used to the darkness she really began to see the complexity and strength but also the fragility of the world just outside her home. The trees of the forest beyond their little yard seemed so solid, with their deep roots buried in rich soil and the rough moonlit bark protecting their trunks, but a hurricane could blow them over, or an axe could fell them; the night-creatures, bug and bird and beast, went about their business as they did every night, as their ancestors had for who knew how long, and yet the slap of a hand could snuff out a mosquito's life; a single gunshot could end a deer, fox, or owl, as could something even smaller, like plague. Others would take their place; she knew that. She had taken enough fluke and crab from the bay to know one was much like the other . . . But were men and women the same? Perhaps so . . . If Lester had died from the polio, someone else would have gotten his scholarship and gone on to become a doctor. If those maniacs in the masks had killed her and Gabriel, someone would have bought their half-finished house to live their lives in it; raise their own families.

Then again, it *wasn't* the same. Weren't they supposed to have evolved from monkeys—not be them? Civilization was something animals didn't have. They ought to be moving forward, not backward.

Ellie rose to go inspect the place where those flames had erupted from the earth. She'd been right—there was no evidence of kindling or wood or anything else that might have burned so fiercely, and for so long. And the ground, too, was untouched, save for a black smear that reminded her less of charcoal and more of motor oil . . .

Or the grease left by those disgusting mushrooms.

Were those repellent growths another piece of this puzzle, whose shape she could not perceive? What was more insane—to accept that it all had to be connected, or to refuse to accept it? She might have been able to deny the masks, or the fires, or Hunter's trick with the moonshine, or everything that had happened with Greene, or that strange occurrence where the air itself seemed to thicken and curdle before queer things happened, but together they added up to something she could not explain, something not a part of the natural world as she had come to understand it.

And really, supernatural or not, this group of masked men had come for her, and they'd said they'd come again—for her, and for others, too. She couldn't sit idly by and do nothing as the noose tightened around all their necks.

It was a terrifying prospect, to accept that some sort of strange phenomenon was at work in the quiet village of Amityville, but it was also terrifying to accept that her father was involved with masked men who murdered people, and she wasn't going to deny that anymore, either. While the man in the mask hadn't sounded like Hunter or her father, there had been four other men standing behind Hunter on that stage—men who'd sat in silence as he performed miracles and played the crowd. And who could say how many new recruits had enlisted after that performance? They were of one mind, as he'd said.

These thoughts were no comfort to Ellie, but comfort was not what she needed. She needed a plan, and the one that came to her was intimidating.

It wasn't the easy thing to do, but she knew it was the right thing.

Ellie didn't know how she would tell Gabriel that she was leaving him—at least until her presence in his life didn't make him a target for further violence. They'd said they'd come back—they'd said she'd leave him if she knew what was good for her. While it felt like giving in to them, a few days away might throw them off the scent. By then, she would have figured out a course of action. At least, she hoped so.

Eventually the sky began to lighten, and the birds she'd heard all her life awoke, and the mosquitoes came back to feast upon her, driving her inside.

"There you are." Gabriel was up, earlier than usual. The tantalizing smell of coffee reached her nose even as she winced to see his poor bruised face. "When you weren't beside me I couldn't get back to sleep. I guess I've already gotten used to you being here."

Ellie accepted a cup of coffee, but set it down on the counter without taking a sip. "Gabe . . . we need to talk."

He stiffened, as if he knew what she was about to say. "What's wrong?"

"I'm going away for a while. Just while I figure out what to do."

"Do about what?"

"About . . ." Ellie didn't know how to start, after hours of working through this in her mind. "About what's been happening here, to us, and elsewhere in Amityville. The attacks, the murders."

"What do you plan to do about them?"

"I want to put an end to it all." She hoped he wouldn't ask her how she planned to do that. He didn't, but what he did say troubled her even more, in a way.

"But why do you think you'll be able to?"

This brought Ellie up short. Gabriel usually expressed confidence in her abilities, not the reverse.

"Well . . . because . . ." Ellie fumbled and then found her footing. "Because I know who they are."

"And who are they?"

"They've got to be that creepy church my pop joined. It tipped me off when the man in the round mask called me 'daughter of the island.' I've never heard that said anywhere except for when I went to that tent revival with Jones. I'd been hoping those clowns were all talk, but—"

"It could just be a few members who've gone into business for themselves, though."

Ellie understood why that would be his hope, but she didn't think that was the case. "Then we still have a problem. Hunter has the right to say what he likes, but if he's actually inciting violence . . ."

"So what are you going to do? Kill him?"

"Gabriel!" Ellie was amazed. "What is this? You don't think I should fight?"

"I think you should take all this to your cop friend and then let it go," he said. "Who deputized you?"

"Nobody, but—"

"And why do you have to leave me to do it? You just moved in." He shook his head. "Ellie, do you not want to live here with me? You don't have to, you know. We're not married yet, and even if we were, you know I wouldn't stop you if you really wanted to leave."

"I don't *want* to leave, but don't you see? I want them to leave you alone!"

Gabriel seemed skeptical. "I'm guessing you're not going to go home?"

"No, I thought I'd go to Rocky's. Pop doesn't know he exists; I've never mentioned him."

"Rocky, huh?"

His tone was not what she'd thought it would be. "What's the problem? You're usually so thrilled when I stop by his place."

"Stop by, sure. Live there? Not so much."

Ellie started to get annoyed. "The only reason you've got a shiner and broken glasses and a cracked rib is me. At Rocky's, I can sleep easy, knowing you're safe, while I figure out a plan."

Gabriel rolled his eyes. "*A plan,* you say."

"Hey!"

"Look." He raised his hands. "I'm not going to lie to you; I respect you too much for that . . . So I have to tell you, I think this is all completely crazy."

Given how often it seemed to be happening of late, Ellie was getting pretty tired of people freely giving their opinions on her life.

"I know you think I should go to the police, but Jones told me he doesn't trust his fellow cops. It'd just be him on his own! I have a duty to help him, I mean, I have a personal connection to a member of this church, and—"

"And he'll ask for your help if and when he needs it."

"I don't think he has much to go on to get, you know . . . warrants and whatever," she began.

"Warrants and whatever. *And whatever.* Come on, Ellie!"

"So I don't know police procedure—so what? Gabriel, they're . . . sorcerers! Or something! They have strange abilities and powers. Didn't you notice last night? What do you want the police to do about *that,* I wonder?"

It was almost a relief to say it, but Gabriel stared at her like her head had just popped off and rolled away.

"*Sorcerers?*" he asked quietly.

She didn't like his tone, but she forged ahead.

"I don't know what you'd call what happened, the way they lit those fires without wood, and their masks, the way they kept changing the more you looked at them . . ."

Gabriel looked extremely worried. "Ellie, I think the strain has been getting to you. They—I can't believe I'm saying this—*they are not sorcerers.* I'm sure there's a perfectly rational explanation for everything that happened."

"But the fire . . ."

"Was just fire!"

Ellie felt doubt creep into her mind again as she realized she alone had noticed what had been really going on. "Gabriel . . . Hunter, at his meeting, he turned liquor into water. I was there up on stage with him, it wasn't sleight of hand. He really . . . *did* something."

"Liquor into water, huh? Like some kind of what, reverse Jesus? Anyway, it sounds like a phony magic act to me."

"It's not, though. I've had a few experiences with people who are a part of this group. Walter Greene . . . he did things."

"Things like . . ."

Ellie was getting tired of explaining. "Jesus Christ, I would have thought with all those trashy magazines you read you'd be a little more likely to see what was in front of your eyes!"

"I read them; I don't *believe* in them. H. P. Lovecraft himself doesn't believe in the supernatural, and here you're telling me it wasn't a bunch of KKK impersonators punching me last night—it was some sort of magus's coterie?"

"Well, when you put it like that, it sounds ridiculous."

"Put it like what—like literally what you're alleging?"

"You don't have to believe me." Ellie felt her annoyance leaving her; a cool calmness took its place. "I didn't believe all this myself, but I can't deny it any longer. I'm not going to sit around waiting to see you become their next victim—not when I can try to stop it."

"You won't see anything at all, not if you're gone! Ellie, I . . ." He ran his hand through his fair hair. "I don't know what to say to you. We're engaged—we're going to be married. At least I hope

we still are. But being with someone means you protect each other
—you get through things together. These days, I don't even know
why you want me in your life. You never let me help, and you don't
seem to want my company."

"I *do* want your help and your company. If you think I'd take
off right as I got here, for anything I thought wasn't important,
then . . . well, then I don't know what to tell you. I'm trying to protect you!"

"I don't need your protection, Ellie. I'm not Lester."

Ellie had tried to remain calm in the face of Gabriel's anger, but
she felt herself getting annoyed.

"What do you mean by that?" she said icily.

"I mean . . ." He shrugged unhappily. "I just mean I don't need
to be defended. I'm not . . . fragile, or . . ."

"He's not fragile," she insisted.

"If he's not, then why do you think I am?"

"I don't think you are!"

"Yes you do, Ellie. Otherwise you wouldn't be cutting out on me."

"I'm not cutting out."

The fight seemed to leave Gabriel all at once. "Look," he said,
"I'm not going to argue with you about this anymore. Just . . . just
go if you want to go."

Ellie sensed that she couldn't convince him otherwise. "Fine. I'll
go for my own reasons, and you can believe what you want. I hate
to ask, but do you mind if Lester stays? I don't think it's a good
idea for him to be across the bay."

"Of course I don't mind." Gabriel was as cold as an iceberg and
just as remote. "I'll take him to school if it's necessary."

"I'm sure it won't be necessary," she said, chillier now too. "But
thank you."

She stalked upstairs after that to angrily pack her bag, furious
at Gabriel. None of this was what she wanted, and it annoyed her
that he was acting like it was.

She wasn't even sure if Rocky would take her in.

Rather than waking up Lester to say goodbye, she opted to leave him a farewell note, slipping it under his door and then tiptoeing downstairs. Gabriel was still in the kitchen, leaning against the counter, his cold cup of coffee between his hands.

"I'll miss you. I'll visit," she said. A thin olive branch, maybe, but she offered it just the same.

"Are you sure that's safe?" Gabriel wouldn't even look at her. "It might not be a good idea to put me at risk like that."

Ellie left without kissing Gabriel, or even saying goodbye. She couldn't. Her throat had closed up too tight from grief; from all the tears she wouldn't let fall. She reminded herself that doing the right thing didn't always mean doing the easy thing, but that was cold comfort as she headed out into the dawn.

6

OSCAR'S GARAGE WOULD NOT BE one of the places that Fin would mourn if her vision came true and Long Island was destroyed. True, Oscar had given her Ellie's address, but he'd forced Fin to endure many unsubtle provocative remarks and minimally veiled lecherous glances before he'd finally done so. As she drove away, Fin marveled to herself that Ellie entrusted that man with her secrets; if Fin had been able to wheedle Ellie's personal information out of him, at least after she'd given him ample time to comment on her legs, her suit, her hat, her manners, and a few other parts of her person, this Oscar character would surely hand any gangsters or federal officers whatever they wanted in a heartbeat.

The Wests' home on Cedar Avenue, on the other hand, Fin hoped would never change. It was a weather-beaten shingle-sided house tucked behind two spreading white oaks that provided shade and privacy. Black-eyed Susans and Indian paintbrushes and other bright flowers rioted outside the front door; behind them, vines of stately ivy climbed the walls. It seemed like a very pleasant, restful sort of place — at least it did until a man with a face like a thunderstorm answered her knock at the door.

Fin took him to be Ellie's father. While Ellie didn't carry about her that look of suspicion and dissatisfaction, Fin saw her in his strong jawline, dark straight hair, and wide but guarded eyes. He wasn't a bad-looking man at all, really; except for his relatively untanned face, he looked like any other Amityville bayman.

Fin smiled at him. "Hi," she said. "My name is Delphine Coulthead. I'm sorry to bother you; I know it's terribly rude to stop by unannounced—but Oscar—you know Oscar, who owns the garage over on Ireland? He said Ellie West lived here, and you see, I'm trying to find her."

She was utterly failing to charm him—that was obvious—but she didn't realize how badly she'd failed until he snarled, "Coulthead?"

It hadn't occurred to Fin that people might find her name notorious after it was printed in the paper, but this man certainly seemed to know of it, and disapprove. "You're the sister of the man who leased the old Samis place on Ocean Avenue, aren't you?"

"I'm his wife," she said, "but—"

"Looking to buy more liquor, even after you humiliated yourself and your family, and *my* family? As if I hadn't enough reminders of my failures as a father, here you are, a living reproach on my doorstep, clothed but barely in city fashions."

The man's physical bulk and unapologetic hostility were intimidating enough that Fin took a step back, clearly to his satisfaction. For a moment, she wondered if she just ought to go home—tell Jimmy she was sorry, that she'd been trying to save face with her story about a vision of the end of the world, move wherever everyone else decided was best, and leave the unpleasant inhabitants of this island to whatever doom was coming for them.

Then Fin's nerves steadied. She'd marched for the vote; agitated for reproductive rights—she'd endured insults and garbage hurled her way by men with faces just like this one's, or men of the law who had wielded their authority like a club. She would not let him frighten her away. There was too much at stake.

"I have *not* come here to buy spirits, sir," she said primly, "but even if I had, your remarks about my clothing and my behavior could not be considered civil by any standard."

"How dare you come to my home and insult me?"

"I'm merely paying a social call; the only insults issued have been yours. Please, Mr. West—let's start over, or shall I wait out here on the stoop for Ellie to discover my presence?"

"Go away," he roared, but Fin stood her ground. "In fact, you may *not* wait for my daughter here. This is my property, and—"

"Robert, who on earth are you speaking to?"

A mild woman who also reminded Fin of Ellie appeared behind where the unpleasant man stood. He half turned to speak to her, but Fin beat him to it.

"Are you Mrs. West? I don't mean to make personal remarks, but you look so much like your daughter! I'm Delphine Coulthead, and I'm afraid Mr. West and I got off on the wrong foot. I'm hoping to speak with Ellie about an urgent matter requiring her attention. Is she at home?"

"Ellie isn't home," said Mrs. West as Mr. West fumed. "I'm so sorry you came all this way to find her gone. Won't you come in and have a cool drink?"

"Harriet—"

"I won't have her standing on the doorstep like a traveling salesman while you shout at her loudly enough for the whole neighborhood to hear," said Mrs. West firmly.

"Better she should stand on the doorstep than enter our home," said Mr. West.

"*Robert.*"

"If you'll have her inside, then you'll have her without me." And with that, he pushed past Fin, stalking off down the street. He had an unsteady gait, Fin observed—a limp that looked to her like an old war injury.

Fin remembered that it was her mention of the Families of Crippled Veterans fund-raising event that had sparked Ellie's anger. Of course it had—she'd all but said Ellie and her family were in need of charity after forcing Ellie to accept a tip she didn't want. Twice then she'd treated Ellie as if she were needy, when Ellie was clearly someone who had read a lot of Horatio Alger books as a child, and still put a great deal of stock in those ideals of hard work and self-sufficiency.

"If you'll forgive your welcome, I'd be pleased if you'd come inside and have that drink," said Harriet, stepping aside so that Fin could enter.

It was a handsome home; everything in it was clearly old, but it was all well cared for. Fin complimented a tall cabinet made of honey-colored wood that was so polished it almost glowed in the low light of the front room. Mrs. West was pleased to have it noticed.

"It's a cutlery cabinet," she said, opening one of the doors and revealing some old silver and more curiously, some implements carved of what looked like ivory. "Ellie's grandfather—Robert's father, I mean—crewed whaling boats, and bought many nice things for his young wife, once upon a time. He also carved the scrimshaw that you see there."

"It's lovely."

"It is, isn't it?" Mrs. West sighed. "The truth is, Mrs. Coulthead, I don't know when Ellie will be home," she said as they continued into the kitchen. "She and her father had a bit of a problem . . ."

"Even after meeting your daughter once, I can see how they'd have their differences," said Fin.

Mrs. West looked relieved to have to be no more specific. She handed Fin a glass of tea cold from the icebox. Fin sipped it; it was good.

"Thank you so much," she said. "You're being very kind to me, especially given, well, everything with the paper and all."

"That seems really more the fault of that dreadful reporter," said Mrs. West. "If people are going to hold some sort of drunken debauch at their house, I'd really rather not know about it. Robert feels differently, and I see his point, but . . ."

"I'm not usually one to poke my nose into other people's business, either," said Fin. They were getting on so well she decided not to dispute Mrs. West's characterization of the party, even if she felt it was a bit harsh. "I know that must seem strange, given that I'm here, but I really desperately need to speak with Ellie."

Mrs. West looked at Fin appraisingly. "She's staying with her . . . husband." Fin was curious why Mrs. West had hesitated, but elected not to press. "You'll have to go around Robin Hood's barn to get there; they like their privacy. Let me just write it all down; there are a few turns, and I wouldn't want you to get confused."

"Thank you," said Fin, and sipped her tea while Mrs. West went into the other room and returned with a scrap of paper with several lines of directions written down in a neat, even, schoolteacher's hand.

"When you see her," said Mrs. West, "will you tell her I miss her? And if you see my son Lester, please tell him . . ."

Mrs. West's voice cracked, and she took a moment to dab at her eyes with her apron. Fin pretended not to notice as she finished her tea. Mrs. West made a feeble protest as Fin rinsed out the glass and set it on the drying rack, but Fin told her not to be silly.

"I made trouble for you. Unintentionally, but I did. The least I can do is not leave dirty dishes everywhere."

"Well, thank you," said Mrs. West, in a polite but guarded tone that made her sound as well as look like Ellie. Long Islanders and their pride! Fin didn't think she'd ever get used to it.

"I really can't thank you enough, and I'll give your regards to your children," continued Fin, with an eye to the door that brought Mrs. West to her feet. She would have been happy to sit in the clean, pleasant kitchen for longer, but she didn't want to be around whenever Mr. West returned. "I really ought to be on my way, though."

"Of course."

Fin found herself once again on the Wests' doorstep when Mrs. West said, "My husband is a good man, you know."

It was difficult to know what to say, as Fin wasn't sure she did know that. So she just nodded.

"He's been disappointed frequently. That makes a body bitter," said Mrs. West.

"Well, I don't know him from Adam, but I'd say he's had more than just disappointment. After all, he has a lovely wife, a nice home ... Your daughter is really quite a go-getter, and I'm sure your son is wonderful too."

"Just the same, it wears a man down, feeling useless."

It was as if Mrs. West were begging Fin to forgive her husband, not just for what had happened today, but for something bigger, something too large to speak about within the solid walls of their house.

"I know all about feeling useless," said Fin, rather than agreeing or disagreeing with the woman. "Thank you again for the tea, and for the directions. I hope Mr. West comes home in a better mood than he left it."

Fin had thought to try to find Ellie tomorrow, but she was now quite determined to see this through and get her answers today. Looking over the directions again, she was eager to get on with her investigation—after all, it was only just past two.

She had plenty of time before she'd be missed. Or rather, she thought wryly as she started up the Ford, before the car would be.

THE OLD FARMHOUSE WAS INDEED REMOTE—or at least as remote as things got in Amityville. She came upon it suddenly, for the ancient-looking house with a sharp and uneven roof was tucked away behind a thick copse, down a bumpy, twisty country road that made Fin worry for the Ford's suspension.

It had a half-finished look about it; the yard was full of old bits of metal and curling wood shavings. Mrs. West had said Fin's husband was restoring and modernizing the place for their life together. Apparently that meant some pretty heavy carpentry, not just clearing out the basement and replacing the fixtures.

It was not Gabriel who answered the door—at least, Fin didn't think it could possibly be him. He was too young, for one, and she didn't think he'd be able to haul much lumber with those slender legs and arms characteristic of polio survivors. No, this must be Ellie's brother whom Mrs. West had spoken about.

"Hello," she said. "My name is Delphine Coulthead. I'm looking for Ellie West . . . Is she home?"

He looked her over with his large, intelligent eyes. "I'm sorry, but Ellie's not here."

"Do you know when she'll be back?"

"I really don't," he said, and seemed a bit troubled.

Ellie was more slippery than an eel. "Do you know where I might find her? I just came from town . . . Her mother sent me here. Said to give her love to Ellie and her brother Lester, too."

"I'm Lester." And then, to Fin's surprise, he said, "I'm not inclined to tell strangers where she is, if you'll forgive me for saying so, Mrs. Coulthead."

It made sense, in a way—the extra attention from the article in the paper surely wasn't making it easy for Ellie to keep a low profile.

Lester was being polite, but Fin was just about done with being obstructed. She tried a winning smile—if that didn't work, she'd chain herself to the front porch until her demands were met.

"I really just need to talk to her about a personal matter. She's the only one who can help me."

This softened Lester a bit. "Well . . . you can come in and wait for Gabriel, if you like. Not sure when he'll be back, though; he's working."

"Gabriel is . . ."

"Ellie's fiancé." Ah, so that was why Mrs. West had hesitated; they were living together without really being married yet. "He knows where she is. I do too, in theory, but it's not on Long Island. She's across the bay. You can't get there by car."

"Oh my." Fin hadn't anticipated a complication of that nature. Of course it would be no problem for Ellie to get back and forth, but Fin? She could go home and get *The Bee's Knees,* but she'd not yet taken a turn at the wheel, and she'd be dipped before she asked Jimmy to take her across.

"There's a ferry," said Lester. "But once you're over there, I'm not sure. I've never been."

No telling how late the ferry would run. Resigning herself to yet more delays, Fin was just about to ask where to find Gabriel when she heard the sound of a pickup.

It rattled to a stop beside her Ford. Two men jumped out— a brawny-looking, fair, blond man with a broad chest and long legs that seemed at odds with the taped-up horn-rimmed glasses perched on his nose, and a wiry black man in coveralls. The latter hung back to look at her car while the one in the glasses strode over.

"Hi," he said. He and his glasses were even worse-off than she'd thought—he had one hell of a shiner beneath a cracked lens. Other than that, he was one of the handsomest men Fin had ever seen outside of a movie theater. "Can I help you?"

"She's looking for Ellie," said Lester. The man's full-lipped mouth tightened at this.

"I really need her help," said Fin, after introducing herself. "I hear she's across the bay somewhere, but I'm not from Long Island ... I know it's a bother, but I just need a bit of direction figuring out what ferry and all."

Gabriel hesitated, then nodded once. "It is a bit complicated. I'll just take you there."

The ferry was in some other village called Babylon; Aaron offered to take them as far as the train station in the pickup. She sat between them on what proved to be a chatty drive. Aaron was mechanically minded, and had lots of questions about her car. She answered them as best she could, wishing she'd paid more attention to Jimmy when he'd brought it home. Apparently, it was quite a fancy machine.

Once Aaron dropped them off, however, it grew quiet and awkward. Fin was grateful it wasn't a long ride, for Gabriel said only what was necessary while they rode the rickety train as it clattered along to a town nearly indistinguishable from Amityville, save for it having a higher proportion of hotels close to the station and streets thronged with tourists, and then walked to the ferry.

He didn't seem surly or unpleasant—just pensive. Nervous, maybe, which set Fin to wondering if he and Ellie had had a falling-out. Surely not, if he'd agreed to accompany her and not just send her with directions.

Fin had taken the ferry across to Jones Beach a few times with and without Jimmy and the rest of them; this one was similar. It had just returned, but Gabriel talked to the captain, and for a fee the old man agreed to take them over in his personal craft if they'd come back by the ferry on its next run.

It was a clear, hot afternoon, and the cool breeze was welcome when they got out on the bay. Gabriel's meditative silence was less burdensome, as Fin could chat with the captain. Shading her eyes from the glare with one hand as she hung onto her hat with the other, Fin listened to him talk about fishing, the tourist season, and the weather as she watched the flat shore of Long Island recede and then turned her eyes to the almost identical flat shore before them. The only difference between Jones Beach Island and Long Island was that as far as she could see there were no signs of human presence beyond the little dock where they tied up and the sand-caked wooden boardwalk that snaked into the thicker forest beyond.

The captain waved goodbye, leaving them alone. Fin eyed the path.

"It's not a long walk," Gabriel said. "The ocean is just on the other side; that's where all the tourists go. We'll head north along the beach a bit. Ellie ties up in a different place, to keep her boat hidden. You're not really supposed to live over here year round, but Rocky's crazy enough to do it."

"Rocky?"

"Todd Rockmeteller."

Fin was quite surprised to hear this. "The poet?"

"Mm-hmm," said Gabriel. There was a tightness in his voice that made Fin wonder if she'd been right, and something had gone wrong between him and Ellie. She just hoped there wouldn't be a scene—Gabriel didn't seem like the type, but you never did know when matters of the heart were involved.

She must have had a funny look on her face, because Gabriel asked, "Do you know his work?"

"Oh yes," she said.

Gabriel couldn't have known how dearly Fin would have liked to have known this information before their windy crossing; she guessed her hair was a mess, and she was sweaty from her long day of running around all over town. Oh well; it couldn't be helped. At least when Gabriel stopped to take off his shoes when they reached the ocean side she was able to surreptitiously check her face in her compact mirror and wasn't too displeased by what she saw. A bit of fresh lipstick and she was at least presentable.

"So you're a fan," said Gabriel wryly, and Fin blushed to be noticed primping. "I'd suggest you take those heels off, though ... they won't be much use on the beach."

Fin ended up shedding not only her heels but also her stockings, which quickly became caked with the smoother sand on the ocean side of the island.

"I guess his stuff is all right," said Gabriel as they trudged along. "That one poem about the demons I liked okay. He probably could have gotten that into *Strange Tales* or even *The Argosy*."

"The pulp magazines?"

"Yeah, they run poetry sometimes. Good stuff, too."

He started to tell her about some of it. Fin was amazed; he didn't seem like the sort who'd go on about wizards in outer space or horrors from beyond the grave. She didn't think she wanted to read about fictional sinister forces while she investigated some that were all too real, but to be friendly she promised she'd check out some of his favorite periodicals.

Long after they'd left behind the final sunbather they came upon a small and shabby dwelling, really more of a vacationer's bungalow than a proper house. It was certainly remote and picturesque, but Fin couldn't imagine living there in the winter — she wondered if it even had modern plumbing or running water.

"This is the place," said Gabriel, a bit of skepticism creeping into his tone. Fin could understand why. She was baffled by the idea that Ellie would come here when that snug little house outside of Amityville was waiting for her.

She half expected yet another unfamiliar man to answer the door when they knocked, but no. At last it was Ellie, in a loose men's shirt with the sleeves rolled up to her elbows and trousers rolled up to her ankles. Her bob had grown out even more, hanging shaggily below her chin.

"Oh," she said, when she saw Gabriel, and then her eyes slid to Fin. "Oh!"

"She said she needed to talk to you," he said, affecting a careless tone that Fin instantly saw through.

"You do, huh?" said Ellie, addressing Fin. The skepticism in her voice was withering, but Fin would not be deterred.

"I'm so sorry," she said. "About what happened, I am. And I'm sorry to barge in on you, but I needed to see you ..."

Shyness claimed Fin for the first time that day. She had only thought about locating Ellie, not how to ask whether the alcohol she had sold them was capable of bestowing visions upon those who drank it.

"You'd better come in, then," said Ellie as Fin hesitated. "Will you come in too?" she asked Gabriel, somewhat hopefully.

"I don't want to miss the ferry back," he said.

Ellie glanced inside, presumably at a clock. "It's not due for another hour."

"Sure, but I figured Mrs. Coulthead here would be going back on it, too . . . It's the last one tonight. I'd better give the two of you your privacy."

Fin felt horribly guilty now, as from Ellie's expression it was clear she'd really prefer for Gabriel to stay.

"I can always take her back over if it gets late," protested Ellie. "You've come all this way. Won't you have a drink at least before you . . ." She trailed off.

"Ellie, I hate to interrupt, but my hair was blown every which way on the boat over. Do you have a powder room?"

Ellie stepped aside. "Of course, I'm sorry. Go through the house and out the back door . . . the little shed . . ."

"Thank you."

Fin took her time, not out of any need, but to give Ellie and Gabriel what privacy she could. When she returned, Ellie was sitting on the rough porch, dirty bare feet dangling above the sand. She was alone, and staring out at the sea beyond.

"He left?" asked Fin.

"He left."

Feeling even more awkward, Fin sat down beside Ellie. "How long have you two been . . ."

"I came out here two—no, three nights ago."

Fin didn't know what to say next, so she sat silently beside Ellie and watched the tide go out.

"So," said Ellie, after a bit. It seemed her ire had departed with her fiancé. "You needed to talk to me?"

"I'm sorry, I did—I mean, I do . . ."

"Go on, then. Don't worry about—" Ellie waved her hand at the footsteps that retreated into the distance. Her anxiety over whatever had happened with Gabriel had softened her up a bit.

Fin took a moment to gather her thoughts. She wanted to present the best case possible for the vision being real, especially after Jimmy and Bobbie hadn't believed a word of what she'd said about that night. Stalling more, Fin reached into her purse and withdrew her cigarette case. She only had two left.

"Do you mind?" she asked. Ellie shook her head, and Fin lit it and took a pull. The smoke curled into her lungs and gave her the energy and strength she needed to speak.

"Like I told you, I didn't even want to have that stupid party," she began. "It was all Bobbie's idea—Bobbie's one of my husband's friends. She used to be my friend, too, but recently . . . things have changed."

For the next few minutes Fin poured her heart out about what had been happening over on Ocean Avenue. Once she'd started she couldn't seem to stop, and so she told Ellie about her growing estrangement from Jimmy and her feelings of dissatisfaction with her life; how she wasn't sure how she'd become the person she was, and didn't know how to change.

She took a final drag on her cigarette and realized she'd smoked the whole thing while talking without even mentioning the worst part of all of this mess. She'd spilled her guts but not the beans about her worry over having had some sort of vision or supernatural experience.

"Anyway, I drank that booze you sold me, and . . . Ellie, something happened."

"Something happened, huh?" Fin wasn't expecting her to sound so hostile. "*Do go on,* isn't that the favored expression of your sort?"

"I'm sorry. I know took my time getting to my point . . ."

"You have a point?"

It had been wrong to bare her soul to this woman instead of

getting right to brass tacks. Ellie hadn't invited Fin's confidence, after all; she'd only agreed to hear out her business.

"Yes, but it's just hard—"

"What's hard is listening to you going on and on about your petty problems!" Fin had yet again unintentionally frustrated Ellie, and she recoiled from the woman's tone. "You have money; you can get a divorce from your husband. I mean, it doesn't even sound like you like him. Same goes for your situation. Don't like it? Leave it!"

Fin was on her feet now. "It's not that simple," she said, getting a bit loud herself. She couldn't endure this scorn, not after enduring so much of it elsewhere.

"Isn't it? I left my fiancé."

"You did?" Fin's empathy won over her curiosity. "Forever?"

"No. I mean—I don't know. Maybe!" She bit her lip, and Fin saw clear as day her anger replaced by that quieter, gnawing worry. "You saw how he was."

It wasn't that Ellie was angry at her—not really, Fin realized. She was upset over some other matter, and Fin was rubbing her nose in it accidentally, just like she'd done before.

"I know I should leave," said Fin, "but it's difficult. Jimmy and I are married . . . we even slept together recently. It's complicated, and he won't tell me what he really wants, and every time I ask him about what he's thinking or feeling, he treats me like I'm crazy for even asking."

"You're not crazy."

"Maybe I am!" Fin didn't know why she shouted it, but she did. "I had a vision after drinking that booze you sold me—a vision of the end of the world. Or at least, the end of Long Island, in a strange way I can't describe other than it involves the earth dissolving into puddles of luminous goo and waves of rainbow scales and heaving mounds of fur and all sorts of odd things. And I think it's real. That's why I came here and told you all this . . . I told Jimmy, and I told Bobbie and Lily and Duke and Edgar, and every single one of them thinks I'm either lying or insane. But I know what I saw. So . . . there," she said, finally calming down a bit. "You sold me the booze, so I wanted to know if you think it's possible that what I saw was real . . . because frankly, Ellie, I have no one else to ask."

Ellie stood still for a moment, and then to Fin's utter relief, she nodded.

"Yes." She said it angrily, but in one explosive moment she took Fin's free hand in hers and squeezed. "I think it's more than possible. Something strange is going on, and it's destroying this place . . . figuratively, if not literally, and I've been banging my head against the wall — figuratively, not literally — trying to — Oh!"

Fin couldn't help it; she embraced Ellie and buried her face like a child in the other woman's surprisingly muscled shoulder as sobs erupted from deep within her. It was such a relief to hear Ellie say yes, after being told no again and again; to hear that someone else didn't think what had happened to her was a joke or a lie.

The tears wouldn't stop. Fin was mortified to sob like a child, but there was nothing she could do. Eventually, Ellie pulled away to hand Fin a large men's handkerchief. That made Fin laugh, which stemmed the flow a bit.

"Thank you," she said shakily, dabbing at her eyes and nose. "I'm sorry."

"No, I'm sorry. I shouldn't have popped off at you like that. I know what it's like to not have anyone to talk to. And I'm sorry for selling you queer booze made by people who — well, we can talk about that later. As you might imagine, it's turning out to be some pretty complicated stuff. All I mean to say is that I didn't mean to sell you anything strange, but I did, and —"

"And here we all are." Fin took a deep shuddering breath. "Oh, Ellie. I'm sorry too, for everything. I've offended you twice now and I never meant to."

"I know. I shouldn't have said what I did. I'm sorry."

"Yes, you damn well should have said what you did; I was being an ass. That's one of the reasons I came here . . . I know far too well that wanting to do good doesn't amount to much if you're not actually doing good. That you'd talk to me at all after that, much less believe me . . . it means so much."

Ellie peered at her. "Why? I've been experiencing strange things, as I said. What if I've cracked up too? What if we're experiencing some kind of . . . mass delusion?"

"Ellie, you're the most down-to-earth person I know." Fin gave Ellie a weak smile. "If *you* think something's real, I'm sure it is."

7

ELLIE STARED AT FIN for a moment or two as she puzzled through this remarkable statement. Down-to-earth? *Her?* Even before the weirdness of the last few weeks she'd felt like she'd barely been keeping it together as she worked herself half to death to send her brother to college. Now that she was seeing and feeling things other people didn't, all bets were off.

To Fin, however, probably she *did* seem to have her act together. It was a little like how to Ellie, Fin seemed to have an easy life.

Fin's situation might not be as dangerous as Ellie's had proven to be on a day-to-day basis, but it was just as treacherous. Wealthy Fin certainly was, and out of touch, but Ellie could not deny that the conditions under which she'd been living sounded depressing and strange. Additionally, she had been through a troubling experience without any support, in part because Ellie had sold her alcohol of unknown, and apparently unknowable, provenance.

Fin lit another cigarette, her last. Acting completely on impulse, Ellie reached for it. She inhaled deeply. She wasn't much of a smoker, but Rocky sometimes had them, and she enjoyed the occasional puff. Fin grinned at her, and Ellie laughed. Amityville might be changing, and her life with it, but the camaraderie that came from sharing a cigarette would probably always be the same.

"Well . . ." Ellie began awkwardly.

"A very deep subject," said Fin, and giggled.

"Jesus Christ," groaned Ellie. "Look . . . all right. Let me just say, and no insult to you, but the important thing about everything you just said is this vision you had."

"I agree. My home life is insignificant in the grand scheme of the universe. What I care about is the island."

Ellie warmed to Fin a bit more, hearing that. She sounded sincere. "Well, it all might be insignificant in some grand scheme, as you said, but it also sounds *terrible*. You don't deserve what's happening to you. At the very least they should have listened to you about the, you know, *vision*," she said, a bit of bitterness creeping into her tone as she thought about Gabriel's dismissive attitude. "And I also think your husband should tell you to scram if that's what he really wants. What's the point of pretending he wants to stay married when he doesn't?"

Fin's lips twisted, but no tears fell from those wide blue eyes. "I'm guilty of the same. I could have left him any time," she said softly. "I have a lawyer. I could have had her figure it all out. She got me out of serving jail time; she could get me out of my—"

"Jail time?" Ellie stared at Fin. She, a member of the criminal element of Amityville, had never been arrested . . . yet Fin had, with her angel-blonde hair and her angel-blue eyes and her little white suit that probably cost more than Lester's lodging for his first semester. The world really was an amazing place.

"Oh sure," said Fin. She was being completely serious. "A bunch of us got ourselves arrested for mailing out pamphlets on family planning."

Ellie boggled at her. "So, not just charity balls, then?"

"Not just. Being arrested scared me, though, and I left that all behind me. What does that say about me?"

Ellie shrugged. "I've never tried to be anything other than what I am now, so what do I know?"

"You know a lot."

"Here I am, sleeping in another man's bed instead of living with my husband-to-be, trying to figure out . . ." Ellie trailed off, not sure how to describe what she was trying to determine. She'd been doing a lot of thinking about the masked men and the island, and still had no idea what to do about any of it.

"So you and Mr. Rockmeteller are . . ."

"Mr. Rockmeteller!" Ellie snorted. "Anyway, Rocky and I, we're just . . . friendly. "

Fin gave Ellie an arch look. "Very friendly, I'd say."

"Gabriel knows. He . . . doesn't mind."

"He seems like a nice man." Fin sighed. "Having things out in the open like that . . . what a relief. I made it with a ukulele player right before I had that awful vision—at the party, I mean. Jimmy doesn't know."

"Was he cute?" Ellie grinned at Fin.

"*Very* cute."

The two women dissolved into more giggles, their shoulders crashing together like waves as they leaned toward each other in conspiratorial glee. Ellie wondered if she'd given up something precious without ever fully appreciating what she was losing when she'd become busy and let her childhood friendships flicker out.

She hadn't had much choice in it, not really. Her father's enlistment had meant they'd all needed to do more around the house to make up for his absence, as had his unexpected return. Rocky, and then Gabriel, had consumed her few free hours after she met them. Friendships were difficult and messy, at least in Ellie's experience, whereas Rocky had been a casual source of stress relief.

And Gabriel . . . Well, the heart had a way of making time for itself.

She knew she ought to be talking to Fin about bigger matters, like those men in the woods, or Fin's vision of the end of the world, but it was just so pleasant laughing with her in the cooling afternoon, their toes in the sand. It had been so long since she'd done anything this frivolous.

The creak of a door and the sound of footsteps behind them brought the two women back to reality. A shirtless, sleepy-eyed man with floppy hair emerged from the house, suspenders holding up his threadbare slacks.

"Oh, company," he said, pleased but confused. "Sorry I didn't hear you down here before. I was working."

"Todd Rockmeteller?" Fin was a bit unsteady as she lurched to her feet. "I'm Fin Coulthead, Delphine Coulthead—at least for now I am, a Coulthead, I mean—and I'm ever so pleased to meet you. I'm a fan of your work."

"Is that so? Why, thank you."

Ellie watched the two of them as they made awkward small talk about *The Ginger-Eaters* and the various poems in *City Songs* and *Sea Songs*. Talk about friendships being messy and complicated . . . Fin hadn't been here even an hour, and it was obvious that she'd immediately hit it off with Rocky. The air practically sizzled between those two as they chatted.

Ellie didn't mind. Moving in with Rocky had been a stopgap. She'd never planned to make it a more permanent arrangement, and after a few days with him, that desire hadn't changed. Rocky rarely woke before noon, long after Ellie could even relax in bed with a book, and stayed up so late she hadn't gotten a good night's rest since arriving. And as for his other habits, well, the stack of dishes in the sink and the layer of dust had become a lot less charming now that she was living there, as opposed to swanning in and out.

When Rocky invited Fin to "come on up" to see what he was working on she demurred, to Ellie's surprise. The woman was practically panting.

"I can't," she said. "I'm already going to inconvenience Ellie by asking her to take me back across the bay tonight. I shouldn't waste her time. We have a lot to discuss."

"What are you two girls talking about, then, if I'm allowed to know?"

Ellie hesitated. She hadn't spoken to Rocky at all about her concerns about the masked men and the strange things she'd been seeing and feeling around Hunter. It had been easier to just omit that whole part. Fin, however, had no such scruples.

"Honestly, I know it's going to sound crazy, but not long ago I drank some bathtub liquor and I had this terrible vision of, well, if not of the end of the world, then at least the end of Long Island. And Ellie seemed to think there was something to what I was saying."

"Ellie, is this true?"

"It is," she said. "I saw a miracle in broad daylight, and masks that changed as I watched them. I saw a man's skin get so hot rainwater steamed off him, and . . . and other queer things." She finally met Rocky's eyes. He looked astonished. "I was afraid to tell you. Gabriel didn't believe me." Ellie felt uncomfortable, like she was betraying her fiancé, so she said no more.

"You ought to have told me, love!" Ellie saw Fin's eyebrows shoot up at the word; likely she didn't realize it was just a term of endearment, not a statement about his feelings for her.

"You mean . . . you believe us?" said Ellie.

"I only write about what's real. I told you that," said Rocky. "I said it was something you and I had in common, don't you remember?"

Ellie did; she'd just interpreted that differently, given the more fantastical elements of *The Ginger-Eaters*. As it turned out he'd really meant it.

"Wait," said Fin. "Are you saying demons are *real?*"

"Let's go inside," said Rocky, glancing at the darkening evening. The insects were getting louder, their chitinous chorus both familiar and unsettling. "It's better to talk about these things behind closed doors."

ONCE INSIDE, ROCKY CONFESSED a part of his past Ellie had never known about, and surely would never have believed before recently: the commune of artists and aesthetes who shared their minds and bodies with a demon from *The Ginger-Eaters* was based on a real one, and he had grown up there among them, but not one of them.

After hearing that, Ellie needed a drink.

"I wrote *The Ginger-Eaters* after I moved to New York," Rocky said to them both as Ellie uncorked a dusty bottle of real Glenmorangie that Rocky had smuggled into the country when he'd emigrated. "That's when I felt finally free enough of the demon's influence to write about it."

Even though Rocky's cool recital of the circumstances of his upbringing made Ellie feel as though her experiences of the past few weeks were not the delusions of an injured mind, it was a lot to accept all at once. Based on what she had witnessed thus far, it was certainly possible that Hunter did possess powers granted to him by some diabolic entity . . . but it all still seemed a little too much like a story in one of Gabriel's magazines.

"The demon my family served was a powerful, seductive being," he said, "innocent in many ways, but still obscene. I never desired to commune with it. I'd seen what it could do—how it changed people without them realizing it. Which isn't to say my family wasn't a happy one. We were, but I never fit in there. I couldn't abide it, wondering all the time if I was actually talking to my mother, or to a demon. That's why I wrote *The Ginger-Eaters*. I'm glad it resonates with the more common sort of experiences people have of losing themselves in a lover, or to a career . . . but I have hoped, secretly, that someone might read it and decide against trafficking with demons."

"But you make it sound so appealing," said Fin. "I mean, the girl . . . She loses a lot, but she gains so much."

"I had to write the story honestly, or not at all. There are always advantages to communing with a demon—but there are too many disadvantages." Rocky's smile was sad. "What are demonic powers to having control over yourself?"

"What indeed," said Fin softly. Ellie wondered what she was thinking about, but when Fin caught her eye, she blushed and changed the subject. "So . . . there really was demonic ginger candy?"

"Ginger *everything*. It was a taste I knew from infancy, though of course they never fed me any of the demonically infused stuff. They never dosed anyone who didn't volunteer . . . though I've often wondered if I received anything while I suckled at my mother's breast. I know she communed with it while I grew inside her; demons do not easily let go of their hosts. In order to be healthy enough to bear a healthy child, she would have needed to keep doing so. And my father, too . . . He was a diabolist. Who knows what lurked within his *donation* to my existence." Ellie had never heard Rocky sound so bitter.

"So you think this liquor of Hunter's is like the ginger?" asked Fin.

"Demons can't physically manifest in our world. To commune with one, a human must consume something into which a demon has been summoned. It's usually a plant—most animals don't survive direct contact with demons any better than we do. But there's always a cost for the human."

"Not for the demon?" asked Fin.

"If there is one, I wouldn't know," said Rocky primly.

"I wonder what the cost to Hunter was." She shook her head. "I'm amazed that he would drink spirits to do *anything*, much less commune with a demon. For one, he's a teetotaler."

"People like him always make exceptions for themselves, in my experience," said Fin, lighting another of Rocky's cigarettes.

"I guess my question is, if he is communing with a demon through liquor, is he summoning it into the booze itself, or distilling it from something corrupt?" asked Rocky.

"It tasted earthy, oily," said Fin thoughtfully, and her eyes went wide. "*Fungal*—and there was that big disgusting protuberance that seemed sort of mushroom-like in my vision."

"Those mushrooms!" said Ellie. "Of course ... They're everywhere, and they weren't around before this summer. I'd have noticed them."

"Mushrooms?" Rocky asked.

"Nasty ones," said Ellie. "Slick, oily things that have been cropping up everywhere. They're full of some sort of liquid that burns skin and smells like kerosene."

"Doesn't sound like the sort of thing you'd want to eat," said Rocky. "I suppose distilling them might make them more palatable?"

"It sounds possible, as much as any of this does," said Ellie. "But ..."

"But?" asked Fin.

"It's just odd that I drank it ... but I didn't have this vision."

"You drank some of it?" asked Fin.

"I did. That's why I sold it to you. The night I ... acquired it, I tried a sip. I didn't have any problem with it; it just tasted like young spirit, maybe a little more harsh than most. I did notice that earthy taste, though, now that you mention it."

"But you believe me?" Fin asked.

"Of course. Why wouldn't I?"

"Because you didn't have the same experience, that's why."

"You didn't see Hunter change moonshine into water, right? But you believe me?" Fin nodded. "Well, there it is. Our experiences are similarly inexplicable."

"'Inexplicable' is the exact word for it," said Rocky. "Demons are fundamentally unfathomable. The one my family summoned had no real goal I knew of beyond expanding the consciousness of its companions—not through any altruism, you understand; just because it pleased it to do so. Just the same, they encountered demons with less warm intentions toward mankind ... There are many, and the one this Hunter character is consorting with seems to be one of those."

"I'll say." Fin shuddered. "In my vision I felt how strongly it desired to destroy Long Island. I just don't know why he — Hunter, I mean — would want that. He lives here."

Rocky stood. "Now *I* need a drink," he said, and took Ellie's cup. "Another round?" he asked her.

She nodded. "When Hunter spoke at his little rally, mostly he talked about rebirth, and change ... not destruction. Cleansing this place." She took a sip, and considered. "Well, that's not entirely true. I've heard him talk about the destruction of 'our' way of life. But he seems to want to take back Long Island for the people he thinks deserve to live here, not destroy it so no one can. Why would he work with a being that wants to make this island uninhabitable? Your vision didn't really sound like the sort of place anyone would want to settle down and raise a family." Ellie shook her head in disbelief, and then something occurred to her. "Could someone be deceived by a demon?"

"Of course," said Fin and Rocky, at the same time. Ellie looked at Fin inquiringly.

"That's what happens in *The Demon in the Deep*, after a fashion ..."

"The children's book?" said Ellie curiously.

"Yes ... her last — Georgiana Baker's, I mean."

"I only ever read *Three Nights at the Cottage*."

"I've never even heard of her," said Rocky.

"She's an American writer who wrote children's books for girls," said Fin. "Her last book was called *The Demon in the Deep*, and it was all about a woman, Miss Depth, who strikes a deal like we've been talking about. She wants to see the truth of the world, understand its inner workings, *its reasons for dealing generously with some and cruelly with others*." Fin always remembered that line. "The demon says it can show it to her ... but the cost is that one day, she'll have to give up her body to the demon. And, well, that happens.

She'd thought the demon meant eventually, but it meant immediately."

"And then what happens?" asked Rocky.

"The book's heroine, a girl named Susan, she tries to save Miss Depth, but she doesn't succeed. Miss Depth disappears."

"What happens to the girl?" asked Ellie.

"Susan never finds out what happens to her friend. And in the end she starts to wonder if she should summon the demon, too." Fin shrugged. "It's not Baker's most popular novel."

"I'd imagine not," said Rocky.

"That certainly sounds less child-friendly than the one I read," said Ellie.

"Anyway, in the book it sort of tells you how to summon a demon," said Fin. "At least, it alludes to it. The woman conjures it into her sister's homemade beach plum jelly."

"Beach plum jelly?" Ellie laughed. "Is she from around here? Baker, I mean?"

"Cape Cod, I think . . . ? Why? Do you have beach plums here?"

"Sure! They get ripe in September. My mother makes beach plum jelly every year. She has her own secret patch of bushes; every woman on Long Island does, I think." Ellie got up and rummaged through Rocky's cabinets for a bit, and then withdrew a jar of something claret-colored. She raised an eyebrow at Rocky. "Still here! Ma would be so insulted." She set the jar on the counter. "Well, Fin, if you want to try some it's right here, and I think it's some of the best."

"I assume it's not *demon*-tainted beach plum jelly," said Fin. "Or demon-tainted Scotch, for that matter. I wish we had some of what I'd drunk! We're talking over something I saw once, and we can't even duplicate my results to see if we can do anything about it. If we're trying to prevent what I saw from happening, it would be better if we could all be on the same page."

"But we can, if we want to," said Ellie. She felt silly for not having thought of it before. "We have the liquor here."

"We do?" Rocky was surprised by this.

"Sure, up in the attic. I wasn't just going to leave it at . . . at Gabriel's house." *Our house,* some voice said softly in her mind, but she really wasn't sure if that was still the case. Between their bloodless farewell the other day and Gabriel's coldness to her this afternoon, she wasn't sure if there was a path back to ever being comfortable with one another again.

Rocky seemed uncertain about this plan. "I don't know, girls. Trifling with demons is always risky."

"But we need to know what's really happening," said Fin, surprising Ellie. "The island—our home is at stake here! If some clue to Hunter's intentions—his *specific* intentions—could be revealed through the vision, we have to take advantage of that."

Fin and Rocky continued to discuss it, but Ellie scrambled up the rickety stair to the attic—Rocky could decline a tipple if he wanted. She grabbed a bottle out of the suspect case and came back brandishing it.

Fin seemed to have convinced Rocky to go along with the plan in Ellie's absence, so Ellie poured everyone a slug of Hunter's booze. She wasn't exactly eager to knock it back now that she was holding it; neither were Fin and Rocky, apparently. They all sat in silence for a bit; then they all seemed to come to their final decision at the same time.

"Bottoms up," said Rocky.

It tasted like Ellie remembered, hot and greasy and earthy. It made her start sweating, but nothing else.

"Maybe a little more?" she asked, but then Fin gasped. Her eyes blazed every color of the rainbow at once, and her skin took on a faint luminous sheen before she stiffened and fainted prettily onto Rocky. Rocky shook Fin's shoulder for a moment, and then his eyes went funny too, and he fell back with a moan.

Ellie watched them for a few minutes, unsure what to do while her lover and her friend lay insensate on the sofa, both gently glowing. Neither responded to Ellie's gentle shakes or verbal calls to attention. Ellie shifted Fin into a more comfortable position and then pried open Rocky's eye. The pupil was a mere pinprick, and the whites were still a neon rainbow of swirling, shifting colors.

With a sigh, Ellie settled in, resigned to waiting out whatever was happening. Rocky's house was full of books, but none of them appealed to her. Mostly she just missed Gabriel fiercely.

She was just about to fix herself a snack when Fin screamed.

Ellie dropped the block of cheese she'd been scraping mold off of and ran over to her. Fin was shaking, convulsing really. Ellie called her name and her friend's eyes flew open, but it was obvious she wasn't seeing what was before her.

"The roots," she said, staring into some unknown beyond. Not only were her eyes ablaze with every color Ellie could name and some she couldn't — little tendrils of light extended outward from the whites, little boneless fingers searching for something unseen. Fin wasn't just gently glowing now; she was practically phosphorescent, and tiny spores or motes drifted from her nose and mouth. "The root of it all!"

"What's at the root of it all?" asked Ellie. She didn't know if Fin would hear her, but she thought it was worth a shot. "What do you see?"

"From the center, they spread, and sprout . . . they grasp, and they tear!"

Fin screamed again then and fell back with a whimper. Her luminous skin began to return to normal as Rocky stirred and then woke. He seemed more bleary than afraid.

"I say," he said, his accent much stronger than usual. "That was most unusual."

"What did you see?" asked Ellie, one eye on Fin, who was again out cold. She handed Rocky a cup of water; he drank it eagerly.

"It was as Fin said. I saw Long Island . . . I saw it break apart and change. I saw something else emerge from the chaos, neither island nor animal. What's to come . . . It isn't a natural disaster, it's . . . I suppose it's an act of God, or *a* god, at least. There is will behind it, terrible will, not whim."

Ellie noted that Rocky, too, seemed completely, unquestionably certain of the truth of what he'd seen.

Fin's eyes opened. "Yes," she said. "And not only that, but it's happening soon. Sooner. It felt imminent this time."

"You said something about roots," said Ellie.

"The mushrooms," said Fin, glancing almost fearfully at the bottle of tainted moonshine, "or whatever they are . . . they're part of all of this. Their roots form a network beneath the earth. Eventually it will be strong enough to break the island into pieces. When they're mature, the transformation will begin."

Fin and Rocky began to discuss their visions, swapping theories about what they'd seen. Mixed feelings aside, Ellie couldn't help but smile as she watched them. It was nice to see how they were just so instantly enchanted with one another. Ellie had never seen Rocky like this—they'd always had a very casual relationship, fueled by desire; this was different. And Fin, too, was clearly quite taken with him—she was smiling more, and looked relaxed and comfortable in spite of the topic of conversation.

For Ellie, however, all this talk of Long Island's destruction had gotten under her skin. They were both so certain it was real, and she believed them even though for whatever reason she had not been able to see what they'd seen. It seemed impossible, and yet it wasn't as if this was the first time she'd felt the sense that her island was changing without her understanding how or why. It had been too easy for too long to pretend that it was just her family that had changed; then Jones had told her about the attacks, and now . . . now the earth itself was no longer familiar. The idea of a silent network of spreading fungal bodies bent on tearing apart her home terrified Ellie even more than the sub-rosa cult of diabolists who were helping it. She knew that the authorities—well, one authority—had been attempting to investigate and curtail Hunter and his cohort. But now she knew that even if they stopped Hunter there was still something else, something yet more insidious, helped by man but independent of man, living and growing beneath the earth, the physical manifestation of the will of something beyond her understanding.

Rocky's shack by the sea suddenly felt a little small for all three of them. Ellie stood, drawing their attention.

"I need a little air," she said. "Forgive me. I think I'm going to go for a little cruise. It's a nice night."

"Do you want company?"

Ellie was grateful to Fin for asking, especially as she was getting on so well with Rocky. She shook her head.

"It's just a lot," she said, "all of this." Fin seemed to understand. Rocky nodded his head, too, but he had that look about him as he so often did, of only half listening. "But would you walk me out, Fin?"

"Sure," said the other woman, rising immediately. Ellie shut the door behind them and took Fin's hands in hers.

"Go for it," she said, squeezing them.

Fin had the decency not to pretend ignorance. "Ellie, I can't pretend I don't like him, but I would *never*—"

"Go for it," she repeated. She meant it. "Rocky and I, we were never exclusive. Obviously. I'm engaged." At least, she hoped she still was.

"I don't want to queer things between us. That's more important to me than having him for a lover."

"I'm telling you it won't queer anything," said Ellie, "and the end of the world is nigh. It's time to do what we want."

Fin hugged her. "I do like him," she whispered. "A lot. He's different than I imagined."

Ellie managed not to say "I agree," and instead nodded back at the house. "Go on," she said. "I need to get out on the bay and think my thoughts."

"Be safe," said Fin.

Ellie nodded and headed down the beach, toward the path that would take her to her skiff. She hadn't said what was in her heart: that, given what they'd just pieced together, Fin's wish for her — or anyone — to *be safe* seemed absurd.

8

ELLIE WASN'T REALLY THINKING as she steered her skiff away from Rocky's, but eventually she realized habit had her heading toward Gabriel's house. *Their* house. Whatever house it was, she wondered for a moment if she ought to chart a different course, but then she decided that if it really was their house she could go there even if things were currently awkward.

Maybe Gabriel would still be up. It wasn't all that late. It would be nice to talk to him—who would understand her feelings about Long Island better? Especially about it feeling unfamiliar, unlike home anymore.

She knew she could hardly just walk through the door and talk to him about all of *that*. They needed to settle things between them, make things right.

That sounded good to her. If Amityville no longer felt like home, she'd like her fiancé at least to feel like her fiancé. She'd longed for him every moment she'd been apart from him.

Ellie had first noticed Gabriel across the ballroom of the Terry-Ketcham Inn in Center Moriches, and after a while he'd noticed her looking. Later, he'd claimed it was her big mouth that had caught his eye that night; Ellie was convinced it had been that she was the only woman in the room wearing slacks, and Gabriel had recently been kicked out of the house for being found in a compromising situation with another boy.

They'd woken up early the following morning, straw in their hair from having had an actual roll in the hay, only to discover they were both in need of a ride back to Amityville. Convenience was never the most romantic reason for seeing a lover a second time—but it didn't hurt, either. And of course, there'd been something else there . . . Ellie smiled to herself as she killed the motor and pulled up to the dock.

Pure chemistry, as SJ would say.

She could hear the sound of Gabriel's wireless through the open windows of the living room. He had tuned in to a fight, and she wished she was in there with him, listening along. Just the same, Ellie hesitated before walking in the back door. She didn't quite feel like barging in, but neither did it please her to knock and beg an entrance.

Ellie's warm feelings faded as she recalled just why she was worrying. She'd not made Gabriel happy—not recently, at least. And maybe not ever, in a few important ways. She recalled his complaints about her refusing to let him help her; her independence made him feel he had no real role in her life beyond the everyday: eating meals together, sleeping together, talking over this and that, making love. That's the sort of support *she* thought was important, but he clearly saw it as incidental.

Ellie sighed and turned away from the house, retreating down the back porch steps, taking care to avoid the middle one that creaked. Instead, she crept around to the side of the house, where Lester's window was still illuminated.

Talking to Gabriel was just too complicated right now, but things were never complicated between her and her brother. She guiltily realized that they'd not talked about what had happened the other night, when he'd so bravely defended her and Gabriel from the men in those masks. She'd just left him on his own . . . or rather, with Gabriel. It was time to atone for that.

She found a convenient pebble and tossed it up at his window, wincing as it rapped the glass hard. When there was no response she tried again, this time with a clod of earth. That summoned her brother to the casement.

He didn't seem surprised to see her when he opened the window. After nodding at the finger she held to her lips he shut it, and appeared as silently as an owl on the back porch, so quickly Ellie briefly wondered if he'd had other late-night rendezvous while she slept, entirely unaware of that side of his life.

"What are you doing, sneaking around this place?" he murmured. "You live here."

"Only sort of," she replied unhappily. Her earlier musings had really gotten her down.

"No, *definitely*. The two of you are absolutely ridiculous and you should be ashamed. You, plural. He's been mooning around the place like a sick dog, and here you are throwing rocks at my window to avoid him. You're both crazy about each other. Just admit it and reconcile."

"I wish it were that easy," she said.

"It *is* that easy," he said, folding his slender arms. "Go up there, knock." Ellie must have had a look on her face, because he scoffed at her, which was not his way. "I won't do it for you — if you called me down here to have me deliver a message for you, I —"

"No," said Ellie. "I called you down here to see if you'd like to go for a cruise out on the bay."

"Oh." When he smiled he looked so much like their father, back in happier days. "I'd love to."

"Need a sweater from inside?"

Lester shook his head. "I'll be fine," he said. "You don't have to worry about me."

"I'm not worried about you," said Ellie. When he gave her a skeptical look, she clarified her statement, saying, "I'm no more worried about you than usual."

"There's the honesty I'm used to," said Lester. "Anyway, let's just go. I'm sure I'll be all right."

Just then, the back door swung open again, revealing Gabriel's silhouette against the lights from within. Ellie wondered if she'd ever really appreciated just how broad his shoulders were, or how narrow his waist.

"Ellie?" he asked, peering into the darkness. "Is that you?"

"Yeah." She approached him, but walked only to the base of the stairs. There was so much she wanted to say, but so little she could actually explain. He hadn't believed her about Hunter; why would he believe her about Rocky and Fin drinking some tainted hooch and having visions? "Just out for a late-night cruise . . . Thought I'd take Lester with me."

"It's getting a little cool . . ."

"I'll be fine," said Lester, exasperated.

Ellie thought to extend the invite to her fiancé as well; it was on the tip of her tongue when he said, "Well, enjoy yourselves," and went back inside.

Ellie stared after him, despairing.

"Go talk to him," urged Lester. "We can go for a cruise any old night."

"Nah," said Ellie, trying not to let her emotions show in her voice. "When's the last time just you and me did something? Let's go."

They clambered into the boat and cruised west, the Great South Bay smooth as glass as Ellie's skiff carried them along. The night was quiet and so peaceful; Ellie looked at Lester and was grateful to feel that familiar understanding between them, powerful and complete. He understood why she'd left; she understood he'd been hurt that she'd done it without talking to him. It was all there, between them, too deep for speech.

"I'll miss you," she said. "I know the city isn't so far by train, but it sure feels like a long way when I'm used to having you so close."

"I'll visit," he said.

"I know. I'll visit too. But it won't be the same."

"I'm sure I'll move back after I'm done," said Lester.

"Don't be," said Ellie. "Who knows what will happen to you once you go? You might end up anywhere—a big-deal doctor in the city, or maybe you'll go off to . . . to, I don't know, Chicago or San Francisco!" She didn't know how to say what needed to be said—that she was unsure there would be a home for him to come back to.

Ellie was just wondering if she could save Lester at least, spiriting him away to the mainland and then coming back to deal with the problem at hand, when Lester interrupted her thoughts.

"What's that?" He was pointing in the distance at a red glow. It looked like fire.

"That's over by SJ's place," she said.

She looked at her brother. She felt like they had an obligation to check on her and see what was happening, but she wanted to know his feelings on the matter. He nodded grimly.

"Let's go," he said.

Ellie killed her motor even earlier than she usually did and rowed up to the concealed dock by her friend's house, wincing every time her oars splished. She didn't want to hurry, but the worrying glow was only getting brighter.

After tying up, she and Lester crept up the slight hill to see SJ's shack surrounded by several all-too-familiar fires. They shimmered in the night, a halo of colors like an oil smear shimmering around each blaze. Staying in the shadows of the tree line they saw several cloaked figures were lurking outside the ring of firelight, their shaped masks making their heads look large and strange; SJ and Aaron stood in the center of them, their backs to the door of the shack. SJ was balancing her large, heavy-looking crossbow on one arm, training it on the man in the circular mask; her free hand grasped her brother's. Ellie found Lester's in the darkness and she squeezed it, hard.

Aaron had a crowbar. Ellie wished she and Lester were armed, even with makeshift weapons; she wasn't sure what exactly they could do about the situation, given that they were unarmed. And outnumbered even with Aaron and SJ: a man stood behind each of the fires as far as she could tell, plus the man in the circular mask.

Ellie couldn't hear what the man in the mask was saying, but SJ didn't seem too entertained by it. Ellie would have bet Lester's college fund that it was a good deal worse than anything they'd said to her or Gabriel.

SJ's crossbow was intimidating, certainly capable of killing one of her assailants . . . but only one, unless she chose to swing it around like a club after. They'd fall upon her before she could get it reloaded. It was more effective as a threat than a weapon.

"Lester," whispered Ellie, "go back to the boat. I'm going to try to help, and—"

"No," he said. "I didn't run away from these men last time, and I won't now."

"You had a shotgun then," she hissed.

"Yeah, well." Lester let go her hand, and after casting around for a moment, found a stout-looking stick that would make a decent club.

"You'll just get yourself killed," she said angrily.

"I won't sit idly by," said Lester. "Aaron is my friend, SJ is his sister, and they wouldn't hesitate if it was us."

Ellie saw in his eyes that she couldn't stop him, and nodded. "If we can sneak up on them and each take out one of them from behind, it'll cause a distraction and increase our odds," she said.

"I agree," he said. "I'll take that one." He pointed with his club. "I'll go for the one to his left."

Ellie figured she'd try to choke him . . . but would she go so far as to kill another man? The last time had been an accident . . . The idea of deliberately setting out to kill someone was overwhelming, but like Lester, neither could she stomach the idea of letting them harm or murder her friends. And better to take the man out permanently than risk him regaining consciousness at an inopportune moment . . .

Ellie was furious at having to think that way, but this wasn't her choice. It was theirs. They came here to do this. Luck had granted her the chance to intervene.

"Ready?" whispered Lester.

Remembering her boxing lessons, Ellie pointed to her temple. "Bring that club down on him here," she recommended.

"The mask, though . . ."

Ellie swore. "Well, just . . . just hit him as hard as you can. It's the best we can do. But please, Lester, if it gets bad . . ." She handed him her pocketknife. "Go back to the boat, cut yourself free, and get out of here? I didn't bust my ass all year for you not to get to college, all right?"

"I promise," he said.

The man in the circular mask was still talking when Ellie and Lester stalked their prey. Ellie wished they had more of a plan than "take them out and see what happens," but she reasoned it was best to act rather than dawdle and risk things getting worse. Right now they had what Gabriel would probably call "the element of surprise."

Between the fire and the moonlight Ellie actually found it fairly easy to pick her way along the edge of the clearing without being seen. Lester did, too; when they were both in position, she indicated to him that she was ready. He nodded.

Once again, that unspoken connection between them served them well. Lester's club came down on the back of his target's head right as Ellie got her arm around the neck of hers. She heard the thunk but willed herself not to look; she was too busy making sure to get her opponent's throat right in the crook of her elbow, hoping that it would put the man to sleep like it had when she'd seen Ed Lewis use it during a wrestling match. They called him "Strangler" for a reason, after all. Gabriel had claimed that match was a fix; she had a wild thought as the man writhed in her grip that if it worked on him, she'd have to tell her fiancé it was real.

And it did seem to be working. He was heavier than her, and stronger, but she'd gotten the drop on him. It was tough to keep him in the grip as he thrashed, but she only had to hold on for a few moments before he fell to his knees. She went down with him, keeping his throat pinched. After a few moments he went limp, but she held on for a few more breaths after that, to make sure.

He dropped to the earth with a soft thud. Ellie wasn't sure if she'd killed him or not until the shape of his head . . . *changed.* It took her a moment to understand that it hadn't been a triangle-shaped mask he'd worn; it had been his actual flesh. She felt sick as she watched it shrink into the more familiar shape of a human head.

Even worse, the head it changed into belonged to Lieutenant Perry of the Amityville Police.

Ellie had seen the man often when making deliveries to Jones. As it turned out, Jones had been right to be suspicious of his fellow officers.

Something collided with her sternum, knocking her back as the wind left her lungs. Ellie's head hit the ground, and she saw stars for a moment—then she saw a foot coming down again. She rolled out of the way and tried to push herself to her feet, but the toe of her assailant's boot caught her on the left side of her torso. She cried out as the pain blossomed inside her, but she managed to keep her wits about her, rolling one more time into a crouch to get away from her attacker, whose mask—no, whose *face*—was diamond-shaped.

Though dizzy, she gained her feet as he came at her and even managed to dance out of the way of a wide punch he threw her way. Keeping to the balls of her feet, just like she'd learned in her boxing lessons, Ellie kept out of his reach until she had her wits about her, and came back in to try for a punch to the jaw.

He ducked. Ellie kept on her toes and dodged again. Her next punch caught him on the general area where his right eye would have been, and he wailed as her fist made contact with flesh and bone, albeit flesh and bone molded into an unusual shape.

Her fist hurt from the strike, but she ignored it; the sounds all around her were maddening, but she ignored those, too, in spite of her worry for her brother, and for SJ and Aaron. Her attacker was reeling; she had to focus on that, so she pressed her advantage, socking him in the gut with her left hand and remembering to rotate her fist, just like she'd learned to and had practiced on her heavy bag at home.

He choked on his wind, and she shoved him hard. He fell on his ass; she kicked him in the groin. Inelegant, but he was crippled enough for her to get her hands around her neck. She choked him until he stopped moving.

Ellie didn't see who he turned into; she was too busy vomiting into the grass. Her side hurt, her hand hurt, and even worse than that, seeing him thrash out his last had been horrible. At least with the first she'd been unable to really see what was happening; this time she'd watched her own hands as they cut off his air.

There was no time for doubt. She looked to her brother, to see that his original target was on the ground, rolling around and clutching his head and screaming. One of his fellows had come to his aid, and he'd wrested away the branch Lester had been wielding. Meanwhile, SJ was keeping the man with a square face at bay with her crossbow while the man with the round mask-face tussled with Aaron.

SJ was holding her own, as was Aaron, so Ellie selected one of Lester's attackers — the one with the club — and ran up behind him. A sharp kick to the back of his knee made him drop the branch, and in a lucky accident it landed on his own foot. Ellie grabbed for it as he hopped.

Once she had his weapon in hand, she hesitated. Her stomach lurched again at the thought of hurting someone else, but then she saw the man on the ground grab Lester's foot, dragging him down, and she knew what she had to do. Her tired arms had some strength left—she swung wildly and caught the side of the man's jaw. He went down hard, and Ellie turned in time to see Lester had gotten out her knife. He gripped it uncertainly, slashing at the man who was hanging on to his foot. Drawing on some deep well of fury inside her, Ellie hit her assailant a second time, on the back of his head, and then went for the one attacking Lester.

"Let him go!" she shouted, striking down at his midsection with the branch. Lester scrambled away as she cracked the man another to the head. She must have hit him hard, or at just the right point, as his skull caved in.

Apparently, she hadn't heaved up everything before; she threw up again, a sour taste that had an odd pungent tang to it, probably from the moonshine.

Wiping her mouth, Ellie heard a panicked "No!" in the distance from SJ.

There was a twang and a thunk and then a scream after SJ's cry, and Ellie turned to see the man with the round face stagger as the crossbow bolt caught him in the back of the shoulder. He did not let go of a dizzy-seeming Aaron, whom he was dragging toward the forest; rather, he redoubled his efforts, in spite of the quarrel sticking out of his flesh.

The square-faced man took advantage of her distraction and caught SJ with a swipe at her side. Ellie ran to help, but SJ did not need it; she swung her crossbow around and struck the man in the neck with the stock. He dropped like a stone.

Skidding to a halt, Ellie looked to the tree line to see Lester, her knife still in his hand, crashing into the underbrush toward where Aaron was struggling to free himself from the man with the round face. Aaron was putting up a good fight, but his opponent was large. Ellie started running, too, and as she headed their way the round-faced man held his hand aloft. It began to glow with a strange light that cast uncanny rainbow shadows on the rough bark of the trees and the spindly branches above them.

"Let you be of some use to this island at last!" he cried as the glow intensified and he reached for Aaron.

In his haste Lester tripped on a root just as he approached them, his hands shooting out to catch his fall. What he caught instead was Aaron, knocking into him, which knocked Aaron into his captor. They all went down in a heap, scrambling at one another.

There was a bright discharge of eye-searing color that made Ellie's eyes water, and she stopped in her tracks. Once it dimmed she rushed toward them in the hopes of breaking up the scene, but she slowed when the three men fell away from one other.

Aaron got to his feet. The man in the mask did too, leaving Lester's crumpled form splayed on the ground.

Ellie watched, limbs leaden, as the round-faced man backed away from her brother as if in horror. Taking a step away from Lester's too-still form he stumbled — limped? — in a way that was all too familiar to Ellie. But maybe that, too, was her eyes playing tricks on her. Surely the man in the mask couldn't be her father . . .

Aaron knelt down, and then stood up again. "He's dead," he said accusingly. "You killed him!"

The man took off into the woods, his first step terrifyingly distinctive. Aaron charged after him.

"Aaron!" SJ screamed, but behind her Ellie saw the man SJ had clocked with her crossbow getting to his feet. He had something in his hand; it ignited and he hurled it at her shack. When it hit the roof it burned with surprising ferocity.

Remembering what SJ had said about her operation's flammability, and seeing how close SJ was to the structure, Ellie grabbed her friend and not the man, physically dragging her toward the water when she struggled.

"Stop," cried SJ, looking over her shoulder. "Ellie, no, I can't—"

Whatever SJ couldn't do, Ellie never learned. The explosion was powerful; she felt it in her bones and stumbled but managed to keep herself and SJ on their feet. Only when they reached Ellie's boat did she let her friend go, but quickly Ellie realized SJ intended to return.

"What are you gonna do?" she demanded, grabbing SJ's arm.

SJ went limp and stopped fighting Ellie; in fact, she just sat down on the ground, staring at her feet.

"I'm so sorry, SJ," said Ellie.

"*You're* sorry? Why?" said SJ. "This isn't your fault."

When SJ wiped her eyes with the back of her hand, Ellie saw her shirt was soaked with blood. A quick inspection showed a nasty-looking stab wound; it was shallow, but bleeding freely. Ellie had no idea how to treat it other than binding it, so she gave SJ her handkerchief and had her press it to the wound as she ripped a strip from the bottom of her shirt and set to tying the dressing tightly about her friend's ribs.

Just then Aaron crashed around through the scrub forest.

"Oh, thank God," he said, sitting down beside his sister. "When I heard the explosion, I—"

"We're okay," said SJ.

"She's *not* okay," said Ellie. "One of them got her in the side with a knife." Her own ribs, while aching terribly now that she was calming down, were nothing to an actual wound. And there was something else—something she had to deal with now that SJ was safe and being tended to. "Aaron . . . I have to go . . . Will you look after SJ?"

"What, you're going back there but you won't let me?" SJ was still full of vinegar, even when injured.

"She needs to see to her brother," said Aaron. SJ inhaled sharply.
"That was your brother." It wasn't a question. "I'm so sorry."

"I'll come up in a minute to help," said Aaron.

"Help?"

"If you can't carry him, I mean. You won't want to leave him there, I reckon."

Ellie hadn't thought of that, so she just nodded and started up the hill. Her feet felt heavier than normal. She was not eager to look upon her brother, take him to her boat, take him . . . where? Where did one take the body of one's dead brother?

Under normal circumstances, she'd go to the police. But that was impossible, given that the circumstances were not normal and she'd just killed one police officer, possibly more. She hadn't really looked at the others she'd killed.

She entered the wood about where she thought she'd find her brother. Scanning the ground, she spied a pale patch and made for it.

She had tried to steel herself against the horror of Lester's body, but it was far worse than she could have imagined. What at first she thought was blood was not blood at all, but a glossy, oily substance that rippled like the bay on a blustery day. It was *consuming* him in some way, absorbing or dissolving his body, she couldn't tell . . . The darkness of the night and the smoke from the remains of SJ's shed made it even more uncanny . . . but not unfamiliar. The flickering firelight behind her seemed to bend with the undulating, oozing mess.

She'd seen light bend like that before, convex one moment and concave the next. Her brother was becoming one of those terrible mushrooms, and at an astounding rate.

She watched helplessly as it grew over Lester's neck and wrists. Just as it reached Lester's face and began to grow over his features, so familiar to her and yet alien in death, Aaron crashed up behind Ellie. He looked to her, his eyes wide in horror, begging her to explain, but before either of them could say a word, in the distance they heard a stranger's voice call, "Over here!"

Glancing over her shoulder, Ellie saw lantern light coming their way.

"We need to go," she whispered. Aaron nodded.

It seemed wrong to leave her brother's body there, alone, but it wouldn't help him if she and Aaron were discovered. They padded their way down to the dock as quietly as they could; there, they collected SJ and piled into Ellie's skiff without a word, after gesturing for silence and pointing up the hill where lights were now everywhere.

Ellie rowed them out of the inlet as quietly as possible, her ribs screaming at her with every motion. When they were safely away from the ruins of SJ's shack and anyone who might be listening for them she fired up her motor, but remained silent otherwise. What could she possibly have to say? Lester was gone and yet here she was, puttering along her usual bootlegging route, knowing she'd never need to worry about earning a dime for his future. Her brother only existed in the past.

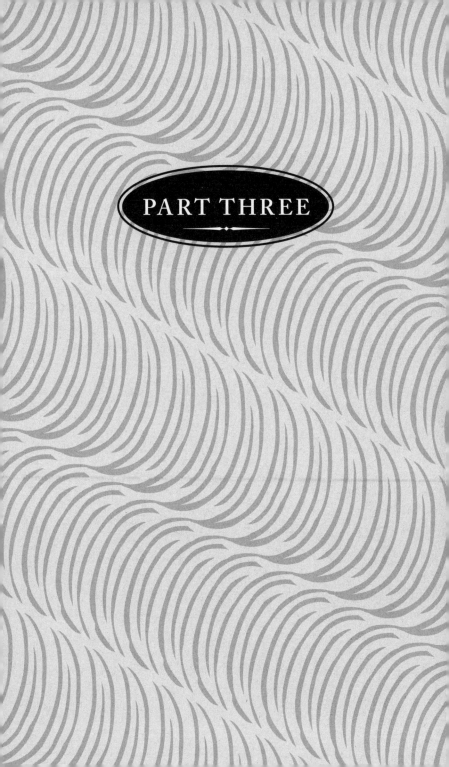

PART THREE

The Demon in the Deep
by G. Baker

ISS DEPTH'S HOUSE ALREADY HAD the cold, empty look of an abandoned dwelling even though it had only been a few days since Susan had woken up on the shore, unsure if what she remembered was real. But in the parlor she found the forlorn remains of whatever Miss Depth had done still sitting out, like a feast no one had cleaned up. There was that odd altar, and upon it, between two waxen puddles that had been candles, sat a jar. Given the deep purple color of the crust still clinging to the sides and bottom, it had once held Miss Depth's sister's beach plum jelly.

Miss Depth had once sadly observed that her sister would never can another batch; she clearly treasured it. Why then the jar should be there was completely beyond Susan. She picked it up, as if it might offer some further clue, and heard a rustle from the paper doily upon which the jar had sat. In pencil she saw *Turn me over* written in her friend's handwriting.

On the other side were a few lines of verse. Susan puzzled over them until she realized it was a descrip-

tion of how to perform whatever ritual her friend had
done at this altar . . . and an invitation.

Take thee these first steps
when you would at last see
what the world seeks to hide.

Susan thought about her friend's white skin and
white hair and black eyes and shuddered. And yet, when
Susan undressed for bed that evening, she discovered
in the pocket of her dress the doily with those strange
verses. She thought she'd cast it aside, but there it was.
In her familiar room, instead of inside that strange cold
house, the sight of her friend's handwriting made her
sentimental. She placed it carefully between the leaves
of the Bible her grandmother had left her in her will.

It was many years before she thought about it again.
But think about it Susan did.

1

E LLIE, I HATE TO ASK THIS," said SJ, "but where are we
going?"

The truth was, Ellie didn't know. She hadn't been
thinking about it as they skimmed away from the ruins of SJ's
shack. Her mind had been a confused jumble of images—Lester falling to the ground; the burning shack; the different ways in
which the men she'd killed had died; the gait of Lester's killer. Ellie looked from SJ to Aaron as if waking from a deep sleep.

"Do you want to go to your house?" asked Aaron. He, too,
looked vaguely worried. "I mean, your and Gabriel's house; I know
home isn't ..."

Ellie shook her head. "Not there." SJ and Aaron looked surprised. "Gabriel didn't believe me when I told him about, well ...
everything we just saw," she said.

"What *did* we just see?" asked SJ.

We saw my father kill my brother, thought Ellie, but she didn't say
that. She wasn't sure it had been Robert West, or at least she didn't
want to believe it. A moment's limp wasn't a lot of evidence to go
on, but at the same time, her stomach knew, her bones knew ... It
was just that her mind didn't want to accept it.

"Demons," she said, not looking at either of them. "They're real
... apparently. People can summon them, and they grant odd powers to their followers. I know it sounds unbelievable, but ... I've
seen what they can do. Now you have too. When the man—the
one who killed ..." She trailed off for a moment, then said, "His
hand, when it went bright ..."

"I didn't see that," said Aaron, looking worriedly at SJ. "I thought
he'd ... I'm not sure what he did, really."

"I didn't see that either," said SJ, "but I know those weren't masks. They didn't fall off. Their faces . . . changed."

"That's true," said Aaron. "Well . . . if you say it's a demon at least that makes *some* sense. I thought I was going crazy when those fires just appeared out of nowhere."

"I thought I was at first too," Ellie said, "and I didn't want to believe it—any of it—but there have been other things, too. You know that article in the paper, the one about the party where it was allegedly some bad liquor that made people go crazy . . ."

"I think calling 'The Prying Eye' an *article* is generous," said SJ acidly, "but sure, go on . . ."

"Obviously that wasn't your stuff. I got it elsewhere. From the people who just burned down your shack, actually. I didn't know that at the time; I just thought it was some moonshine. And I drank some; it didn't affect me that way. But it seems to affect others . . . gives them visions and things."

"Visions of what?" asked Aaron.

"They see Long Island being destroyed by . . . by the same sort of mushrooms that just . . ." She took a moment to breathe, not wanting to say aloud Lester's name, while Aaron explained to SJ what had happened to Lester's body, and then continued. "Apparently this demon wants to remake this island into something other than what it is, for reasons none of us really understand. Our working theory—as much as it *works* at all—is that it's using a local group to . . ." She trailed off.

SJ and Aaron exchanged a look after too long a moment had passed without Ellie continuing. "Ellie?" asked SJ.

"Sorry, sorry," she said. "I just realized where we need to go."

Ellie wasn't completely sure where Officer Jones lived; she just knew it was north of Grace Court, on Bennett Place. If they headed out that way, she assumed they'd see his truck outside. The idea of getting there—stealing through the streets of Amityville at this hour of the night, with Aaron and SJ in tow . . . Likely no one would see them or raise any alarms, but recently, Amityville hadn't felt like the safe place it had always been.

Then again, had Amityville ever *really* been that safe of a place? Would SJ and Aaron have ever felt comfortable running around after dark here in the center of town, where the houses were closer together than the trees and the eyes peering out of windows might not assume that two black people had any business being in the area? Long before Hunter, there had been the mindset that had made his message resonate so strongly. Ellie felt ashamed that she'd never thought about it before.

But wasn't the arc of the universe supposed to bend toward justice? She'd read that in school, where she'd sat beside black students . . . and yet, the three of them were stealing along dark streets late at night, years later, after one of those former students had just had her business burned to the ground by hateful bigots.

The only encouraging part about any of this was that they might be up against a demon, but its servants were mere men. Men could be killed, as they'd just proved—and Rocky had said that demons *needed* people in order to work their will in the world.

Stop the people; stop the demon.

"So . . . where are we going?" SJ asked again as they reached the boatyard.

"Officer Jones's house," said Ellie as she killed her boat's engine.

"Oh, hell no," said SJ. "I'm not going to some cop's house in the middle of the night; I don't care who or what's trying to destroy the world. I can't help if I get my ass shot before I have a chance to say 'Hello, Officer, how are you this fine evening.'" She said this last in such an accurate imitation of a snooty white person that Ellie actually laughed.

"Jones is all right," she assured SJ, sobering at the thought of talking to him, telling him all that had happened, including what had happened to her brother. "I promise he's not like that."

SJ frowned. "Didn't you say one of the men who blew up my house was a cop?"

"Yes—but that's exactly why Jones has been investigating this on his own," said Ellie.

"Doesn't seem like he's been doing too good a job of it," muttered SJ.

Ellie didn't want to get into an argument. "I understand why you don't trust him, but I hope you trust me enough to know I wouldn't take you somewhere you'd be shot on sight. I really think he's the best chance we've got right now. He'll believe us, take us seriously, plus he knows first aid," she said, her eyes drifting to SJ's side.

"All right, all right," said SJ. "Let's go, then."

They slipped through the streets of Amityville as the moon sank low. It wasn't a long walk—nothing was too far away in their little village—but the dark shadows and the specter of what they'd seen made the half-mile seem a lot longer. The last few minutes were the worst, as Ellie peered at every house on Bennett before she finally spied Jones's familiar pickup and sighed in relief.

"We're here," she whispered.

"Goody," muttered SJ.

Ellie pleaded with SJ with her eyes; SJ shrugged in annoyance and went to wait in the gloom beneath a spreading oak with Aaron as Ellie went up to the door. She knocked softly, her heart seeming louder than her gentle taps, but when that brought no response she knocked properly.

Jones answered the door in slacks but no shirt, looking extremely confused. He held a lit candle in a candlestick, like Wee Willie Winkie; the light made her eyes water as she tried not to stare at his hairy chest.

"Ellie?" He rubbed at his eyes. "Have you been in another fight?"

"Yeah." She looked up and down the street. "I have friends with me. We need shelter, and one of them is hurt. Can we come in?"

"Of course." He stood aside; Ellie motioned to Aaron and SJ. "You're all welcome here. I did a bit of field medicine when I was in the service. Who needs patching up?"

"Me," said SJ, with less than her usual surliness. She seemed pleased by their polite reception. "I got stabbed."

"I've stitched up a friend once or twice . . . but not recently. Still, let me take a look. I'll be honest if I think we need to get you to a doctor."

At the word "doctor," Ellie's strength left her and she slumped against the cool wall of Jones's little house. The sensation the word evoked in her was intense and raw and dangerous. She tried to distract herself by looking around while Aaron explained to Jones much of what had happened.

It was funny—Jones didn't seem like the sentimental type, or religious, and yet there was a dusty-looking statue of the Virgin Mary on a shelf, and old photos hung everywhere, many of short, brown-skinned, dark-haired people beneath tropical trees. She spied a picture of two people standing outside a Catholic church —the man tall and pale, in the dress uniform of a military man; the woman short and darker, in an elaborate wedding dress.

It was uncomfortable being in Jones's house—observing his life beyond him being a cop on the take who would flirt with her a little sometimes. There was nothing embarrassing, per se—his house was tidy enough, and clean, but it was just so strange to think about him living here, sitting on his sofa reading a book, bringing a girl back here for lovemaking, or cooking himself a solitary dinner. Well, it didn't look like he did much of that, given the terracotta pot perched on a windowsill, containing what had once been oregano but was now little more than a fossil.

"I think I can clean this up for you and stitch it," he said, retreating into another room to get a kit, "but you should have it looked at. In fact, I'm surprised you came here; shouldn't Lester be better able to— Wait, what's happened?"

Ellie wasn't in Jones's line of sight; it must have been something about Aaron's and SJ's expressions that alerted Jones to the situation. Ellie closed her eyes and merely listened as they explained more, with Jones making exclamations here and there.

She heard a creak as he walked over to her. "Ellie," he said softly. "You don't have to look at me . . . you don't have to speak . . . but I'm sorry."

Ellie nodded, fighting back tears she wouldn't let fall. Jones didn't try to touch her; she was at least grateful for that; he just pressed his own handkerchief into her hands and let her be.

"You did the right thing, coming here," he said thoughtfully, his voice farther away; he had rejoined SJ and Aaron. "It will be helpful, especially when it gets out that a cop's been killed. I bet it was Ellsworth . . ." Jones trailed off for a few moments, then said, "The biggest problem now is figuring out what they'll do next, especially if the plan is, well, destroying the island. And frankly, we still don't know for sure that Hunter is behind all of this. All we have is circumstantial evidence."

This annoyed Ellie. "It's *circumstantial* that those creeps in the woods called me 'daughter of the island'?"

"That's basically the definition of it. An odd turn of phrase isn't proof," said Jones. "It could be a coincidence."

Ellie thought, *I could just ask Pop,* but didn't say it. He had no reason to tell the truth. Even if his lie about Hunter was a lie of omission, he'd lied . . . lied that his cult was just a church, that Hunter was a simple man with good ideas he respected. She had no idea if killing his own son—if that had indeed been her father—would change him or not.

"I don't think it's a coincidence" is how she summed all this up.

"I don't think it is either," said Jones. "Remember, I was there with you at the rally; I saw what you saw. I'm not doubting you, any of you—even the wilder bits with the masks and the fires and whatnot. But if we're wrong—if we go after him and it turns out it *is* a coincidence—how much time will we have wasted if the end of the world really is nigh?"

Ellie looked to SJ, whose expression had gone from skeptical to considering as Jones spoke.

"So what do you think we should do?" she asked.

"I'd say we need to gather our forces," said Jones. "We need to get everyone who's with us in one place."

"Who else is with us?" asked SJ.

"Gabriel," said Aaron.

Ellie's stomach rolled over. Aaron seemed so certain, but she wasn't.

"We need to give him another chance, Ellie," said Aaron. She nodded.

"Let's head to his place," said Jones. "My fellow police officers might come here if I don't show up tomorrow, and I don't want them finding you. Anyone else?"

"Fin and Rocky," said Ellie.

"Where are they?" asked Jones.

"Oak Beach."

This caused some consternation for a time—everyone seemed to have a different idea of whether Ellie should go now to retrieve Rocky and Fin, or come back to Gabriel's with them and then go get the others the next morning. Ellie let them argue as she mulled it over in her own mind. On the one hand, she longed to see Gabriel. The memory of his arms made her yearn for his touch, and she hated the idea of SJ, Aaron, and Jones telling him that his friend and almost-brother-in-law had been killed horribly in a way that beggared belief.

That said, gathering everyone together had to take precedence. Not only that, but there was no guarantee that when they saw each other they'd have the sort of reunion Ellie hoped for . . . It wasn't like he'd rushed down the porch steps to embrace her the last time she'd shown up at his door.

"I'm going to Oak Beach," she said. "I think it'll be best if we not backtrack. If our goal is putting our heads together, it ought to be with the two people who've actually seen this demon's plans."

"Let me finish up with SJ's side and we can go," said Jones.

"There's no need for me to wait. I can get back to my boat in a jiffy, if you're all right with it?" she said, looking from SJ to Aaron, who shrugged and nodded, respectively.

"I've no desire to stop you," said SJ.

"Be safe, Miss West," said Jones. "And keep the handkerchief."

"Thank you," she said.

"Nothing to thank me for, other than the handkerchief—and you can bring it back to me after this is all over with. Laundered, please."

IT WAS EARLY ENOUGH in the morning that by the time Ellie was heading back across the bay it was a little lighter in the east; by the time she was approaching Rocky's shack the sky was a bright fiery orange that made Ellie think of that old bayman's adage her father had taught her: *Red sky at night, sailors' delight; red sky at morning, sailors take warning*. Well, she'd take the warning, but she wished all she had to worry about was a storm.

Given how Fin and Rocky had been looking at one another before she left, Ellie assumed they'd had a nice night together. She wasn't upset by this; she just didn't particularly want to walk in on Rocky doing to Fin what he liked to do to her. Too bad; that was a risk she'd just have to take.

Rocky left the front door unlocked most of the time, and indeed he had done so last night; Ellie eased her way inside and cocked an ear, listening. All was quiet and largely how she'd left it—even the jar of beach plum jelly was sitting where she'd placed it on the kitchen counter. Ellie resigned herself to waking up her friends, but when she stepped on a creaky board she heard a muffled groan from the couch and looked over. There, to Ellie's surprise, was Fin, snuggled in a blanket, her flaxen hair spilled out over the armrest and a moth-eaten pillow.

"Ellie?" she asked, blinking in the early-morning shadows. "You came back! I was worried. I waited and waited . . ."

"You did?" Ellie was amazed by this, until Fin blushed.

"I mean, I was awake the whole time . . ." Ellie snorted, in spite of everything. "Where were you?

"Fin, we need to talk. A lot has happened. Last night . . ." Dizzy, Ellie sat down beside Fin. It was all finally catching up to her. But this was no time to feel sad, or tired, so Ellie haltingly related the events of her night.

"I only met him once, but he seemed very kind," said Fin, her voice thick. "I'm so sorry. I can't imagine how it feels."

"You don't know the half of it," said Ellie.

As she continued, Rocky came down in his pajamas. He usually couldn't function without a cup of coffee, but Ellie's talk of Lester being consumed by or absorbed into one of those awful mushrooms woke him up quickly enough.

"That certainly sounds like some sort of component of a greater ritual," he said thoughtfully.

That. Ellie felt more than a little annoyed to hear her brother's death referred to in such a way. Probably Rocky didn't mean anything by it, so she let it slide.

"There must be something to it—something connected with the demon," Rocky continued. "Your policeman friend said there were disappearances before this last attack. Is that right?"

"A few that we know of."

"Hmm, yes. Difficult to say, then, when the next incident will be."

"Incident!" Ellie couldn't help herself this time. "This wasn't an *incident*. This was a calculated attack. A murder."

"Yes, of course it was, I just—"

Ellie stood. "No matter what it was, in the end, I came here to bring you both back with me. We're all meeting at Gabriel's house to strategize and figure out how best to stop them before the next *incident*."

"Of course," said Fin, immediately on her feet. "Let me just go get my things together. I don't have much."

Rocky, however, said nothing. Both women turned to look at him, but he remained in his chair. He looked very serious.

"This isn't my fight," he said, and the heavy silence that followed felt strange in the bright morning light.

"Not your fight?" It was Fin who spoke first, to Ellie's surprise. "What do you mean? This is your home."

"It is where I live," said Rocky diplomatically.

"How can you say that? I've not lived here long enough to write one poem about Long Island, much less give a talk at a local library about writing a whole book of them. I thought you loved this place! Your poetry made me want to see it before I'd even come to visit . . . and once I did, it was my guidebook. How can you have written all that you did about this island and yet not want to step up and help it now that you have the chance?"

"I'm sure it's difficult for you to understand, but—"

"You know more about demons and diabolists than any of us," said Ellie, but he would not meet her eyes as she spoke to him. "We need you. Please come."

"No." He stood, shaking his head. "I came here to retreat from the world; it doesn't agree with me. When I'm out there, I'm lost. I can't go back."

"You can't retreat from the world forever," argued Ellie. "No one can. Looking away from something doesn't make it disappear. I'm learning that the hard way right now."

She was speaking from her heart now, but she could tell from Rocky's body language that she wasn't getting through to him.

"These people—the ones who killed my brother and burned down my friend's house—they're not the same as your family back in England. From what you told me, your family seemed content to live their lives without bothering anybody. These characters, they're not interested minding their own business." She was pleading with him now. "No one other than us knows what they're up to. If we won't help, who will?"

Rocky stood up. "All I can do is wish you good luck, Ellie."

"All you can do?" She finally raised her voice. "Rocky, who's to say it will stop with Long Island? You might not be safe here! You might die with everyone else—and even if you don't, what will you do? What will you do without the *ferry*?"

He didn't reply. He just left the room. He didn't even look back. Ellie's anger erupted out of her in the form of one word.

"Coward!" she screamed after him.

"Ellie," said Fin, taking her hand and squeezing it, "let's go."

"He's a coward!" she said, suddenly painfully aware that this was simply Rocky's way, and had always been. For a long time she had believed his aloofness was a result of his artistic nature; his dizzy ignorance of reality had seemed necessary, something that allowed him to create. Now she saw him for what he was: someone who took what he wanted while giving as little as possible. She was astonished that she hadn't been able to recognize it before.

"He *is* a coward," said Fin gently, "and he's not worth another minute of your time. I'm disappointed in him, too, but we have more important things to do than worrying about some minor nature poet backing down from a fight."

Fin was right. Ellie nodded at her new friend, who also looked extremely unhappy—unhappy with an undercurrent of real annoyance in her expression that made Ellie aware of just how keenly Fin understood the stakes.

Ellie grabbed her mother's jar of beach plum jelly off the counter; the dust atop it still framed her lone fingerprint from when she'd grabbed it the night before.

"I'm taking this with me," she said.

"You should," agreed Fin. "He never deserved it. He never deserved *you*."

"Let's not go crazy," said Ellie. She didn't bother to shut the door behind them. "Deserve had nothing to do with that."

"No?"

"No, just desire and convenience. But I appreciate you saying what you did."

It seemed strange that they giggled their way to her skiff, but the way Ellie figured it, they might as well laugh while they still could.

It was when they reached the little dimple of shoreline where Ellie moored that Fin said, "So what's our plan? I mean, I know we still need to talk everything over with everyone, but are we going to fight these *diabolists*, or . . . ?"

Ellie sighed. "Probably."

"Can we make a stop, then? Before we head that way?"

"Where did you want to go?"

"My house." Fin didn't sound all that excited by this, really. "I want to get my bow and arrows."

Ellie had a lot of feelings about the idea of going after Hunter and his acolytes like Robin Hood hunting down the Sheriff of Nottingham, but Fin had an air of determination about her that she didn't want to crush.

"It's so early," said Fin as Ellie helped her into the boat, "we won't even see them; they won't be up. I can sneak in the back; I have a key . . ."

"Sure," said Ellie, as she hopped in after. She was feeling even more tired, but in a wakeful, anxious way. "I just wish I knew what you think you'll be shooting at."

"Don't we?"

Ellie shook her head. "Not for sure. Talking to Jones, he thinks we don't have enough reason to go after Hunter, but he's a cop, and—"

"Wait, *Officer* Jones?"

"You know him?"

"He's the one who talked to me after the incident with the liquor," said Fin. "He was very kind to me. I appreciated his candor, even if he did laugh in my face."

"That's definitely Jones," said Ellie. "What was he laughing about?"

"I pretended not to know from whence the booze had come, but as it turned out, Jimmy and Bobbie had already squealed."

Ellie was unimpressed to hear she'd been betrayed by Jimmy, but also unsurprised. "I'm sure he thought that was a riot."

"Oh yes."

They zipped along toward Fin's place in the morning sunshine, the breeze cool on their faces but promising more of August's oppressive heat. Ellie watched Fin as she sat in the bow, her blonde curls bouncing in the wind. She turned around and smiled, and it was the most genuine thing Ellie had ever seen. Fin was not quite a Hollywood beauty, but in that moment she could have broken America's heart on the silver screen. Or at the very least sold them Lysol or hot dogs.

Fin had really opened up to Ellie the day before . . . and because of her bravery, even in the face of Ellie's scorn, they now had some small idea of what they were doing. Or what they were up against, at least. Ellie figured it was time for her to do the same.

"Fin." Ellie took a deep breath, and for the first time, spoke aloud her fears. "I think my father was the one who killed my brother. I don't have a lot of evidence—he was disguised—but after he did what he did . . . when he backed away from Lester's body . . . he moved in a certain way that was very familiar to me."

"Because of his injury," said Fin, surprising Ellie before she remembered Fin had stopped by her house. "Oh my goodness. Ellie, that's— What do I even say?"

"I don't know what to say, either, or how to feel, or what to do. I called Rocky a coward earlier, but I'm just as bad. My friend SJ, she shot the man who killed Lester. I'm afraid if I go home, Pop'll have some big wound in his shoulder, and I won't be able to doubt myself anymore—I'll know."

"But at the same time, he might have information we could use."

"I thought of that too, but I'm afraid he'll lie to us, if we ask. He's been loyal to Hunter this whole time; there's no way we can make him tell the truth."

Fin got a strange look on her face as Ellie said this.

"Maybe we could make him tell the truth," she said slowly.

Ellie laughed, but it was a dry, hollow sort of sound. "I've never been able to make my old man do anything."

"Yes, but . . ."

Ellie peered at her friend, who was once again seized with that powerful, enthusiastic energy. Ellie wondered what it would have been like to march alongside her for suffrage. She had probably been a sight to be seen.

"What are you thinking?" she asked.

Fin blushed, then blurted out, "Why not fight fire with fire? What if *we* summoned a demon?"

It was obvious Fin was serious, but this was even crazier than her idea of using a bow and arrow to fight these face-changing, fire-summoning demon-worshippers. Sometimes it was the duty of a friend to listen and support, but this wasn't one of those times. She had to put a stop to this idle fancy.

"Fin, that's absurd."

"It might sound that way, but I'm serious. What if we summoned a demon and used it to help us? Miss Depth in *The Demon in the Deep* summons one to see the truth of the world, and—"

"*The Demon in the Deep* is a children's book."

"But Rocky's poetry was real . . . or at least, it was based on real experiences. Real *demonic* experiences."

"Fin . . ."

"How could it hurt to try?" Fin reached into Ellie's bag. "Look, we even have the beach plum jelly! And in my copy of *The Demon in the Deep* . . . Please don't look at me like that, Ellie. Listen—in my copy, the author, she inscribed it to me personally when I met her, and the inscription, it said that everything in the book was true, just like in Rocky's."

Ellie pulled a face at the mention of Rocky. "That doesn't mean anything, Fin. Lots of books for children have little fake magic spells. Do you think we should also try to buy some silver shoes for everyone and say 'There's no place like home' in the hopes that we all get transported to Oz?"

She'd gone too far, and she saw it in Fin's wounded expression. Remembering all Fin had told her of her life, she repented immediately.

"I'm sorry," said Ellie. "I'm frightened of what's to come, so I want us to keep our feet on the ground . . . and I just really don't think it's feasible for us to summon a demon."

"Hunter did."

That was true. Ellie had to concede that point, at least.

"All right. So let's say it's possible," Ellie said. "What would happen to you—to us? Rocky said there was always a cost. What will be the cost for you? Didn't you say that this Miss Depth doesn't do so well at the end of your book?"

"No . . . but none of us are going to be doing well if Hunter succeeds. I think it's worth a shot. What if it works? Think about what we could find out." She was begging Ellie with her eyes. "You wouldn't accuse your father, even just to me, if you didn't have good reason to think it was him. I also know if you thought he'd talk to you about it, you would have gone to him by now. He's the best lead we've got unless you just want to go to Hunter's house, break down the door, and . . ."

"It just seems like a huge waste of time," said Ellie, but at Fin's expression, she sighed. "Then again, how much time could it really take?"

"It won't take long to grab my gear and my copy of the book," said Fin eagerly. "We can skedaddle right after."

They were in sight of Fin's house. Fin climbed awkwardly out of the boat as Ellie tied up—she really was jazzed. "Come on," said Fin as Ellie lingered over the knot. Time was indeed of the essence, but Ellie had never been inside a house this nice before. While she was curious about how these people lived, she was uneasy, too. She felt out of place here—she always did, even when she was selling rich folks the liquor they wanted. After all, it's not like any of them had ever invited her in for a drink.

With a flush, Ellie realized that Fin had been the first to do that. And look how that had gone.

Ellie and Fin crossed the lawn, their footprints revealing the dark green of the grass beneath the silver of the dew and spiderwebs. It was so peaceful here on Ocean Avenue, where the lawns were so manicured, and the boats had no peeling paint. This time of day everyone was still inside, either asleep or just eating their breakfasts. The sounds of working people had not yet intruded —

only the birds and insects and the whispering of leaves and the lap of water against wood and stone.

And yet, even so, there at the edge of Fin's lawn Ellie saw the telltale black smear of those foul mushrooms. In fact, as she looked closer, they were sprouting everywhere, at the base of the rose-bushes near the house, and at the edges of the gazebo where she and Fin had once drunk a glass of iced tea together. Beautiful this place might be, but money and class would not save it. It would be destroyed too, if they failed.

2

THE HOUSE WAS QUIET as Fin collected her archery gear from the closet with all the athletic equipment and raided the larder for a bite to eat. One of the servants bustled in to start breakfast for the household as they were tearing in to some bread and butter, which made Ellie stiffen up. Fin was on good terms with them all, however, and Ellie visibly relaxed when Lucy didn't seem to think there was anything strange about Fin being there making coffee.

"Will you be eating with everyone, Mrs. Coulthead?" she asked as she gathered plates and cups from the cabinet.

"No, thank you," Fin said as she handed Lucy a cup of coffee with cream, just as she knew the older woman liked it.

"Sugar, please," said Ellie as Fin poured a second, and then added a surprising amount on top of what Fin had already stirred in.

"Enjoy it," said Fin, after taking a sip of her own. "I'm going to go get a few things from my bedroom."

It wasn't until after Fin surprised Jimmy out of a deep sleep that she realized she had forgotten he'd be there, in their bedroom. Recalling where she'd spent much of the previous night, she blushed.

"Kid?" he said. "Is that you?"

"I'm sorry if I worried you. I was out and it got late so I just stayed where I was."

"Okay," he said blearily. "We were just surprised when you didn't bring the car back."

Jimmy mentioning the car ameliorated a few of Fin's feelings of guilt, as did his report that they were surprised, not worried. It was odd, but even after just one night away from it, their bedroom didn't feel like hers anymore.

Ellie was right; she needed to leave. This situation was not working out for any of them. She was done, and the realization made her feel happier than she had in a long time.

"I'm sorry to wake you," she said. "I'll get the car back when I can, but I have a busy day ahead. I'm only here for a moment."

"Wait, no . . . Don't go."

Fin paused with her hand on the door of the closet. "I have to; I'm sorry." Without further discussion, she opened the closet, selected a bag, and then put her sturdy brogues in there, along with some fresh undergarments and her favorite sporty dress.

Jimmy sat up in bed, watching her. "This is important, Fin."

Fin reemerged and went for her bookshelf to grab *The Demon in the Deep*. "What is?"

Jimmy swung his legs over the side of the bed and grabbed his dressing gown. "Well . . . last night, we decided we're moving, and—"

"We?" asked Fin wryly.

"All of us. It's not our fault you weren't here to discuss it," said Jimmy.

Fin suspected that her absence the previous evening actually had had quite a bit to do with the timing of this conversation, but she did not choose to mention this. "What have you all decided?" she asked.

"We'll head to Martha's Vineyard for the rest of the summer, and then go on to Lisbon. Doesn't that sound fun? Imagine it, kid —Spain, in the fall!"

"Lisbon is in Portugal," said Fin.

Jimmy's expression curdled. "Well, wherever it is, we're heading there. You could at least pretend to be excited."

Fin had been casting about the room for a few extra odds and ends she knew she'd want—candles, matches—but she paused at this, and looked up at her husband.

"Why?" she asked, genuinely curious.

"Why? Why what?"

"Why should I pretend to be excited? I mean, I am for you—if you are excited about Portugal, hard cheese if you had your heart set on Spain—but I'm not moving. I'm staying here."

"What?"

Fin took a step back. "Shh," she said. "People are sleeping!"

"Don't shush me," said Jimmy, not lowering his voice at all. He was really upset, which surprised Fin. She hadn't imagined a separation would bother him all that much. "You want me to be quiet when you tell me you're not coming with me? What do you want, a divorce?"

The word shocked Fin, even if she'd been contemplating the idea. "I . . . I suppose I do."

"Christ, Fin!" Jimmy started to pace angrily, like a tiger in a cage. "Really? After all this time?"

"Jimmy, you suggested I see a psychologist because I wasn't *fun* anymore." A calm had come over her, in the face of Jimmy's anger. "You're not happy with me, nor I with you."

"How could I be happy with you? I barely even see you! You never wanted to do anything here. What was I supposed to do, stay home with you all the time?"

That was what tipped Fin over into anger. "No, I didn't want to go out with you. It was mortifying to have everyone ask me if I was your cousin, or your sister!"

Jimmy blushed now, looking absolutely appalled. "That's not my fault!"

"Maybe not, but you certainly never made an effort to help fix the situation. You left it to me to insist you and I were married. Want to imagine how that felt for me?"

Jimmy scoffed at her. "When did you start caring what other people think, huh?"

"It's not that I cared what they thought. It's that I cared about how I was being treated."

There was a knock at the door, and then it opened without further warning. Bobbie was there, in her dressing gown, and behind her was Edgar, and behind him, Duke and Lily. They must have been even louder than Fin had thought.

"Everything okay, Jimmy?" asked Duke.

"Where was *she* all night?" asked Bobbie, not even looking at Fin.

"Still not speaking to me?" said Fin. Bobbie ignored this; apparently, the answer was yes.

"She didn't say where she was," answered Jimmy.

"She was with me," said Ellie.

Fin felt a rush of gratitude to her friend for appearing at that moment, especially as the reactions from the rest were so amusing.

"We were out on the bay enjoying the evening," Ellie continued, when no one spoke, "and as we were closer to my house than hers when we finished up, she stayed over."

"And who are you?" asked Jimmy.

Ellie stared at him, brow furrowed. "We've met," she said. "Though it's reassuring to know you couldn't identify me in a lineup."

"Oh! You're the one who sold us that bad booze!"

Now Ellie looked as pissed off as anyone else. "It wasn't bad, it was just . . . unusual."

"Unusual," said Bobbie, who apparently had no problem speaking to anyone, unless it was Fin. "It made us *notorious*."

"Well, no. Serving it at a party is what made you notorious," said Ellie.

Only Fin and Edgar laughed, but that was enough to infuriate Bobbie.

"You think it's funny!" she snapped, shooting Edgar a look that sobered him up quickly. "I knew it. I told Jimmy you weren't sorry for ruining our lives here, and here you are *laughing* about it."

"Oh no! Not *laughing!*" Fin surprised herself by back-talking, but then again, she no longer had any reason to be afraid of what might happen if she spoke out. "That's bad—not like, say, deciding to relocate without asking everyone involved their opinion."

"Oh, come off it, Fin. We would have talked to you if you'd been around, but you aren't. Ever."

Astonished, Fin stared at her friend—former friend, she supposed, finally comfortable considering her such. Hadn't she been around? Hadn't she stayed home when they went out—hadn't she sat with them as they talked? Hadn't she been just outside, shooting arrows at targets, while they sat inside coming up with these plans?

"I've been here," she said. "Apart from yesterday and last night, I've been here more than any of you!"

"You're only making my point for me," said Bobbie, with a toss of her hair. "You hardly do anything with us, and when we're here, you're always elsewhere . . . if not physically, then mentally."

"And looking about as miserable as a wet cat," added Lily. Edgar laughed again.

"It's true," said Jimmy. "I've never seen you unhappier than you've been on Long Island. I know you don't want to, but I think moving away from here, starting fresh . . . It could really be good. For all of us."

Fin could see in everyone's eyes that they were all in agreement. She honestly didn't know where to start when it came to refuting this. Their version of their collective history was unnerving because it was so inaccurate to her own experience, but they were all so certain of it. It was disorienting that it was her memory alone that diverged from their narrative.

"I do think a fresh start will be good for all of us," said Fin. "I'll just be making mine elsewhere."

"Well, if that's how you feel, I'll call my lawyer right now," said Jimmy, pushing past Edgar as he stormed out of the room.

"This has been delightful," Fin said directly to Bobbie, "but I'm under a bit of a time constraint. I'm going to jot down a forwarding address. Would you make sure my things are sent to me, please, when you move?"

"You're *so* dramatic," she said coldly.

"Be that as it may, I'd still appreciate it," said Fin, feeling rather amazed at herself for keeping her cool. She peered out into the hallway, past Lily and Edgar, who was looking at her respectfully, to her surprise. "Ready, Ellie?"

"Sure," said Ellie. Then turning to the rest of the group, in that hoity-toity voice she'd used on Fin more than once, she said, "It's been a *real* pleasure meeting you all."

FIN WAS GRATEFUL FOR ELLIE'S taciturn nature as they walked side by side out to her boat. The scene with her future ex-husband had given her a lot to think about, and she wanted to read over the important bits of *The Demon in the Deep*: the inscription, and the bit where Susan inspects the remains of Miss Depth's summoning spell.

In a strange way, Fin was actually looking forward to this.

"So that's the book, eh?" Ellie finally broke the silence. Fin nodded and handed it over, opened to the front page. After a moment, Ellie said, "I'll admit that *is* an odd way to inscribe a book to a kid."

"It really is."

It occurred to Fin that in the book, the demon actively solicited Susan—she wondered then if G. Baker in turn had been soliciting *her*. Thinking back on that day, the way she'd been unable to lie . . . Given what Rocky had said about the powers bestowed upon diabolists, it fit. In fact, given the plot of *The Demon in the Deep*, Fin couldn't help but wonder if it had been someone—some*thing*—else inside Baker's skin at that book signing, so long ago. The demon had worn Miss Depth, after all.

Fin knew she shouldn't look for demons everywhere. But then

again, knowing they were real and considering the inscription—*"let this book be a lantern to light your way . . . If you use it as such, it will guide you. Just know that everything in it is true"*—a little paranoia seemed fair.

Whether G. Baker had encouraged her, or whether it was all coincidence, Fin had to walk the path she was on. It didn't matter how she'd gotten there.

"You know . . ." Ellie was grinning at her. "I'm not sure what I want more—for me to be right that this is all a lot of nonsense, or for you to be right, and for it all to be real."

Fin smiled back; apparently Ellie too felt the expectant mood, like Christmas morning.

Ellie took them into a small, sheltered cove and anchored offshore. Fin didn't see how they'd get to the spit of beach until Ellie stripped off her coveralls and shirt. After tying them into a little bundle, she left them on her seat and dove right in to the bay in just her underthings.

She popped up, water shining on her bare forehead. "You can swim, can't you?" she asked. "Seems like the sort of thing they'd teach you in that girls' school."

"Sure I can swim," said Fin as she shimmied out of her wrinkled frock. Before diving in, she tied the matches, the candle, the book, and everything else into her slip. "But I've never really done it in open water . . ."

"You'll be fine," promised Ellie. "It gets shallow closer in; we can walk most of it."

The water of the bay was so warm it was like a bath, but also refreshing . . . Fin was amazed that with all the exploring she'd done around Long Island, she hadn't actually done much swimming. She had when they'd all gone to Jones Beach to get some sun and be seen in it, but the water hadn't been this warm. Today it was truly delightful; she wished she could forget her troubles and spend all day in it.

They held their bundles high above their wet heads as they swam to shore. The water in the cove was quieter than the bay itself, so there was minimal splashing but a lot of laughter—a good reminder of what they were fighting for.

While she'd seen plenty of images of witches dancing naked in their heathen sabbats, Fin pulled her dress back on once she was dry. She wasn't so interested in reviving that particular myth today, and anyway, most of those seemed to be at night, when there was less risk of sunburn.

"Right," she said. "Let's get this over with."

Ellie still seemed quite skeptical of the whole affair, but in a good-natured way—she helped Fin out by reading both the inscription and the passages aloud and discussing what some vague descriptions might mean, translated into an actual attempt at a summoning. What they ended up with was a little altar made of two stones and a flat piece of driftwood; upon that were two candles and the jar of Ellie's mother's beach plum jelly. A circle drawn in the sand with a stick completed their preparations.

"It certainly looks witchy enough," said Ellie.

Fin understood Ellie's doubts, but she also knew they were on the right track. She couldn't say how, but she felt in her bones that something would happen today. She just didn't know *what*.

"I guess it's time," said Fin, after a deep breath that did little to soften the hard knot of anxiety in her stomach. "Do you want to try with me?"

Ellie shook her head. "I'll watch and try to help if something goes wrong."

Fin stepped gingerly inside the circle and knelt before her makeshift altar. She pried open the jar cap with her fingernails, the satisfying pop sending a shiver down her spine.

As Fin lit the candles, clouds began to gather where before it had been a bright and sunny day. She had lived on Long Island long enough to know that the weather was quite variable this close to the sea, but there was something uncanny about the way the clouds were just *there* all of a sudden, thick and clotted and ominous. The light that filtered through them was strange, more like winter sunshine than summer, and though the day was warm, Fin shivered.

The wind picked up—a cold wind, not a cooler breeze on a stormy summer day. As she thought about her need to really know the truth, the jar began to feel significantly heavier in her hands than it had before.

With the spoon she'd stolen from her house Fin took a bit of jelly and then stuck it in her mouth. There hadn't been any specific instructions on how to eat the stuff anywhere in *The Demon in the Deep*, just that the demon required a "sweet" offering, and she wasn't quite sure what to expect.

For a moment, she simply enjoyed the flavor, wild and tangy and tart. As it melted on her tongue, like lightning striking sand she felt her mind divide, and just as quickly it fused, re-forming into something new. Her eyes lost the ability to focus, but she could also see something new—a blurry shape before her, small and more like condensed vapor than anything solid. She wasn't sure how she knew, but she knew she wasn't *really* seeing it. It didn't actually have any presence; this was just a trick of her mind to give her eyes something to focus on.

Finally, said the demon, but it was impossible to tell if her ears were actually registering sound, or if it was all inside her mind. Only its irritated tone kept her from flat-out marveling at it. *I thought you'd never summon me. And even after I practically begged you to.*

Fin wasn't sure what to say to that. Its voice did seem familiar to her, or maybe it was just its presence.

"We've met before," she said. "You were . . ."

Georgiana was still mostly herself, then, it said. *But . . . yes, I was there.*

"Watching?"

More than that, it said. *After all, she meant her book to be a warning.*

"A warning . . ."

Georgiana wouldn't be the first of your kind to make a choice and then doubt whether she was right. She wanted to write something while she was still herself that would stop others from taking the same path. And yet, here you are.

"Here I am," she agreed. "It's true, I might regret summoning you, but I'll regret it more if I do nothing and Long Island and its people perish."

She hadn't told Ellie this, but there was a more personal side to Fin's desire to save this place. The truth was, there hadn't been a day since she'd promised Judge Glasser that she would never again mail illegal materials across state lines that she hadn't regretted her shift to safer forms of activism. Here was her chance to do something direct, something real, something that would genuinely help people.

Oh, I know all about the situation. It sounded profoundly unconcerned. *Usually, our kind work on the small scale, but not,* and it said a word in Fin's mind that caused her physical pain. The sounds were nothing her brain could process, neither consonants nor vowels, no sibilants or familiar glottal stops. It seemed to last forever, too, but then the world returned to normal. She raised her fingers to her nose to find it was dripping blood. Her stomach settled, but her muscles felt sore and spent, as if she'd been doing some unfamiliar task for hours. *No indeed, only the dramatic will satisfy—*

"Don't say that name again!"

Oh, of course. Forgive me; sometimes I forget the limits of the human mind.

Fin didn't think that was the case at all, for it sounded amused rather than contrite. Well, Fin wasn't here to amuse it—she needed information.

"So, given this demon's penchant for the dramatic, you understand why it's important for—"

I understand much, my dearest Delphine. It couldn't smile—it had no lips—and yet she felt it.

"If I ask you to explain it to me, will you tell me the truth?"

What is true for me may not hold true for you, it said, *but as you already know, I can control whether or not others tell you the truth as you mean it, and that makes all this worth your while.*

It *had* forced her to tell the truth when she was young and eager to meet her favorite author.

It was this revelation that made Fin finally take a step back from what she had done. She could not possibly understand the entity she had willingly called into this world—no, not into this world . . . called into her *body*. She had summoned it and consumed it; what was before her was mere illusion. Everything happening was inside her mind.

Before this thought occurred to her, this had still seemed a bit like an adventure—something she could do to help in an unwinnable fight against an unknowable evil capable of unimaginable destruction. Now, she knew that the stakes were also quite personal. Even if they saved the island, she would never be the same.

True, it said, its tone tinged with irony. *If.*

It could also, apparently, read her mind.

"Is it possible?" she asked it, knowing it would know what she meant.

To save the island? Of course it's possible. If you act quickly you may yet avert disaster.

"How quickly? How do we—"

Let's not get ahead of ourselves, Delphine. Fin bit off her questions; it would quite obviously reveal what it would reveal in its own time. *We've just begun discussing things. For example, we haven't decided what you will do to make attempting to save this island worth my while. And before you ask, no, it's not worth it to me on what you would consider moral grounds. The potential loss of life is inconsequential, to me and to the universe. Plenty of islands have been swallowed*

*by the sea since I first became aware of your world and my own ability
to observe it.*

"I had no idea demons were so galling, or I might have reconsidered this entire plan," she replied. "All right, then—what must
I do?"

There it is, said the demon, sounding pleased. *The reason I
marked you as my own. Even all those years ago you displayed that
cool ability to see the ridiculous in things. One needs it to deal with demons . . . at least, to deal successfully with us.*

"What does *successfully* mean to you?" she asked. "To me, it
means saving the island."

*Then that is your truth, and we will treat it as inviolate. I will help
you, Delphine, but you must give me something in return.*

"Name it."

Yourself. Fin had nothing to say to that, so after a moment it
continued. *It is the same cost for everyone. You are no different than
Georgiana. I want you, Delphine.*

"You want me?"

*Yes. I enjoy living as a human, when I can, and since humans need
me, I frequently get to indulge.*

Fin hated herself for hesitating, but she did. This was not what
she had come prepared for. She barely knew who she was, and this
demon was now asking her to become someone else.

*I can't go making exceptions or everyone will think they're entitled
to one,* it said. *But, I don't consider myself cruel, or at least not overly
so . . . Since you have been so lost to yourself for so long, I'll promise I
won't take my rights immediately.*

"That's what you told Miss Depth, too."

*True, but I have no desire to engage in this endeavor of yours. Sav-
ing this island is nothing to me. I will grant you what gifts I can give
you—what generous gifts I can give you—to complete your task with
my blessing while I attend to other matters, and then . . . Who can say?
I'll come for you eventually, in ten days, or ten years . . . It's so easy to*

lose track of time, don't you think? Maybe you'll live a long life and die of natural causes before I get around to it. I can be forgetful, like anyone else.

"Would you say you think you'll come for me in closer to ten days or ten years? I'll trust your answer, whatever you say, given that you're a demon of truth . . ."

Is it wise to get cute with me, do you think? She did not, and it knew that. *Indeed. So, what will it be, Delphine? Your life, or everyone else's? What matters more? Were you telling the truth when you said you wanted to save the island, or was that a lie?*

"It wasn't a lie." Fin knew that much. "Tell me of these generous gifts?"

The gift of truth, what else? Fin felt more blood dripping from her nose, and she realized she hadn't blinked her eyes during their entire conversation. She couldn't. She wondered what Ellie was thinking, watching this.

Ah, yes . . . Ellie. That girl is trouble, said the demon thoughtfully. *She is becoming anxious; we should finish up soon. I'd try to recruit her, too — she's also quite capable — but she's immune.*

"Immune?" The word conjured up the memory of getting her diphtheria vaccination the previous year. "Immune to what?"

I mean she cannot be swayed by demonic influence. That's why that liquor you've all been drinking had no effect on her.

"But she said she's been seeing things that others can't . . ."

There was a grudging respect in its tone now. *Her immunity allows her to discern the truth in different ways than I can provide. This happens sometimes . . . Some of your kind are particularly sensitive to our influence, while others cannot be touched by us. It makes her useless to me . . . but likely quite useful to you, in your coming fight. The quintessence of that which would destroy this island is change, and its servants can ensorcel and bewitch with their words, bringing people to their side. It's easier to do when the message is . . . palatable . . . but your comrades must also beware.*

"Thank you for the warning," said Fin.

Then we have a deal?

"I have one more question."

"Let's have it." The demon now sounded bored.

"Why on earth has Hunter spent his time recruiting people to his cause if the island is going to be destroyed?"

Hunter has chosen to believe a lie of his own creation—that the change and destruction he beheld was metaphorical, rather than physical. This demon he has summoned—it is not in its nature to dissemble. All this time, he has simply needed to perform whatever ritual was revealed to him by his master, but instead he recruited an army to rule that which he thinks he will create. What he will create, however, will be death for himself and life unlike what your race has seen before.

"I can't let it happen," said Fin, the first thing she'd been certain about in this entire conversation.

Then why are you hesitating? Take a look at your life as you've lived it. Do you really think you'd be any worse off with me in control of it?

That stung, but it was a truth demon, after all. Fin thought for a moment about how she'd been so eager to do something important with her life, the paths she had taken with their detours and dead ends . . . and accepted her fate.

She didn't even have to say it; the demon knew.

I'm glad you made the right choice, it said. *I'll leave you to it. Remember, to your kind, truth is often subjective . . . But when an individual confesses their personal truth, they will reveal much to you. You will see through all lies, including the lies people tell themselves. Just keep a bit of that delightful jelly on hand . . . You'll need it. If I'm not a part of you, inside you, I can't help you.*

Fin gasped and fell backward onto the beach. She rubbed at her sandy eyes; when her hands came away bloody, she screamed.

See you soon, it said.

Ellie was there, standing above her, shaking her. "Fin!" she cried. "Are you all right?"

"I . . . talked to it," she said. "I saw it—I mean, I saw something, and it told me . . ." Fin didn't know where to begin.

"Fin," said Ellie, using a big handkerchief to wipe at her face, "you had a bit of the jelly, and then you just . . . froze. What happened?"

Now that it was all over, she wasn't quite sure.

"We did it," she said. "We summoned it, and we can use it. We should go talk to your father right now. We should—"

"Slow down," said Ellie, dabbing at her face with that big handkerchief. "You're not well."

"Listen to me," said Fin, grabbing Ellie's hands with her bloody ones. "He can't lie to me. You can, because you're immune. That's why Hunter couldn't seduce you; that's why the liquor didn't give you visions. It can't affect you; demons can't affect you. It's just who you are."

"Fin, you're talking a million miles a minute."

"That's because there's no time! We have to figure out what's going on. The demon said we can still save the island, but we have to act quickly." Ellie didn't look convinced, so Fin thought fast. She couldn't compel Ellie to tell her the truth, but the demon had said that she would have an easier time seeing through lies. "Tell me something. Tell me something and don't tell me if it's the truth or a lie; just tell me something I wouldn't know and let me show you what I mean."

Ellie looked confounded by this demand, so Fin latched on to something she'd earlier noticed.

"Tell me how you feel about that cop—Jones."

Ellie went red as a boiled lobster, which Fin could have seen through without any help at all. "Never mind. Please just believe me, Ellie! I mean, why would I be bleeding from the eyes and the nose if something hadn't happened—if something hadn't changed?"

Ellie looked skeptical. "But what if we go and he's not there?

What if we go and *everyone's* there? We can't take them all on, and what if they capture us, or . . ."

"Have they traditionally gathered at your house?"

"No, but . . ."

Fin's mind whirled like a pinwheel. "Why would they all be there, Ellie? There's no reason for them to be. Plus, didn't you say you thought your father was shot with a crossbow bolt? If that's true, and I believe it is, likely he's just recovering, sleeping off his long night. And if he's not there, your mother will be, and we can get her to tell us where he is. We need more information about what's happening, and it seems to me that the most reliable way of obtaining it is to go to your house." She peered at Ellie. "You're afraid," she said, seeing it clearly.

Ellie's expression became mutinous. "I am not!"

"You are." Fin could see it as clearly as she could see the sand, the skies, the trees. "It's all right. I'm proposing we find out if it really was your father who killed your brother. That's terrifying."

She had made Ellie angry, but she was also now seeing the truth so clearly she couldn't help but speak it. The odd thing was, she had no idea if the demon was helping her or not. She still felt strange, but the thoughts seemed to be occurring naturally from within her own mind. Then again, the demon was inside her mind, after a fashion . . .

She couldn't do this, not right now. She had to go with her gut.

"I'm sorry," she said. "I didn't mean to . . ."

"No, I'm sorry," said Ellie, with a shake of her head. "You're right. I mean, of course you're right. I *am* afraid. But I also think you're right. We have to go talk to him." She sighed. "I just wish I knew for sure if this was going to work."

"It will work," said Fin. "Trust me."

It wasn't until they'd swum back to the boat and were under way that Ellie asked the exact question that Fin had been dreading answering.

"Rocky said that when you deal with demons, you have to give something up," she said. "There's a cost."

"Sure," Fin replied, as casually as she could.

"I wonder what Hunter gave up," said Ellie, and Fin relaxed for a moment, until she continued. "What did you give it?"

"Nothing of value," she replied. As far as she was concerned, that was the truth.

3

I T WAS STILL EARLY AS Ellie tied up at the boatyard at the end of Ketcham Avenue, but a few of the usual suspects were already there, huddled together, no doubt grumbling about the weather, the look of the bay, the day's tasks. She knew it was impossible she and Fin would get by them without being hassled; she did not usually arrive with anyone, much less a bedraggled but proper-looking lady with salt-crusted hair and bloodshot eyes. So she came prepared to answer their questions as blithely as possible.

She needn't have. They scarcely looked up as Ellie and Fin passed them by, so intent were they on their discussion, until Fred spied her and said, "It's Ellie. Hey, Ellie! You were up on stage with him! With Hunter!"

"So what if I was?"

"Well, what do you think?"

"About what?"

"About this?" He handed her a little flyer. It said:

TONIGHT, AMITYVILLE PRAYS!

Friend, tonight is the night we've been waiting for.
We have done our work.
If the faithful act as one, it will be in strength
that we call for the change we need.
Tonight, I entreat you: add Long Island to your
prayers.
If it was there already, pray twice.

This community has been reeling. Pray that it shall be steadied!

This community has suffered. Pray for peace!

The time is now, if we all act! Our voices WILL be heard!

Yours in fellowship,
Rev. Joseph Hunter

Ellie looked to Fin. The circumstantial evidence against Hunter, as Jones might say, was becoming overwhelming.

"So?" asked Fred.

Ellie had not prepared for this sort of inquiry—only to answer who Fin was and why she looked so disheveled. She opened and closed her mouth, unsure what to say—she believed that *something* would happen tonight if Hunter willed it, though of course not the direct touch of the hand of God. And yet she could not foresee it going well if she were to tell these men a tale about demons, magic, and the end of the world.

"Where did you get this?" asked Fin.

Eyes slid to Matthew, who stuck his chin out defiantly. "It was in my mailbox this morning. Don't know who put it there."

"Tell me the truth," said Fin.

Ellie didn't feel a tightening in the air, as she did whenever Hunter did what he did, but she did shiver. Fin's voice was strangely compelling as she spoke, and Ellie wasn't the only one who noticed. The men all stood a little straighter, most of all Matthew.

"I went to Hunter's revival, and put my name and address down on his list of sons of the island," he said. "I told him myself he could count on me."

Ellie's doubts about Fin's experiment with the demon left her, replaced by a strange terror. It was obvious from Matthew's expression that he hadn't wanted to confess this, but had felt compelled to do so.

"You said you hadn't gone!" said Fred. "You said you'd changed your mind!"

"Why would you lie about that?" asked Fin, in that same strange way.

"Because I knew what you'd all say—what you'd all think of me, just for the crime of wanting to protect our society," answered Matthew. "Because your wife's mother is Irish," he said, looking at Fred, "and you're marrying a Polack," he said to Ellie, "and the rest of you were so unpleasant about my interest in Hunter's philosophy. Anyway, he said after the meeting that we must feel emboldened by our success, but still not be *too* eager to tell the world who we are. He said our message will inspire fear in the weak as it inspires courage in the strong."

"So you think I'm weak?" Fred said, understandably pretty annoyed by this. "Weak because I married my Clara?"

"Because you do not see how corrupt our society has become," said Matthew, his bold words—or rather, Hunter's words—at odds with the terrified look on his face. "Because you have not just allowed—you've *encouraged* worms to gnaw at our community's roots. You have welcomed the stranger at the expense of your neighbor."

"I went to elementary school with Clara," said Fred. "You didn't move to Amityville until you were twenty-three."

"It's not just about Amityville," said Matthew. "It's about all Long Island! Too long have we tolerated what we ought to cut out. But no longer."

"Yeah? What are you gonna do about it?" asked Ephraim.

"Pray," said Matthew. "We're going to pray for God's intervention, just like it says in the pamphlet. The time has come to get everyone on our side, so that we may come together after God has answered us. Through our faith, our society will finally become free."

"Thank you for your honesty," said Fin, and gave him a brilliant smile. "But we must go now—we have an appointment elsewhere. Enjoy your morning."

Ellie did not think that was likely.

"WHY DIDN'T YOU ASK HIM more questions?" asked Ellie as she and Fin trotted up Ketcham Avenue.

"If he'd known about anything more than the prayers he would have said so." Fin glanced at her. "Still skeptical?"

"Not after that display." Ellie sighed. "A month ago I wouldn't have believed in any of this."

"I know. But you and I both know that if he'd had a choice, that man wouldn't have shared any of that with his friends this morning."

"Yeah, something tells me he's not happy right now," said Ellie.

"That's his problem," said Fin coolly. "Nobody forced him to go to that meeting."

"But didn't you say Hunter could manipulate people's minds, as you can make people tell the truth?"

"He can, but the demon said it was easier if people were already sympathetic," said Fin. "Didn't you say Jones went with you to that meeting? Is *he* going to be praying along with everyone tonight?"

Ellie conceded the point. "I didn't think about it at the time because I didn't understand what was happening, but yes . . . Hunter mesmerized him along with the rest of the crowd. To no lasting effect, though, it seems."

"Exactly," said Fin grimly. "I think you have to want to believe what he's saying for it to last."

Thinking over what Fin said, Ellie felt a flutter of nervousness as she turned down the familiar street to her house. It looked as it always did, small but well cared-for. It was hard for Ellie to accept that inside, her father might be recovering from a crossbow bolt to the shoulder, but she acknowledged that her unwillingness to believe in that possibility was, in part, how things had gotten to this point in her hometown.

Of course Ellie had known the Klan had a presence on Long Island, but it always seemed like something other families had to deal with. Perhaps if she'd responded more aggressively to the occasional eyebrow-raising things her father had said over the years she could have prevented all this — stopped him before he'd gotten to this point. But with everything else she'd had to deal with, and her desire to preserve peace in her home where she could find it, it had been easier to let it slide.

"You okay, Ellie?" said Fin.

Ellie had paused, weighing whether they ought to knock, or just barge right in the back door as she'd done all her life. She decided on the back — she wasn't interested in standing on the step, waiting to see if someone would answer the door.

"I'm all right," she said, but when she heard how crisp she sounded she walked back her statement. "Actually I'm a wreck. This isn't going to be pleasant. Even if he's fine, and wasn't part of that attack last night, he's still a part of Hunter's entourage, and he won't have any kind words for me."

"You were on my side when I hashed that all out with Jimmy and the rest," said Fin. "Of course I'll be on yours now."

"Given everything you're able to do, you'll be a lot more helpful than I was," said Ellie.

"I really can't explain how much it meant to me to have you there," said Fin.

"Well, all right," said Ellie, her mind alighting on Gabriel in that moment. She'd given up many a chance to have him do just that . . . How different would things be between them right now if she'd afforded him the same chance she was giving Fin?

"Are you ready?" said Ellie, unsure if she was prepared to see what she might see . . . But then again, she would never truly be ready.

"I am," said Fin.

Ellie's house was cool and dark inside, and very, very quiet. A look around the corner revealed no one in the parlor. Her stomach clenched. If her father was in bed at this hour, he was either deathly ill or grievously wounded. Even when he hadn't been fully healed from his training injury he'd still gotten up every morning, gotten dressed, and come downstairs, if only to sit in his chair.

She motioned to Fin to follow her, pointing upstairs. Fin nodded. She looked as uncomfortable as Ellie felt.

They heard low voices as they approached Ellie's parents' bedroom.

"You ought to let me call a doctor," said Ellie's mother. "You're still bleeding."

"I'm fine. And I don't want to explain how I got this."

"You don't have to explain." Ellie's mother sighed. "At least let me go to Ellie and Gabriel's and bring Lester back."

"I'll see you in hell before I ask him for help!"

Ellie exchanged a look with Fin, who nodded. They didn't need a demon's power to draw the obvious conclusion. It had indeed been him last night—what else could they be talking about? And more than that, he hadn't told Ellie's mother what had happened.

Ellie stepped into the room. "That's not the real reason you won't let her go to Lester, now is it?"

"Ellie!"

They said it in unison, like people in a play. Harriet West stood up; her husband did not.

"You didn't tell her." Some part of Ellie knew that this was not the most important part of the conversation they needed to have, but at the same time it was so outrageous she couldn't let it slide even for a moment. "She doesn't know, does she?"

"Know what?" asked Harriet, looking from her daughter to her husband. She said it again, more urgently this time. *"Know what?"*

"Why are you in bed, Pop?" asked Ellie. "What's wrong?" She strode over and pulled the bedsheet away from his shoulder. His pajamas were open to the navel, and she saw the binding for a compress right where SJ's bolt had struck the man who'd killed Lester. "Now how on earth did this happen? Did he tell you that, Ma?"

"He said he was walking home last night from his meeting, and a"—Ellie's mother used a hateful word that Ellie had never heard spoken in their house before, and had never expected to, certainly not from her mother's lips—"shot him in the back, right out of the blue. Can you imagine that? What this town is coming to, I just don't know."

"That's not true." That was Fin, who had sidled in and was standing with her back to the Wests' wardrobe. "Tell her the truth, Mr. West. Tell us all."

Ellie shivered, and not just because of the tone of Fin's words.

Her father's face was still a mask, but now it was a rictus of fury. He was clearly struggling against Fin's order, but he could not resist it in the end. "The truth is, I was shot while my associates and I attacked a degenerate—a moonshiner—at her home."

"Robert!" cried Harriet, and sat back down on the edge of the bed, her hands pressed to her mouth in horror. *"Why?"*

Ellie's father looked horrified too, though for different reasons.

"And why won't you be asking Lester for help?" Ellie knew this was cruel to both of them, but she couldn't—no, didn't want to—stop herself. She wanted to hear him say it.

"Lester is dead," said her father. "I killed him with my own hands."

This time, Ellie's mother could not even say her husband's name.

"It was an accident," he added. "I meant to kill . . . someone else.

I had to, as one of the generals; I was the only one who hadn't helped in our grand plan to establish the vessel's nodes all over Amityville . . . But Lester knocked him out of the way."

"Nodes? Vessel?" Ellie pressed him as her mother stared on in mute horror. "What do you mean?"

Her father sat up straighter in bed. "The vessel is the physical manifestation of the god's holy energy that will cleanse this land. It is like a fungus; its roots reach beneath the earth, bubbling up here and there, but its reach is not infinite. It requires help to put down larger nodes from which the smaller tendrils can emerge and spread—help in the form of blood sacrifice."

Ellie wasn't sure what she'd been expecting to hear, but it wasn't this. She had no idea what to say.

"Excuse me," Fin said as Ellie mulled over all of this. "What god is this exactly?"

"If the God we were taught about in church exists, he has abandoned us," said her father. "Just look at what he has allowed to happen to his world!"

"So," said Fin, "you and your associates, you think you're worshiping some sort of *god* that has commanded you to kill people . . . and it's supposed to help change this island for the better." Ellie appreciated her friend's skepticism; it helped her feel like she wasn't completely insane.

"Worship is for the weak," answered her father. "Men of vision, men of integrity—we act."

"So if Lester became a node, how many others have already become . . ." She couldn't quite say it, thinking of what she'd seen.

"He was the sixth. There will be a seventh, tonight. Hunter will do it—the final feeding that will make the vessel strong enough to grant us our desires at last."

Hunter. It was actually a relief to hear the man's name mentioned. Ellie realized in that moment how little she'd trusted herself. Her experiences, being unique—at least as far as she knew—

had seemed insignificant and untrustworthy. A clearer picture had begun to emerge over the past day and a half, but only now did she feel that she ought to have trusted herself.

But enough was enough. "So you're telling us that a god has asked you, Hunter, and some friends of yours to sacrifice human beings to help out some sort of fungus that will cleanse Long Island of undesirable elements." Her father nodded yes; Fin's demon had been right. He'd been duped. The big question now was, did Hunter believe what he'd told her father, or did he know the truth? "How will this god do it?"

"It is not for weak men to know," he said.

"So it might just kill us all. You don't know. You could have been hoodwinked by Hunter, hoodwinked by this god."

"No, Hunter has shown me that which it showed him. I know of what I speak!"

"And what did you see?"

"I saw the earth, consumed in fire and water—a metaphor for what Long Island has become. I saw it change, into something new and magnificent—a paradise, where men might live in peace, uncorrupted by the city, undiluted by outsiders."

"I've seen this vision," said Fin. "I didn't see a paradise. I saw death and destruction and madness."

"Perhaps undesirables see their fate, while the worthy see theirs," said Robert coolly. Even now, laid up in his bed with a wound from a quarrel in his shoulder, three women staring at him in mingled disbelief and horror, he was still so amazingly certain. Ellie wondered: If they prevented this final death and thus the chaos promised by the demon—if they were able to destroy it—would her father let go of this madness? How much of this was Hunter's hold on him, and how much was his own choice to embrace hatred and fear?

"What did you see?" said Fin. "Tell me what you saw exactly. Did you see people living in harmony?"

"Not exactly," said Robert, uncertainty creeping into his voice for the first time. "Hunter interpreted it for me. For all of us. He says he is privy to a greater amount of information, due to his connection with the god."

"Hunter's connection . . ." Fin looked thoughtful. "It's the liquor?"

"He distills it himself. Those of us he selected to be his generals also have partaken of it, to see and to understand."

"Hunter is a teetotaler," said Ellie. "You were so embarrassed for him to hear I was bootlegging."

"What is good for the few may not be good for the masses. Hunter does not drink to excess; he is no sot. He is a man of measured appetites—a man of vision, of strength. I cannot imagine doing what he has done . . . sacrificing what he has sacrificed . . ."

"What has he sacrificed?" asked Ellie.

"That's his business," said Robert.

"Tell her," commanded Fin.

Ellie's father looked as furious as an injured man unable to sit up in bed could look. "Hunter's wife was sick, dying. He began to research cures that doctors rejected, and discovered that men have the ability to contact gods. Not the God you hear of in church. Real gods, with real powers. The one he reached . . . it had no ability to cure his wife, but it did offer answers to other questions. It showed Hunter that like the cancer that was eating his wife from within, our home had become polluted, weakening us, sickening us, and—"

"Yeah, yeah," said Ellie. "That's great, except this isn't a god. It's a demon—at least as I understand it. You've been duped. You won't have this island for yourself if you succeed—you'll destroy it, and yourselves in the process. So cut the pretend piousness and tell us what happened."

"Yes, tell us," intoned Fin.

"It asked him for a sacrifice. Seeing that the doctors could do nothing for his wife, it was decided that she would give her life for the island."

It was decided. The words chilled Ellie. She tried to keep from imagining the scene. It was too horrifying to be believed.

"The power it gave him in return was a boon to him and to the island. He could change the world with just a touch of his hand or a word from his mouth. He set to work, tirelessly, recruiting neighbors and strangers alike. Tonight he will be rewarded—we all will. Tonight, our future will be secured."

"Let's talk about tonight," said Ellie. "What exactly will happen? What do everyone's prayers have to do with it?"

"The prayers are to give those who survive a sense of investment in their future homeland," said Robert. "Right now, men feel no sense of connection in this place. They do not feel as if anything they do affects anything for the better. The act of praying and seeing those prayers answered will give them satisfaction, and they will work harder to rebuild and make things the way they ought to be."

"So their prayers don't actually matter?" asked Fin.

"Not for what will happen tonight, when I and the rest of Hunter's generals convene where the original vessel lies sleeping. There, he will give the vessel its final feast, and all we have longed for will come true. The nodes are connected; the sacrifice will flow through its tendrils beneath the earth. Its strength will spread to every corner; its power will be more any man can imagine."

The nodes were connected . . . If that was the case, a "sacrifice" might not be the only thing that could flow beneath the earth. Something deadly, like poison, might too . . .

"Where is the vessel, and what's the easiest way to get there?" asked Fin. Ellie caught her friend's eye; they seemed to be on the same page.

Ellie listened carefully while her father rattled off how to find the original fungal growth. Apparently it had been growing in the small wooded area behind Hunter's house. The easiest way to get to it was via an old smuggling tunnel. Ellie was familiar with these; they were all over Amityville. This one, however, led from the shed on Hunter's property right to that which he had summoned.

When her father finished his recitation, Ellie was ready to leave, but her mother surprised her by asking another question.

"Who is supposed to die tonight?" she asked.

"I don't know," said Robert.

"You don't?" prompted Fin.

"I don't; I really don't," he answered. "I just know it will be to-night, after the moon is down and the night is dark. We—"

"*We* nothing," said Ellie. "You're not going anywhere. You know we're onto you and your plans; you know we want to stop you; you even know we know how to get there quickly and easily."

"He won't be going."

Ellie's mother wasn't looking at her, or at Fin—she was look-ing at her husband.

"Harriet!"

"I've listened to you, Robert—now you listen to me." She was pale, but there was steel behind her words. "Given the state of our family, and the world, I've done what you asked and given Hunter a chance . . . But you never told me what else I'd have to give him. You killed our *child*, Robert. And you never told me that you were involved with gods or demons, never told me that Hunter had any strange abilities. Has he changed *my* mind, Robert?" She might have said more, but she began to cry.

Fin merely looked at Robert. "Yes," he admitted.

Ellie didn't like to see her mother cry, but remembering what Fin had said about how that mind-changing stuff worked a lot better on people who were eager to accept what Hunter had to say, she had no words of comfort for her mother.

"If you're with us," said Ellie, "go get some rope."

They tied him to the bed by his good arm—loosely, but securely. He could turn over and sit up, but with his bad shoulder bandaged tightly to his side, he could not untie it. It would hold him . . . and Harriet would, too. She promised, and Fin assured Ellie that she was telling the truth.

Ellie wasn't sure what to say to her mother before they left, so she didn't say anything. She wasn't ready to forgive her, and she wasn't sure she ever would be.

What they needed now wasn't forgiveness, anyway. What they needed was a plan.

4

ELLIE'S FEELINGS WERE HOPELESSLY MIXED as they tied up at the little dock behind Gabriel's house. *Their* house, she reminded herself for what felt like the thousandth time . . . and yet, after their interaction the night before—had it really been just the night before?—she was uncertain about their future.

She was certain about what she wanted, though. She wanted to live here, with Gabriel, in Amityville . . . but she had no idea if that would be possible, in part because of what she'd done to their relationship, in part because she doubted they could save the island.

She and Fin agreed that they didn't just need to take out Hunter —they needed to destroy the "vessel." And they needed to do so tonight. As to *how* to do either of those things, well, for that they needed to consult with everyone else.

"What's going on, do you think?" asked Fin, pointing to everyone bustling about Gabriel's front yard. Intrigued, Ellie trotted up to find they were not the only ones who had recently arrived. SJ and Gabriel had just pulled up in the pickup, and Jones and Aaron were helping unload some sacks from the back. SJ, though upright, was moving gingerly; that she was letting other people work while she stood by told Ellie the state of the wound in her side.

"You're all very busy," said Ellie. "What's going on?"

SJ nearly jumped out of her skin. "What is *wrong* with you?" she snapped. "You could give a girl a heart attack!"

"I think you'll be happier to see me when I tell you where I've been," said Ellie, "and who I've brought."

"Another little doe-eyed white girl?" SJ, who was shorter and slighter than either of them, looked Fin up and down in such a derisive way that Ellie wished she'd taken the opportunity to tell Fin not to take anything SJ said personally. But that proved unnecessary—SJ noticed Fin's archery bag and relaxed.

"You shoot?" she said.

"A little," said Fin. "Do you?"

"Crossbow," said SJ. "Slower to reload, but it packs a hell of a punch."

Ellie was grateful for Fin's private-school decorum in that moment; she didn't in any way reveal that she knew too well what that crossbow could do.

"I bet" was all Fin said. Ellie was grateful that Fin was leaving it to her to tell the group just how much a part of this her father was. "Can I try it sometime?"

"Might snap that little wrist of yours," said SJ. "I'm not interested in trying yours; I've shot enough recurves to know they're not for me."

"Fair enough," said Fin.

"Ladies, if you don't mind . . ." Jones stood off to the side, mopping his brow with a handkerchief, the sight of which made Ellie's hand track to her own pocket. "We're trying to get this truck unloaded and sure could use the help."

"What is all this?" asked Ellie as she walked over.

"Sulfur and a few other things," said SJ. "We were talking over . . ." She trailed off momentarily, presumably out of respect for Ellie's feelings. ". . . what happened, and, well . . . if these, you know . . . *mushroom-thing*s"—she looked askance again at Ellie, but Ellie really just wished she'd get on with it—"if they're important to these creeps' plans, then we all figured we'd need to knock them out."

"Early this morning we went out and poked around the ruins

of SJ's shack," said Aaron. "There wasn't anyone there, but the, you know. It's already grown much larger."

"And there were more of the smaller ones, too," said SJ. "They're getting to be *everywhere*. We figured if we could kill off the big one, maybe the little ones would have a harder time of it . . . and if it works, we can try to find out where others are."

"We're basically mixing up a big batch of my mama's fungicide."

The sound of Gabriel's voice was like slipping into a warm bath, but Ellie slowly raised her eyes to his, afraid of what she'd see there. His expression, to her dismay, was unreadable — she could not even divine if he was happy to see her.

"Fungicide," she said, marveling at their good fortune. She and Fin had discussed something similar as they cruised over. "That's just what we need!"

Fin coughed into her hand. "What Ellie's trying to say is that we know the location of the central, ah . . . well, let's just go with 'mushroom-thing'; it's as good a name for it as anything else, really. We've learned that there are other ones, like the one you saw last night, but there's a central one, too. It's here, in Amityville, and we have good reason to think if we destroy the original one, the rest, large and small, will die. They all connect back to the one in Hunter's back yard."

"Hunter, huh?" said Jones.

"Yeah, Hunter," said Ellie. "Someone close to him squealed. I don't know if that's still *circumstantial*, but tonight they're going to feed this mushroom-thing another human sacrifice," she said, her face going red. "And then . . . then it's over for us. It'll set off some sort of reaction that will consume the island."

"That's not circumstantial, that's hearsay . . . but it's my day off," said Jones. "I believe you. It's time to do what needs to be done."

"If we put our heads together, I bet we can figure something out." Aaron eyed the truck. "Let's get all this into the shade and then we can talk about it."

"Into the shade . . . ?" asked Ellie.

"Sulfur shouldn't get too hot," said SJ. "Once it's unloaded, all that's left is to figure out what best to do with it all, and when."

"What do you mean?" asked Aaron as they set to it.

"I mean . . . do we go for it now? Or later?"

"I'd like to know more about this sacrifice," said Jones.

"I can answer a little about that," said Fin.

Ellie made to follow after everyone as they trooped into the house, but Gabriel held her back a moment.

She didn't know what to say, and he didn't seem to either. So much had happened since they'd last seen one another.

"Ellie," he said, and for whatever reason the sound of him saying her name opened her mouth, and she found she couldn't close it until she'd said her piece.

"Gabriel, I'm sorry," said Ellie. "I never meant to exclude you. I've been trying and failing to establish some control while everything's been so chaotic, and doing everything myself and keeping it all to myself seemed like the best way to do that. But I realize now I should have let you help. I was just afraid you would see me differently, after what happened with Greene, and all I wanted was for you to look at me the same way you always have, because . . . because I love you, and I want you, and I want to live here with you and I worried you wouldn't want that if you knew who I was, or at least what I was capable of."

"Oh, Ellie," said Gabriel. "Thank you, but please don't apologize for any of that, not right now! I wasn't asking for an apology, I just—I loved him, you know. Lester was like a brother to me. And I'd said that awful thing about him . . ."

Gabriel was crying now, and more than ever Ellie wanted to comfort him, wrap her arms around him, but she held herself back.

"He didn't hear what you said," she assured him, "and there's no reason to think about things we said to one another in anger." She felt they ought to wait to mourn Lester until after they'd saved Long Island, because if they failed to do what needed to be done, they'd be beyond mourning him. But she didn't say that—Gabriel's feelings mattered too.

"But it's not just that," he said. "I didn't believe you about all the . . . about all this being real. It just seemed so absurd; I mean, it still does, but it looks like you were right and I was wrong. I should have listened to you. I should have thought about how you must have really seen something weird if you were saying all you did about masks and strange fires . . . I mean, it's not like we fight over who gets to read the most recent issue of *Amazing Stories* when it comes in."

"I've really missed you," said Ellie. "It was so hard, not running to you last night . . . or when I saw you this morning."

"You could have."

This was news to Ellie. "I didn't know."

"Want to give it a whirl, just to stay in practice? It's easy to forget how."

Ellie flung herself into Gabriel's embrace, holding him as tight as she ever had. His chest was warm and solid and familiar.

"I love you, Elizabeth West," he murmured, and then pushing her to arm's length, said sternly, "but don't you ever again dare send people to my door in the wee hours of the morning to tell me all kinds of horrible things. I couldn't believe you didn't come yourself. I needed you with me when I heard about Lester, and the rest of it too."

Ellie pulled back, the old sense of annoyance she'd felt with Gabriel's seeming inability to understand returning too soon on the heels of their reunion. "I couldn't," she said. "I had to move quickly, and I think my choices have been borne out."

"You're right; I know you are ... You just don't know what I went through—"

"And you don't know what *I've* been through! Rocky and I ... I doubt I'll ever see him again. He knows all about this stuff—what we're dealing with, I mean—and he still refused to come and help us, just walked away because it 'wasn't his fight' or something. And not only that, but I just helped Fin summon a demon of her own, and it's given her the power to make people tell the truth."

"*What?*"

"If you want to start believing me, start here. It's all true; I saw it. We used it on my father, to find out what we found out about the central mushroom-thing and all that, because he—he's the one who killed Lester."

"*What?*" he said again, even more incredulous.

"*Shh,* I don't want to talk about it with everyone. Not yet, at least. But it's true ... I recognized him. He moved in a familiar way last night, and when I confronted him he literally couldn't lie, so ... he couldn't deny it." Gabriel's mouth was hanging open; Ellie looked away. "I'm not telling you this for sympathy," she said. "I'm telling you because obviously things have been ... unusual of late, but I also can't guarantee you that I won't ever again need to be free to do what I think is right without talking it over first. I didn't think I could afford the time to come back and tell you myself. Would you really have wanted me to show up, tell you what had happened all in a rush, and leave again?" Gabriel shook his head, conceding her point. "I didn't think so. I left that to Aaron and the rest because I had to, not because I wanted to."

"All right, Ellie. I hear you. But I need you to hear me when I tell you that I can't bear to only be a part of the good parts of your life. I need to be your partner ... or nothing."

"I need a partner, and I couldn't bear to have you as nothing. I'm sorry I left you alone when you needed me, but what I did, I did for us as well as everyone else who lives here. If we die, we can't be together, and I want to be with you."

He kissed her then, and it was wonderful. Ellie had a moment's worry that her breath would be terrible after her long night, but if it was he didn't seem to mind. He, too, seemed simply happy to be there, with her.

"Are you two going to come inside and figure out how to save the world," said SJ, "or are you just going to stand outside necking?"

Ellie and Gabriel fell apart like two guilty teenagers. Leave it to SJ to put the finest point possible on something. Ellie didn't know if she was more embarrassed to be called out by SJ or by the expression on Jones's face, for he was there too, that one eyebrow quirked and that smirk on his face.

"Aw, SJ, leave the lovers be," he drawled, never looking away from Ellie. "Who knows if they'll get another chance to make it."

"Chances'll be a hell of a lot better if we *do* something," muttered SJ, pushing past Jones back into the house. Jones gave Ellie a lingering sardonic look before beckoning to her with a crooked finger before he too walked off.

"I guess, uh . . ." said Ellie.

"Yeah," said Gabriel. He looked after Jones with a contemplative expression. When he noticed Ellie watching, he grinned.

"He seems nice" was all he said, before swatting her playfully on the bottom to get her moving. "I can see why you like him."

"I don't . . ." But she stopped herself before she told a lie.

"I like him too."

Inside, things were much less confusing; or at least, differently so. Fin had been telling them about her adventures over a bottle of liquor—early in the day for it, but desperate times and all that. Fin invited Ellie to chime in, but frankly she was happy to let her friend take the lead. Fin had more of a way with words anyway, and had also slept at least a little the night before. Ellie had not, and sitting down on Gabriel's familiar sofa made her aware how tired she was. She let herself drowse against his solid bulk as Fin finished up relating everything.

"Hey," said Gabriel, shaking her a bit. "Wake up. We're trying to figure out what to do tonight."

"Sorry," she said, rubbing her aching eyes and rousing herself.

"Not at all," said Fin. "We knew a little sleep would do you good, but we're about to make some decisions and thought you'd want to be a part of them."

"I still say we don't wait for night," said Aaron. "This mushroom-thing—the vessel—if it's all connected, poison should poison it regardless of whether or not we dump a bunch of sulfur and other stuff on it."

"Yes, but how quickly will it die?" argued SJ. "We need to kill it, not set it back a little. Pouring poison when it's . . . blooming, or whatever Fin says happens in her vision, that seems like the fastest way to make sure."

"But also the riskiest. If we wait for them to be almost successful, they might, you know . . . succeed."

"Yeah, but we're talking about poison coursing through some sort of subterranean fungus for *miles*," said Jones. "We need it to take effect as quickly as possible, especially since we don't know where the other nodes are. We don't want anything to survive."

"Or we could kidnap one of the cultists, and ask." Aaron had a point. "I mean, we know this Hunter person is at the center of it all, and we know where he lives. We grab him, and then she"—he cocked his thumb at Fin—"makes him tell the truth about the rest of the deaths once we've got him."

"It's not a bad idea; I just don't know if we can barge into Hunter's house in broad daylight and 'grab him,'" said Jones. "No telling who's over there, how they're armed, what's in that house we'd have to contend with . . . Out in the open, at least we can see where we're at."

"It's true," said Ellie, and thinking of Hunter's odd daughters, said, "at the very least he has his kids in there with him, and I don't want to hurt *them*. At least, not his daughters. His oldest son is one of his generals."

Thinking of his daughters, Ellie wondered if their oddly similar appearance was yet another manifestation of Hunter's abilities. He had changed the faces of his cohorts into masks ... Had he practiced on his children? She had seen little of the Hunter girls until recently, and had no idea what they had looked like before Mrs. Hunter had sickened and her husband had started down this path.

"But how can we even know when they'll be ready to perform the ritual?" Aaron still wasn't giving up.

"The tunnel," said Fin. "We'll all go in through the tunnel, and listen in."

"Or," said Ellie, "*I* could go in through the tunnel and distract Hunter while you all sneak up on the outskirts, sort of like Lester and I did the night SJ and Aaron were attacked. We surprised them, and I think it helped ... I can't see how it wouldn't work even better this time, since Fin and SJ are good with their bows, and I assume you're competent with a gun, Jones?" He did not deign to respond to this, but then again she hadn't expected him to. "Once you've picked off a few of them, in the confusion we can throw in all the fungicide and mop up the rest."

The silence that followed reminded Ellie that her friends might not be quite so casually comfortable with murdering a bunch of strangers as she'd become. As it turned out, that's not why they were stunned.

"Don't be ridiculous," said Jones, the first to recover his wits. "You're not going in there alone."

"But I'm the only one who can," said Ellie. "Hunter can't bewitch me. I can hold out for as long as it takes for him to get the mushroom-thing ready to bloom, without falling under his spell."

"He can't *bewitch* you?" asked Jones.

"I forgot to tell them that part," said Fin. "Ellie's immune to demonic influence. For whatever reason, they can't affect her."

"Too stubborn, is my guess," said Gabriel. Ellie glared at him as Jones laughed. "Regardless, you're not going in alone."

"I'll go with you," said Jones. "These cowards will most likely balk at killing a cop no matter how many of my coworkers were or are in his inner circle." He chuckled. "I'll plug my ears with wax like in *The Odyssey*. He won't get to me."

Gabriel didn't fight him on this, to Ellie's surprise. "You definitely shouldn't do this on your own, Ellie," he said. "Not when there's no need to."

"Pop said after moonset was when they'd act." Ellie leaned forward, excited again. "We can't know how long after moonset, but if I'm there, I can holler when the time is right."

"It's a plan," said SJ doubtfully, "but I don't know. I still say we light the thing up after we poison it, just to make sure."

"Didn't you say sulfur gas could suffocate us all?" Aaron poked his sister. "I'm all about saving Long Island, but I'd like to be alive to appreciate my efforts."

"We'll just get away from there and we'll be fine. I can light a rag and shoot it with my crossbow, or Fin here can do the same if for some reason I can't."

"I can't let you," said Jones quietly. "I've seen what sulfur gas can do."

SJ stared at him for a long moment. "All right," she said, and argued no more.

"We also don't know what would happen," said Fin, in an attempt to revive the conversation. "If poison or blood could spread to its extremities, why not fire?"

"Couldn't travel underground," said SJ matter-of-factly. "It'd go out."

"Under normal circumstances," said Fin, "but we're talking about demons here."

This reminder brought them all up short. Ellie looked around the room at her friends, contemplated their various expressions. Gabriel looked determined; Aaron, doubtful. Jones mostly seemed distant and thoughtful. Fin was the hardest to read — Ellie couldn't tell what she was feeling. She'd been different ever since the summoning, cooler and more confident, but she also seemed to have the bright, intense look of someone who was worrying. The odd thing was, Ellie got the sense that whatever it was, it wasn't what they were all worrying about.

SJ was obviously just annoyed by it all. *"Demons,"* she muttered. "The nerve of these people."

"So . . . we're agreed?" asked Gabriel. "The plan sounds good to everyone?" He looked to Aaron. "I want us to all be on the same page."

"I'm not going to side against my sister," he said with a shrug. "If we come through this, I'd never hear the end of it."

"Time to mix up the fungicide, then," said SJ, with palpable glee. At first it seemed strange to Ellie that she'd be excited about any of this . . . But then again, she got to play mad scientist and also destroy the plans of the men who'd burned down her business and home. Of course she'd be pleased.

As it was Gabriel's mother's recipe, he joined SJ when she went outside to mix the chemicals. Fin, Jones, and Aaron remained inside to discuss tactics and strategies for their part in the plan. Sensing she would not be missed, Ellie slipped away from the sitting room and went upstairs to Lester's bedroom.

She eased open the door, and a little sound escaped her, part gasp, part moan. The room was as her brother would have left it if he'd just stepped out for a moment. The coverlet on the bed was perfectly smooth and the pillow crisply set on top, the desk neat and tidy, all the pencils and pens in one cup, his eraser right in front of that. The only thing out of place was the open textbook on his desk. He'd been reading about the types of fractures of bones and how to set them.

It was too much for Ellie, and she sat down on his bed. Jones's handkerchief came in handy again, but large as it was it could not contain her tears. Once she began to cry she could not stop, and casting it aside she gave in entirely to her sorrow, lying down on Lester's bed and burying her face in what had been his pillow.

"ELLIE."

Ellie startled awake, disoriented and confused. It was dusk outside, and her body was a mass of aches and pains in strange places. It was warm in Lester's bedroom, but Fin's hand was cool on her shoulder.

"What time is it?" she asked. "I must have fallen asleep."

"We all did. SJ wanted to test out the fungicide, but since we have no idea if that would alert the demon to our plans we decided to rest a little instead. Aaron's cooking now; come and eat."

Ellie's stomach didn't much like that idea, but it was still a good idea to get up and move around before their endeavor. Moonset wouldn't come until deep into the night, after eleven; they had time.

Even before she entered the kitchen, Ellie had reconsidered her aversion to food. It smelled good—*really* good. Aaron had fried some fish, and Gabriel had made dumplings. As she entered, SJ was pouring lemonade out of a pitcher. For a moment, Ellie thought about her promise to have SJ and Aaron over for dinner; this wasn't how she'd imagined it, but it also wasn't so bad. Jones was even folding the napkins as he set the table.

"What can I do?" she asked, coming up behind her fiancé.

"Grab the salad," said Gabriel.

"Salad!"

"We have a garden, you know."

"Right." Mostly, Ellie was amazed by the idea of something wonderful and nourishing coming out of the earth after all this talk of demonic tendrils, but she didn't say that. The mood in the room was good, almost festive, and she wanted to enjoy these moments: the light conversation they had over the meal, the taste of food, the feel of company in the house.

Everyone remained surprisingly cheerful as they ate, and as they cleaned up, and the feeling continued even as they loaded the fungicide and everything else they thought they'd need into the back of Jones's pickup—everything else being Fin's and SJ's bows and ammunition, as well as Aaron's grandfather's Civil War–era sword. He'd spent some time sharpening it with a whetstone earlier that day.

"I guess it's time," said Ellie as she checked once more to see if her flashlight was working. She looked up at Gabriel. "Good luck."

"Good luck, huh?" He lifted her chin with a finger. "How about—"

"I love you," she said, and stood on her toes to kiss him.

"You better come back," he said. "I have plans for us."

"Plans, huh?"

"A man has needs."

That he could think about something like *that* at a time like this . . . It was at once outrageous and deeply comforting. Clearly, Gabriel believed they would win.

"I'll do my best," she assured him.

Jones said, "Ready, Miss West?"

Ellie nodded. She and Jones were going to walk, in order to approach Hunter's house as quietly as possible. While his daughters and younger sons would probably be abed at this hour of the night, the sound of an automobile would be much more noticeable than two sets of footsteps.

"Goodbye, everyone," said Ellie.

"We'll see you soon," said Fin, taking Ellie's hands in hers. Ellie squeezed back. She didn't know what to say; she wasn't any good at mushy stuff, but Fin seemed to understand. Maybe it was the demon inside her seeing the truth of Ellie's soul, or maybe they were just friends. It didn't really matter.

Behind Fin, SJ just shrugged.

"Hey," Ellie said to SJ, after letting Fin's hands go, "thank you—"

"Don't you dare thank me," snapped SJ. Her dark eyes flashed in the light from Jones's truck's headlights. She was not smiling, and there was no warmth in her expression. "This is *my* island I'm saving."

"It is," agreed Ellie. "Then I'll just say . . . stay safe. You're my oldest friend, SJ, you know? Who else is going to keep me from getting too big for my britches if you're not around?"

"I'd think your future husband ought to be in charge of that."

"Look at him," said Ellie, glancing at Gabriel. "Do you really think he has what it takes?"

SJ didn't crack a smile, but her derisive sniff said volumes. "Go on now. It's time."

Ellie had taken many a moonlit walk in the woods around the old saltbox, but never had the trees seemed so thick or the night so dark. Even though the moon was still visible over the tops of the trees, and the night sky was clear, the air itself seemed thicker, harder to see through, almost like fog.

"I wonder how many people are praying like Hunter told them to," whispered Ellie.

"Makes me more than a little uncomfortable," said Jones. "That flyer . . . it was being passed around more than it ought to be, I guess, if even you saw it too. Someone showed it to Gabriel at the hardware store. It's good SJ had chosen to wait outside . . ."

"I can only imagine," said Ellie. "She'd be in jail right now."

"Who knows, maybe we all will be by the end of this," said Jones. "I can't imagine they'll give me my job back, at the very least."

"Why, were you fired?"

"No, but I didn't come in today."

"I thought you said you had the day off."

"I lied. Easier than arguing with everyone. Anyway, I can say I was sick, but if people find out I broke into someone's property and killed a bunch of men, claiming *demons* made me do it . . ."

"I'm guessing there aren't going to be any survivors to squeal on you, if we win," said Ellie.

Jones glanced at her. "That's cheerful."

"It's the truth."

"I know what they're capable of." His tone was mild, but Ellie knew exactly what he was thinking about. She hadn't mentioned it, but Jones didn't seem the same without the prick-eared mutt walking beside him.

Before long, Hunter's house came into view beyond the low fence that marked off his property, and the all-important shed on the north side; beyond that was the small, dark wood where lurked their objective. Fin, SJ, and the rest would be coming at it from the other side. They had a longer walk ahead of them, and a more treacherous one, for they did not know what guards Hunter had posted, if any.

A single light shone out into the darkness from the second story of Hunter's house. Jones cursed when she pointed at it, but Ellie wondered silently who it was, sitting there, waiting . . . and for what. What did he or she believe—that a glorious new era was

soon to be ushered in? Or were they anticipating the end of everything and unable to sleep from fear?

"We'll have to be extra quiet," murmured Jones. "Glad we didn't
take that ride."

"They brought us a pot roast," said Ellie, thinking back.
"Hunter's daughters, I mean. Weeks ago, right after all of this
began." But as she said it, Ellie knew that's not really when all
this had begun—that was only when it had begun *for her*.

Jones was short and had put on a bit of weight since his military days; even so, he hopped the fence and scampered across the
lawn like he did it all the time. As she watched from the shadows
he picked the lock on the shed door with unsettling speed, then
waved for her to come along after him.

As for Ellie, she managed to snag the leg of her coveralls getting over the fence. The sound of tearing denim was terrifyingly
loud in her ears and she paused, straddling the fence and feeling
like an idiot, but there was no apparent reaction from the house.
She exhaled, relieved; it was so late even the cicadas had gone to
bed, so there wasn't much noise that would provide audible cover
if she caused a ruckus.

"Real smooth, Miss West," said Jones as she eased the shed door
shut behind them. Ellie didn't even glare at him; she was too busy
looking at the damage to her pant leg in the dim light that filtered
in through the lone dirty window. There was a big gash in the fabric, but her thigh had escaped with just a scrape.

"Just flash that at Hunter; he'll see the error of his ways and we
can all just go to bed," he said. "I know it'd change my mind."

"About what, though?" asked Ellie. Jones didn't reply—not that
she'd expected him to. "Come on; let's find this trapdoor."

They didn't have to look too hard; it was actually in plain sight.
Streaks in the dust on the floor revealed some crates off to the side
had been recently shifted.

"There may be someone down there," murmured Jones. "I know

you said that your, ah, *contact* would only confirm that Hunter and his gang would be there tonight"—Ellie wondered if Jones refused to call them generals for some service-related reason or if he just thought it was a stupid title for them—"but who knows. He may have a few healthy young men standing guard. After all, if his brass is still alive, who did you and SJ and Aaron kill the other night?"

Ellie's stomach went cold. "I hadn't thought about that."

"You okay with killing more of them?"

"I wasn't *okay* with killing any of them."

"Nothing's changed since then for you?"

"Are you stalling because you want me to go down there first? Because if so, step aside."

"Just being polite," he said, his grin a crescent moon in the dark night of the shed. "Especially since 'ladies first' doesn't seem to be appropriate here."

At that, Ellie sidled in front of him and descended into the darkness. Her legs felt a bit weak; her nerves were getting to her. She was sweating, too, though the tunnel was cool.

"How about you use that flashlight, Miss West," he whispered.

"What if it alerts these *healthy young men* you're so afraid of?" She was afraid of them, too, but pretending as if she wasn't helped her ignore her quivering legs and queasy stomach.

"Then we fight," said Jones.

The tunnel was mercifully quiet as they crept along, the light from Ellie's flashlight bobbing along ahead of them like a will-o'-the-wisp. It was a longer passage than she had anticipated, and more damp. The sound of dripping water was unsettlingly loud in her ears. Ellie shone her flashlight onto the bare earth of the wall. The mushrooms bubbled out of the ground here, too—oily smears that gleamed strangely.

"Kill your light," said Jones, and Ellie almost jumped out of her skin.

She did, and then asked, "What's wrong?"

"Nothing, just look."

There was a faint smear of light up ahead, and another ladder. Beyond, she could hear men's voices.

"Jones," she whispered.

"Hmm?"

"If we make it through this ..."

That eyebrow! It always made the little hairs on her arms and the back of her neck prick up, but she remembered how heartened she'd been that Gabriel seemed to think they'd make it through this. And Gabriel's expression when Jones had been teasing her earlier ...

"Let's you and me have a talk. One we should have had a long time ago, I think."

"A talk, huh? That big handsome fiancé of yours gonna be all right with you having *a talk* with me?"

"I'm guessing he'll request it."

That threw Jones for a moment, but then he shook his head and muttered something Ellie couldn't quite hear, but sounded a lot like *"Figures."*

Ellie held a finger up to her lips, and then pointed to the square of light above them. The end of the passage appeared to be just a rough-hewn hole in the earth, as many of these smugglers' tunnels were. But they were definitely in the right place. It was not moonlight that puddled on the floor by their feet, it was torchlight, and they could discern various sounds of activity—footfalls, mumbled calls, and once, the patter of something that sounded like seeds hitting the earth.

"I don't like how long this is taking," murmured Jones at one point. "They could come down here at any point and rumble us, and then all of this will be for nothing."

"Not for nothing," said Ellie. "None of this is for nothing."

Her heart started to pound when she heard Hunter's voice in

the near distance. Straining to hear him, she climbed a few rungs of the rough ladder, until Jones hissed at her and tugged at her pant leg to stop.

"Is the salt circle complete?" Even when Hunter wasn't performing he was frighteningly compelling.

Ellie couldn't quite make out what the response was, but it seemed to be in the affirmative. It was maddening, not being able to hear clearly—though she knew she ought to be grateful that Hunter's supernaturally clear voice let her hear anything at all.

"If there are any breaks . . ."

In the response, Ellie only heard the word "check," but Hunter seemed pleased.

"Good, good. And what of Robert? Is there still no sign of him?" After a pause, breathless on Ellie's part, Hunter said, "Did you go by his house?" He was clearly not pleased. "How disappointing. I know he was injured, but his absence is really quite strange. Well, no time to worry. If his allegiance has shifted he will not survive the night. The problem will take care of itself. But I hope that is not the case. Robert has been a valuable colleague."

The voices got louder—they were walking toward where Ellie and Jones were hiding. Ellie ducked back down the ladder and out of the light, fearful of being seen.

"He might have told someone of our plans." The voice was a youthful one.

"Even if he has, they will not be able to find us. You assured me the salt circle was complete. If it was done properly, we will be invisible to any prying eyes—and anyway, our guards are already patrolling."

"Guards!" whispered Ellie.

"*Shh,*" said Jones, but neither did he look pleased.

"I must make myself ready," said Hunter. "The time grows close."

"Are you sure you have to be the one?"

"The vessel's demand was clear—each sacrifice must be of special significance. We have chosen well so far, but now it comes down to it—and what is a more significant sacrifice than my showing it my own willingness to die for this island? I know you and the rest of my generals will see everyone through the transition, providing guidance and leadership."

"I know, Father, but—"

"You will do a good job in my stead," said Hunter. "You are my son—you will protect your brothers and sisters and see this task through."

Ellie was amazed that Hunter was planning to sacrifice himself; then again, from her first encounter with these people she'd pegged their actions as pure madness. It was simply becoming apparent how many different forms that madness had taken.

Once Hunter and his son had wandered off again, Ellie and Jones conferred. Neither was pleased.

"Guards, and some sort of demonic protection," said Jones fretfully. "I should go; I should try to find the others, and tell them what we heard."

They heard Hunter call for attention, his compelling voice rolling over the forest like the distant thunder of a summer storm.

"There's no time," said Ellie. "Trust Fin. She can see the truth, remember?"

"Let's at least take a peek," said Jones, unable to contain his fidgeting any longer. "We need to see what's going on."

Ellie agreed; the very minute of whatever would happen that night was upon them. She crept back up the ladder and poked her head up just enough that she could see. As her eyes adjusted, she motioned to Jones to follow her; they were within the clearing, though just at the tree line—Hunter and his colleagues had gathered inside a smaller circle of torchlight that cast enough shadows that Ellie hoped they'd not be noticed.

Hunter was there, wearing his own face but dressed in loose red robes. He'd belted them in the middle, and on his left hip hung a small empty scabbard; on the other, a bottle that swung from a leather thong. She could see it was full of a clear liquid—probably not water.

In his hand, Hunter held a wicked-looking knife, both curved and serrated, as he stood before an enormous, oily fungal excrescence. It came to the men's shoulders and was bigger around than her skiff was long—not only that, but it appeared to be pulsing gently, or perhaps rippling as some unfelt breeze passed over it. When small, the mushroom-things were disgusting; but this one was unspeakable. Ellie couldn't bear to look upon it for long; it was too unnatural, especially when she remembered that it had been given life by the death of Hunter's wife and then glutted itself on the blood of human sacrifice.

Hunter's generals were also robed, their faces undistorted by whatever strange power Hunter possessed. Ellie recognized some of them from the rally she'd attended. For their part, they were holding copper bowls that glinted orange in the torchlight.

The entire scene was incredible, like something she'd see on the cover of one of Gabriel's magazines. There was even an enormous tree behind Hunter, whose spreading branches were occasionally illuminated by distant flashes of heat lightning. Ellie had always found those pulpy illustrations more silly than terrifying, but now, for the first time, she could really appreciate the horror those artists were attempting to evoke. And yet the scariest part wasn't these men's uncanny appearance, but why they were there, and what they were planning.

"What fools men are," said Jones.

"At least Pop's not out there with them," muttered Ellie.

"What?" She could feel Jones's eyes on her. "The Robert he was talking about was your father?"

Ellie had forgotten Jones didn't know. "I'll explain later."

"You bet you will."

"Generals!" cried Hunter, and Ellie felt the tightening in the air that meant something demonic was about to happen. She wished she knew where her friends were — and what weapons these men might be carrying under their robes.

She wished a lot of things, actually.

"Look," said Jones. The fungal mass was heaving now, like some awful, formless creature in its death throes, until slowly, so slowly, it began to unfurl from below, or perhaps from within like an umbrella.

"That's what Fin said would happen. See you, Jones," she said.

Jones grabbed and squeezed her hand before she could run off. "Looking forward to that talk later," he said, holding her gaze for a long moment. "Don't stand me up."

Ellie scrambled for the tree line after hopping fully out of the tunnel, crouching in the underbrush to observe. Hunter was standing before his enrapt comrades, intoning some final words. As he did, she crept through the shadows of the underbrush, circling around to get behind him. Every twig-snap or leaf-rustle made her heart leap, but no one noticed her.

Just as she got into position Hunter raised his knife. The enormous fungus spread wider, its cap separating into flabby petals that glowed from beneath. Ellie took a deep breath and ran into the clearing.

"Stop!" she shouted as loud as she could, and then whooped like a cowboy in a Wild West show as a signal to her friends as she barreled straight at Hunter. He looked extremely surprised, to say the least, and took a step back.

Ellie thought it all through; her plan had been to knock him down and get his knife-hand pinned so that he couldn't cut himself or anyone else until Gabriel, Fin, SJ, and Aaron arrived to finish what she'd started.

But she never reached him. Something hit her from the side, and she went down hard on her arm, her leg twisted beneath her. The last thing she saw was a flash of red cloth as one of Hunter's generals loomed over her.

5

ELLIE SCREAMED AS SHE STRUGGLED against her captors, remembering too well the last time this had happened. Her thrashing, then as now, had no effect.

"Let me go!" She was being as loud as she could, hoping that the sound of her voice, her panic, would alert her companions to where she was if they hadn't found the clearing yet. She trusted in Fin's abilities, but with all the torches around, and the way she'd been carrying on, it felt strange they weren't there yet. The wood behind Hunter's house wasn't that big. They should have found her by now . . . unless something had happened.

"Will someone gag her already?" snapped Hunter. "And you—make sure she came alone."

Ellie resisted as they tried to force something between her teeth until her lips started to tear. As a sweaty sock was forced into her mouth she wondered why Jones hadn't come to her aid, at the very least. After all, he'd insisted on coming along to help her if she needed it—and boy, did she need it.

Ellie heard a shot ring out, and then a shout. She tried to look around to see what was happening, but her captors held her fast.

"Cease your struggling," said Hunter, the air tightening around them as he spoke, but Ellie didn't listen. He put a hand on her head, and the feeling intensified, but again she shook it off. "My goodness," he said. "You *are* willful."

"I found the shooter," said one of the robed men, pushing Jones down on his knees before Hunter. His wrists were tied behind his back, and his nose was dripping blood. "Didn't want to kill him; he's a cop. But he killed Ernie—shot him right through the eye. I snuck around behind him and clobbered him, though. Never heard me—he had these in his ears." The man opened his hand, revealing the wax pellets.

"Curious," said Hunter. He looked unsure of himself for the first time, which made Ellie inclined to think he hadn't told his inner circle about his ability to change or control minds. "Well, I suppose we shouldn't marvel at the lengths some will go to avoid hearing a word of truth or righteous thought."

Hunter sheathed his knife and grabbed Jones under the chin and lifted his face up. "My generals! It is not too late for another miracle. Help me. Pray as I do that this man will step up and see the light," said Hunter. "Let him see the path before him, as we have. With our recent losses, another recruit on the force will help us keep order after our success, after all."

The robed men all bowed their heads, but Ellie did not. She watched on in horror as Jones's expression softened and his eyes glazed over.

"Your faith is strong," said Hunter to his fellows. "I think we've succeeded. His heart has been touched."

"And my eyes now see," said Jones, his voice free of its usual irony or detachment. Ellie wanted to believe it was an act, but she knew better. "Let me help!"

"No need to keep his wrists bound now," said Hunter, satisfied. "But this little interlude has given me an idea. Our numbers have grown—it's true. But why should we reduce them, even by one?" Hunter turned back to Ellie, his eyes wide and wild. "The vessel demands sacrifices of significance," he said. "I thought to use myself to satisfy it, but here before me stands one who has been a significant thorn in my side in my efforts to create a better world. Why not make our savior's final meal be one who has set herself against it, in spite of the advice of her elders and her betters—indeed, even her own *father*?"

Ellie squirmed harder in her captors' grasp.

"Come now," said Hunter, putting one pale hand on Ellie's

cheek. "You would have died in the coming cleansing anyway. Instead of a meaningless death, you will be the catalyst for a new era of hope and peace — something I would think even a scofflaw like yourself would see the value of." Then, to Jones, he said, "Bind her."

Ellie tried to catch her friend's eye, hoping to find some sign he was secretly still in control of himself. But no; his vacant eyes had none of their usual sparkle, and he bound her wrists behind her without a word. That's when Ellie really knew he was bewitched; she figured that even if Jones had been acting his heart out, he couldn't have resisted making some sort of joke about tying her up once Hunter's attention was elsewhere.

Hunter was assessing the area. "Find something to tie her to," he barked. "If she thrashes, she'll waste her precious blood."

"What about that tree?" said one of the men. He pointed up at a stout branch that reached out nearly over the mushroom-thing. Hunter frowned, but then seemed to judge it suitable.

"String her up by the ankles," he advised as they tossed one end of the rope over the branch. "We can't have her kicking."

Her world literally upside down, Ellie felt hope abandoning her, flowing out of her as her blood soon would. They had failed; she could see no way out of this. As she watched the hideous undulations of the mushroom-thing begin anew, she was strangely reminded of the way the bay would lap against the side of her skiff as she tied it up. Soon there would be no bay, no boat, no Ellie West, and neither would there be anyone else alive to remember them or mourn their loss.

AFTER THEY'D WANDERED THROUGH THE WOOD behind Hunter's house for far too long, Fin realized she'd been played for a fool. This town was so small, it was impossible for it to contain a forest of the size they'd explored. Hunter had somehow managed to conceal his location within the wood. Of course he had. He had the power to change, to misdirect and deceive—she really ought to have figured out his trick more quickly.

"*Hurry,*" urged Gabriel as Fin searched in her pack for the jar of jelly.

"I'm sorry," hissed Fin. "I'm not exactly thrilled about this situation, either!"

"I know, I know." Gabriel scanned the darkness as Aaron and SJ urgently conferred on some matter just out of earshot. "I'm sorry. I'm just worried."

"She'll be all right. It's Ellie—and she has Jones with her."

A few mouthfuls of the warm, runny jelly and Fin felt her connection to the demon strengthen. It wasn't like in *The Ginger-Eaters;* no voice spoke to her, reassuring her that all would be well; no soothing presence gave her guidance or instructions. Instead, she just saw the truth of their situation—how precarious a position they were in, and how slim were the chances of their success, especially now that their timing was off.

Fin did not speak these words aloud. It didn't matter—they had decided on a course of action, and Ellie was relying on them to follow through with it.

She also now saw the importance of the disagreement Aaron and SJ were having. She listened in as she peered through the darkness, looking for any clue as to where they might find their friends, but could only discern a few words and phrases: "who cares," "do what's right," and most ominously, "we'll die."

"I'd rather not die," said Fin mildly, sidling up to the siblings. "I know you're eager to kill them all, but we may be able to do that fairly well without exploding a huge pile of sulfur."

SJ looked startled, and she readjusted her grip on the bag she had slung across her back—not her quiver, a different bag, whose contents were unknown to Fin. Aaron and Gabriel carried the fungicide, so she knew it wasn't that.

"The important thing is the island," said SJ. "We need to do what we need to do to, not just to keep *us* safe, but everyone. If this scheme of poisoning the mushroom at exactly at the right moment doesn't work, I'm lighting it up." Her expression was full of admirable determination and understandable anger. "It's under our *feet*, Fin. We've got to get it out by the roots, no matter what."

By then, the jelly was hitting Fin hard, and she could see a lot more clearly through the darkness of the night. Specifically, a subtle flickering behind SJ's right shoulder that hadn't been there before.

That was where they needed to be. But she also saw someone prowling around out there.

"SJ," she hissed, *"get down."*

"What?"

She pulled the other woman down into the cover of the brush. "There's a guard," she said. "Look."

Aaron and Gabriel were not looking their way. Fin rustled a low pine branch to try to get their attention. It worked. She pointed towards where the man was patrolling the shadows.

"I'm gonna take him out," said SJ, readying her crossbow. "I can see well enough."

"You sure?" whispered Fin. She knew they would have to kill people tonight, but now that they were at the very moment of it she felt sickened by the idea.

"I gotta try. If I miss, he'll know we're here . . . but there's four of us and one of him."

"We think. There might be more of them out there. He might sound an alarm."

SJ stood and aimed, handling her heavy crossbow like it weighed nothing at all, and loosed a quarrel. The scream that followed the twang was loud and terrible — and it didn't stop.

"Shit," said SJ.

"We need to shut him up," said Fin, and leaped out of the

bushes. SJ took a moment to cock her crossbow again, but she still arrived at the man's side about the same time as Fin did. Together, they found him writhing, a bolt protruding from just under his clavicle. In the dim light of the wood, his robes looked like the color of blood. Fin was trying to figure out how best to hold him still to gag him when SJ just kicked him in the stomach. He choked on his air and fell silent trying to catch his breath.

Aaron and Gabriel trotted right up behind as SJ set down her crossbow and began fishing for something in her pocket.

"How many of you are there?" asked Fin, drawing on her well of demonic power to make him to tell the truth.

"On patrol? Three. All in all? I don't know exactly, but many more than you," said the man when he'd gotten his wind back. "We are legion, and in the reckoning to come you scum of the earth will die, perishing in a wave of righteousness that will—" But they never found out what the wave of righteousness would do, for SJ slit his throat.

Fin gasped, and Aaron was sick all over his shoes. Gabriel just stared.

"What?" said SJ.

"I was interrogating him!" said Fin.

"You said to silence him!"

Fin elected not to argue the point; there were other voices in the wood now. As SJ cleaned her blade on the dead man's shirt, two more men emerged from the trees. One held a hand-axe at his side, the other a shotgun. When he spied them, up it went.

"Duck!" shouted Fin.

The report from the shotgun blast was deafening. In the smoke and confusion, Fin nocked an arrow. As she raised her bow, she noticed how strange her vision was—not only could she see through the dark, she could also discern where exactly she needed to take aim to kill the man with one shot. In fact, she had options—she could go either through the eye, or through his jugular.

She chose throat.

As she drew, her muscles locked into place and she could feel her body lining up exactly as it should. She'd experienced a similar sensation a few times when she had really devoted herself to her archery practice at school, but nothing like this—never had she felt this kind of clarity, or this level of surety.

She fired. The arrow flew true and the man went down almost silently, emitting only a bitten-off gurgle before falling to the earth like a sack of wet garbage.

SJ came over to see the damage, and gave Fin a respectful look. "Nice shooting."

"What about the other one?" Fin asked.

"We got him."

Fin glanced over. Aaron was in the midst of being sick again, and Gabriel was wiping his hands. She didn't ask how they'd done it; it didn't matter, not really, and they had no time. It was already past moonset.

"We need to go," Fin said, pointing into the distance, where she saw that faint telltale flickering of firelight. "There."

"Then let's do it," said Gabriel, shifting his pack on his back.

"Take the gun," said SJ, pointing to the shotgun on the ground. Gabriel had brought his, but Fin saw the wisdom of a backup. Aaron shook his head, but she stamped her foot.

"Do it," she insisted. "We might need it."

Fin motioned to Gabriel, and they left the siblings to discuss the matter further. Together they crept through the forest until they came to the edge of what, to Fin, appeared to be a ring of light. A clearing—and one, it seemed, that was invisible to Gabriel, given his confused reaction to her motioning for him to stop and be silent.

As SJ and Aaron caught up, Fin tried to discern what exactly was happening beyond the strange barrier that distorted the clearing. It was a bit like looking at someone across a dinner table through a cut-glass goblet, and she couldn't hear anything at all.

"Are you sure about this?" murmured Aaron as Fin edged closer. "I just see more forest."

"I'm sure," she whispered.

She took an arrow from her quiver and poked at the barrier. It slid through with no resistance.

"Huh," she said, and peered up—there was nothing obviously creating the illusion in the trees. But looking down she saw little crystals shining in the light. Something about them looked out of place, and she picked one up.

"What is it?" she murmured, turning it over.

SJ took it from her and boldly tasted it. "Salt." She looked disgusted. "A salt circle. We really are dealing with demons."

"What are we waiting for?" Gabriel hissed, almost vibrating with an eagerness to get on with it. "Can we go in there, wherever there is?"

"I *think* so," said Fin, uncertainly. She really wasn't happy being the resident demon expert here, given that she had less than a full day of experience with the topic. She'd just have to trust her instincts—they were being informed by a demon of her own, after all. "I think if we destroy the salt circle it'll destroy the barrier . . . but it also might let them know we're here. We can't catch them at the right moment if we interrupt them before they get started."

"It's long after moonset," said Gabriel. "I'm going in. I can't take this any longer!"

"All right," said Fin, and stuck out her shoe. With the toe, she mussed the dirt and salt, dragging it through both until no grains remained in the line of the ring.

To her, it looked a bit like a curtain parting at the beginning

of a Broadway show; she wondered what it looked like to everyone else. Unfortunately, what it revealed was nothing anyone could
ever show on a stage.

Beyond the bulk of the monstrous glowing mushroom from
Fin's vision, Ellie hung by her ankles from a stout tree branch, her
bound wrists dangling above the earth. She looked unconscious
or at least insensate, her face redder than the robes of the men
who stood about her in something approximating a circle, holding bright copper bowls. Beside her Hunter was chanting, a knife
in his hand. They hadn't noticed yet that their presence had been
revealed.

No, Fin mentally corrected herself: There were *four* men in
robes . . . and one in slacks and a button-down shirt.

"Jones?" Gabriel boggled at him. "How could he? That son of
a—"

Fin grabbed him by the shirt. "It's gone wrong, can't you see?"

"I see he's betrayed us!"

"I'm taking the shot," said SJ, leveling her crossbow at Hunter.
Fin couldn't blame her, but at the same time, the mushroom wasn't
fully open.

"Wait! We need to wait until the very last moment—and Gabriel, look at Jones. He's not himself! Look at his nose!"

"Then he's our enemy."

"When the mushroom-thing gets a bit bigger you and Aaron
shoot at them with your shotguns—just not at Jones! Then we
can run for it and hit it with the poison, like we discussed."

The mushroom was opening, splitting into flabby petals. Rainbow whorls rose to the surface of the cap, like phosphorescent jel-
lyfish beneath a roiling sea. Ellie stirred in her restraints as Hunter
approached with the knife.

"I'm taking the shot," said SJ.

Ellie's ankles ached terribly where the ropes held her, her feet had gone numb, and her dangling arms felt like they were on fire. She did not see how matters could get any worse. Then Hunter cleared his throat.

"General Jones, step forward!!"

Jones was slow to respond, but he nodded and stepped forward holding a copper bowl. "The f-first offering!" he cried, almost tripping as he approached. Ellie wondered if he was trying to resist Hunter's power, but it didn't give her any hope. If he was, he was losing.

Hunter lifted his arm high. Ellie saw the flash of the blade and closed her eyes, expecting the next moment to be her last, but she opened them again when she heard a whizz followed by a scream. Something hot and wet spattered her face and neck; she couldn't see what. She couldn't see anything that was happening—the angle was all wrong—but her heart leaped when she heard the blast of a shotgun from the edge of the clearing. Upside down, Ellie saw smoke, and a robed man fell to the ground. Hunter's scream turned into shouting, but a second blast drowned out his instructions to his colleagues.

From where she hung, Ellie saw Aaron emerge as if from nowhere. He threw aside his smoking shotgun and charged into the center of the clearing, sword in one hand, the sack of fungicide thrown over his shoulder. Ellie had never seen anything so wonderful in her life, and felt the stirring of hope in her breast.

She twisted in her ropes a bit, to try to see Hunter. He was bleeding—she could see the darker stain spreading on his robes —but he was still reaching for her with that knife. Her abdomen screamed with the effort, but Ellie rallied herself, twisting this way and that from where she hung by her ankles. He might kill her still, but she wouldn't make it easy on him.

"Be still!" snarled Hunter. In the heat of the moment he had apparently forgotten he could not force her to do his bidding, but others were not immune to his powers. "Grab her!" he commanded Jones, who dutifully moved to obey.

"HOW DID I MISS?" fumed SJ as she reloaded her crossbow. Fin didn't have an answer; she had been waiting for the smoke to clear enough for her to see, and when it did, she knew what to do.

"You're aiming too high!" hissed SJ.

"Nope," said Fin calmly, and loosed her arrow.

It was a shot she couldn't have made on her best day back when she'd been practicing every afternoon at school, under the tutelage of her archery instructress. The odds against it were incredible, with the smoke and the confusion and the distance and writhing away from Hunter's knife. But Fin could see the pattern of the rope's sway and adjusted her grip accordingly, felt her muscles shift and align within her body, and took the shot.

The arrow frayed the rope as it sliced through it, and Ellie swung free, coming down hard on top of Hunter and Jones, who were both trying to wrangle her as she twisted in the air.

As Fin reached for another arrow, she assessed the situation. The man Gabriel had shot was down, lying still on the earth a few feet from the undulating fungus, a worrisome dark stain spreading toward it. Fin headed in that direction now that Ellie was free, lest any of the spilled blood reach the entity that craved it. She didn't know if just any old blood would be considered an offering or sacrifice, but she thought it best to keep everything away from it.

As she approached the mushroom-thing, Fin saw that Jones had scrambled out from beneath Ellie, but another of the robed men had fallen upon him and they were now fighting. Either his trance had been an act all along or he'd awoken from it—regardless, she was glad she'd stopped Gabriel from shooting at him.

As she reached the man who was bleeding out near the fungus, Fin heard the unmistakable throaty twang of SJ's crossbow and a yelp of pain. Fin kept her attention on rolling the man in the robe away from the center of the clearing and scraped at his blood on the ground with her shoe until it was hopelessly mixed with dirt in a little hollow. Only then did she look up to see that SJ had gotten her man this time, and was now crouching over him; she'd apparently had the same idea as Fin about keeping any blood away from the brightly glowing fungal body.

Looking around, Fin could no longer see Ellie and Hunter. Gabriel was dumping the contents of the sack onto the fungal cap as Aaron kept a robed man back with his cavalry sword. They seemed to be doing all right, considering, but Fin was worried about her friend.

The good news was that Ellie had disentangled herself from Hunter and her face was turning back to the right color. The bad news was that Hunter was now drinking deeply from the bottle that had hung at his waist. He swallowed the last of its contents as Ellie pushed off the last rope from around her ankles.

Fin's enhanced perception told her that she couldn't do much to help Ellie; jumping into the fray right now would achieve nothing. Having no skill at fisticuffs, it would be better for Fin to stay back and hope for a clean shot at Hunter.

As she nocked another arrow, it occurred to Fin that she had no way of knowing if this really was the best course of action, or just the demon's gift making self-preservation seem like reason. She brushed the thought away—she had to trust her instincts.

She did not trust her eyes, however, when she looked up and saw Hunter's face change shape. His jaw unhinged like a snake's as his mouth opened wide. Ellie had leaped atop him and was punching him just as it happened; her hand skittered across too many teeth that were all suddenly too large for Hunter's mouth. She yelped and fell back, knuckles bleeding from jagged cuts.

Hunter grinned at Ellie, but instead of leaping to his feet he planted his hands on the ground. The earth itself began to undulate like the mushroom cap beyond, and beneath Fin's feet grass turned to fur and leaves to scales; bright colors emanated from beneath his palms, spreading like oil away from him.

"Get down!" cried Fin, and Ellie either heard her or had the same thought. When her friend dropped to the roiling earth, Fin took a running shot at Hunter's eye as he regained his feet; a great inhuman shriek from the other side of the altar distracted her, and the arrow struck Hunter in the ribs.

Hunter roared, and his too-large tongue lolled out of his mouth. At first, Fin assumed he was in pain, but as she retrieved another arrow she saw he was looking at his beloved mushroom.

The fungicide seemed to have worked. The cap had begun to smoke and bubble, and the pulsing rainbow whorls had lost their luster. Fin felt a flutter of hope when the stem snapped; it hit the earth with a thump that sent a wave of earth rolling outward toward Fin and Ellie and Hunter and everyone else as if they were all standing upon the sea, instead of on solid ground.

Then the cap burst.

The oily fluid inside the mushroom splashed everywhere. Some landed on Fin's hand; it smoked and burned and she couldn't rub it away when she tried to wipe it off on her dress—it clung to her skin like oil, and began to bubble and sizzle. Her shriek of pain was not the only one.

ELLIE SAW THE MUSHROOM CAP hit the earth, but her surge of satisfaction was all too short. It shuddered like a dying thing and then erupted noxious effluvium that spattered everyone within its fell radius. Her left arm took the worst of it—the pain was intense, like a terrible burn—and then a strange roll of earth, like a wave of dirt and grass and fur and leather and feathers, knocked her on her ass.

She wasn't the only one. As she tried to get to her feet, she saw Hunter had already regained his.

"You!" he snarled, pointing at her.

Hunter, too, had been baptized by his creation, but he seemed beyond caring that his distended face was smoking and boiling; some had gotten into his eye. Regardless, he came at her again, tongue hanging out of his mouth like a wolf's, his enormous teeth gleaming.

Holding her frizzled left arm close to her body, Ellie thought about her boxing mentor and what he'd taught her all those years ago; she thought about her attempts to practice what she'd learned on the heavy bag she'd saved up for but never really used as much as she'd hoped to. Well, she hadn't known then that she was training to save more than her own life in a fight. Even so, as she danced in close and struck Hunter in the throat with a jab, she was grateful for the time she'd been able to put in—and all the fights she'd listened to on Gabriel's wireless.

Too quickly Hunter recovered enough to come at her, his teeth gruesomely lengthening even more as he approached. Ellie was winding up for another punch when something zipped by her ear. She startled back from him as he swatted, bearlike, at an arrow that had embedded itself deep in the meat of his cheek, but it stayed there, black blood welling in the wound.

Ellie approached cautiously as he flailed, throwing quick punches at his body to avoid his slavering maw and the shaft of the arrow. She struck him in the chest, in the gut, and then she got him with an uppercut to the jaw that sent him reeling, jaw hanging open. Feeling encouraged, Ellie went in for another jab, this time aiming right at his mouth, but as she did, she saw her error too late to correct it.

Hunter caught her fist in his teeth and chomped down.

Ellie screamed in spite of herself, but she could not get herself free. He worried at her fist like a dog with a bone, and she felt her fingers breaking as her skin ripped. The pain was tremendous and she pushed at him with her free hand, but he brushed off her feeble efforts.

Ellie swayed on her feet. She was tired, she was sore, she was weary, but even when her knees buckled he still hung onto her fist with his awful maw. She looked up in despair and saw Hunter's eyes gleaming at her so brightly that her own began to water. Spots dotting her vision like she'd been staring at the sun, the fight went out of her.

FIN SHOUTED AT ELLIE to hang in there as she planted her feet and stretched through her shoulder blades, but her friend was obviously beyond hearing. Her muscles tightened as her vision became wholly focused on Hunter's left eye. Everything else faded away as she held her shot, waiting for Ellie to fade or duck down, knowing the agony her friend must be in and hating every second of it, but only when Ellie's head fell back did Fin loose her arrow.

It struck true. When he howled Ellie fell free at last, hitting the earth with a thud as Hunter staggered back, drooling from his enormous mouth, his arms swinging in a dead way that made Fin feel queasy. She watched the monstrous man flail, eager to make sure he was not just dying but dead, until a cry distracted her.

Aaron was writhing on the ground as SJ dabbed at his eyes, attempting to wipe away the caustic smoking grease from his face as Gabriel and Jones scrapped with the youngest of the would-be acolytes. Neither of them were looking so good: Gabriel's face was all but obscured by the fungus's toxic secretions, and Jones's nose was definitely broken—it was dribbling blood all over his mouth.

"Father!" cried Hunter's son, breaking away from them both.

He started running as Hunter swayed one more time before crumpling to the earth. Fin nocked an arrow, but before she could loose it a twang followed by a thunk left a quarrel buried in the boy's side. Veering to his right, he collided with one of the torches; both fell to the ground.

The boy's robe caught. He slapped at the flames as he screamed, rolling away into the bubbling mass that had been the enormous fungal body until several pounds of explosive sulfur had destroyed it.

"Get *up,*" said SJ, hauling her brother to his feet. "We gotta get out of here!"

"Come on," said Fin, rushing to Ellie's side and grabbing her by her unmangled hand. "Ellie, we need to go!"

"Fin?" Ellie looked confused, like someone waking from a dream.

"Come on! On your feet!"

"Where's everyone else . . . ?"

Fin was actively pulling at her friend now. "They're coming," she said, not sure if this was really true or not. "Let's *go!*"

They hadn't gotten far when a bright blue light and a truly amazing heat radiated out of the clearing. The noise of it was incredible, and the blast knocked them off their feet; Fin pulled Ellie down and rolled them both behind some bushes and they waited there, hands pressed over their ears, until the wood was dark again. When all seemed quiet, Fin still heard a faint lingering ringing that she could not shake, as if they were surrounded by mosquitoes.

"We're alive," said Fin, amazed, and squeezed Ellie's healthy hand. "We're alive, and we got them, and the earth isn't breaking apart under our feet."

Ellie looked confused. "We're alive?"

"We're alive. We won."

Ellie sat up. "But where's everyone else? We need to find . . ."

She fell backward with a whimper as she tried to get up by putting weight on her broken hand.

Fin took a moment to eat another spoonful of jelly, though the gift of uncannily sharp vision didn't help her much right then. It was Ellie who heard the rustle that proved to be SJ and Aaron.

"We need to wash this stuff off him as soon as we can," said SJ, by way of greeting, as she looked worriedly at her brother.

"We need to get out of here, period," said Fin. "Someone will notice that explosion."

"Will you take him for me?" SJ was looking right at Fin. "I have something I need to do."

"What's so important?" asked Fin. She looked worriedly to Ellie. "We need to find the others and get out of here."

SJ pointed to her sack. "I came up with a contingency plan in case something like that happened; I thought that if that abomination *did* get lit up one way or another it might be good if I brought some pieces of equipment from my old setup—broken glass and other things. I figured if I strewed it all around, anyone who came around might think it was just a moonshining still that exploded."

"And on Hunter's property," said Ellie, coming to a bit at this. "That's brilliant, SJ—you always were the smart one. When they hear Hunter's a hypocrite, all those people who showed up for his speech won't be so keen on his ideas!"

SJ stared at Ellie. "Are you kidding me?" she said, though more gently than she usually spoke to Ellie. "They won't care!"

"But—"

"Discrediting Hunter won't change anything for anyone—they'll still agree he made a lot of good points, say he's only human ... They'll justify it to themselves somehow. What's important is to stop questions from being asked—well, more than need to be. After that explosion, fools will come around to see what went down—cops, feds ... the mob too, probably. If they see a bunch of glassware and bottles and whatever else, they'll say c'est la vie. Hopefully it'll stop them from looking too close at that oil slick back there, too."

"You're right," said Ellie. "I should have thought of that. After all, it didn't bother my father. Why would it bother anyone else?"

"Your —"

The conversation was bitten off by the sound of someone crashing through the underbrush. Fin reached for another arrow, but it was just Gabriel and Jones. Neither was looking their best. The right side of Gabriel's face blistered and charred beneath a dark smear, and Jones was absolutely covered in blood, but they were alive.

"Meet you at their place," SJ said to Fin, jabbing her thumb at where Ellie and Gabriel were gently embracing before trotting off. Fin briefly despaired at the prospect of getting back to the little saltbox without attracting too much attention, but thankfully cooler heads prevailed.

"The pickup won't be far from here," said Gabriel, looking at Aaron, "and we've gotta drive. He's in no condition to walk."

"I agree. I can talk our way past anyone who stops us," said Jones, gingerly dabbing at his face. "No one will have any idea what's going on yet, so I should be able to cover for us easily enough."

Fortunately, they passed only one car on their way back to Ellie and Gabriel's place, and it was just some old rattletrap Ford with a stranger behind the wheel, not a police vehicle. If anyone was out and about, investigating the explosion, they weren't coming from the same end of town.

The little house had never looked more welcoming, even in the dark of night and with all the lights off. No one said anything as they climbed out of the pickup, helping one another where needed, and the silence continued as Fin, who was the least injured of them, got some water boiling so they could all clean their wounds.

Fin didn't mind the silence as she sponged off Aaron and then started on Jones. She had a lot on her mind. They'd saved Long Island . . . but she was curious to see how much things would change and how much they'd stay the same. In the back of her mind lurked the thought that she would not be able to enjoy the results of their success. Sooner or later, her bill for helping in this fight would come due, and she would have no choice but to pay it in full.

6

ELLIE WINCED AS GABRIEL DABBED iodine all over her mangled hand. Hunter's teeth had torn her flesh to shreds in places, her knuckles were badly bruised, and her middle and ring fingers were both broken. Gabriel's big hands held her firmly as he worked on her, but she knew she'd need to see a doctor —and soon—if she wanted to keep the use of her hand.

Lester used to talk about how all animals had distinctive bite patterns. She wasn't looking forward to answering questions about the size or strength of the teeth that had mauled her. Not for the first time did Ellie long for her brother, and not just for his doctoring skills, of course.

SJ ambled in like it was just any night. "Hi. Good to see you're all relaxing," she said, though Ellie saw how her eyes lingered on her brother. "As for me, I only just escaped. Someone was coming to investigate the scene just as I was finishing up." Ellie was surprised when SJ submitted to Fin's nursing without a word. "Not sure who. They didn't see me, though. I was in the bushes hiding Hunter's body." When everybody just stared at her, SJ sighed. "I couldn't just leave him there out in the open like that—his face was still all ... *wrong*. By the time anyone finds him, hopefully he'll have decomposed a bit and there won't be enough left to raise any suspicions about ... well, whatever. Everybody here knows what I'm talking about."

No one said anything after this for several long moments. Then Fin stood and poured SJ a drink.

"Thank you," she said, and after she finished it all in one gulp, Fin poured her another.

"Hopefully your burns will heal up fast," said Jones, looking at himself in the hall mirror. "I can say this happened in the line of duty—checking out some tip when I tripped and fell or something—but as for you all, we should probably figure out some kind of cover story."

Ellie's eyes flicked to her fiancé's face. They'd cleaned it and salved it and bandaged it as best they could, but there would be scars. Aaron, too, would not go unscathed, but at least his eyes seemed all right.

Gabriel tied off the bandage around her hand, and Ellie winced.

"Everyone who wants to stay tonight, please feel free," he announced. He put his hand on Aaron's shoulder; Aaron had not spoken since they'd come back; he had just allowed people to tend to his wounds, content to stare silently off into nothingness. Ellie couldn't blame him—while she felt they'd done the right thing, the scars this night left on them would not all be visible. "We have enough space to make up some beds."

"I'll clear up room for someone else by heading home," said Jones. "I'm close enough."

"So's our aunt's place," said SJ.

"Oh, *please* stay," said Ellie, sliding off the kitchen counter where she'd been sitting.

It didn't feel safe, and while she sensed that Amityville would never feel safe for her again—at least, not like it once had—she didn't want to see their group dissolve, not so soon after they'd gone through everything together. Deep down, Ellie got the sense that SJ's earlier statement was correct—Hunter's followers wouldn't change in the wake of his demise and any potential public disgrace that might follow. Surely that meant they all needed to stick together, not drift apart.

"Really, there's room for all of us," she said, "and tomorrow . . . Well, I was thinking we'll need to rest and recover. I thought maybe . . . I don't know, we could have a clambake or something, in the evening. It'd be no problem; I'm sure my traps are full. I didn't check them yesterday, and I could probably catch some flounder. Anyone who wanted could come out with me. It might be nice ..."

"It does sound nice," said Aaron, finally stirring from his reverie.

SJ looked inclined to object until Gabriel chimed in. "My folks should have potatoes and sweet corn up at the farm, too. I could run up and grab some." When Ellie started to protest, he grinned at her from under his salve. "She'll see my face sooner or later. Hell, maybe she'll have some old-world remedy for burns that'll save my pretty face for you," he said, and chucked her under the chin.

"I do love your folks' sweet corn," said SJ. "Can Georgia come?"

Ellie recalled the pretty girl she'd met in SJ's shack, what felt like years ago. "Of course. Why not?" she said. But as she said it, she finally realized what SJ really meant. She was asking if she could bring a date. Jesus Christ, was she thick sometimes. "I'd love to see her again," she added, just in case her face had betrayed her sudden understanding.

"I've never been to a clambake," said Fin. "What is it?"

"Oh, well, first we'll dig a pit down by the water for a bonfire — Hey, maybe that could be our cover! We could say—"

"I'm going to bed," said SJ. "Go on and talk about your party plans as long as you like, but I'm pretty tuckered out after saving the world."

"Here, let me get you some bedding," said Gabriel. Aaron followed them upstairs, still listless, but perking up a bit.

"Well, I'd be pleased to attend this clambake ... even if I wasn't going to impose on your hospitality in other ways," said Fin.

"Stay as long as you need," said Ellie, though she anticipated Fin would land on her feet pretty quickly. Her friend had changed so much in such a short period of time — even now, when they were so comfortably relaxed together, she seemed reserved, thoughtful ... even grave.

"I think SJ has the right idea," said Jones. "I'll come back for your little party if I can, but I want to sleep in my own bed."

Ellie was disappointed, but she didn't say so. No mushy stuff with Jones; that had always been the rule between them. She did see him to the door, however.

"Drive safe," she said.

"Don't you worry about me, Miss West. I'll be all right."

"I know you will. Drive safe anyway."

Jones put on his hat. Ellie imagined him taking it off and hanging it up in his quiet, empty house, with the dead oregano plant on the windowsill and all those photographs of people long gone. He didn't even have a dog to come home to anymore. While she knew that wasn't because of her—or at least, not because of anything she'd done—she felt terrible about it.

"Stop by tomorrow," she urged him. "Please? If not for me, then for the sweet corn. It'll knock your socks off."

He leaned in close to her. "You really want me to come, don't you?"

Ellie felt her skin tingle. "Don't *you?*" she asked, trying to play it cool. "It's not so far to drive for a free meal."

"When you put it like that, how could a man resist?" He tipped his hat at her. "Good night, Miss West."

FIN WAS HAPPY TO TAKE the couch, bolstered with a few extra pillows and a blanket or two. SJ had put Aaron in Lester's old bed, and had decided to bunk on the floor beside him in case he needed her in the night.

After making sure everyone was all right, without appearing to fuss over them too much, Ellie and Gabriel went up to their bedroom hand in hand. It was the first moment they'd really and truly been alone together in . . . well, even if it had only been a few days, it felt like far longer.

"Miss me?" said Gabriel, after shutting the door behind them.

"A little," she said, and then shook her head. "So much. I can't do it, Gabriel—I can't be away from you. You're always on my mind, and your name's always on the tip of my tongue. Even times when I've been with . . . other men"—Ellie blushed, amazing herself that she could still be shy about such things—"I always think about you, about how you might be pleased by hearing about the things I was doing."

He took her in his arms then, and kissed her. "What a good little wife you'll make," he said, and then tweaked her on the nose when she pulled away from him in mock outrage. "Oh, come on. You know I missed you too."

"Did you?" Ellie wished she had Fin's power to discern the truth.

"Oh, I was furious at you. I'm not too proud to say it . . . or pleased at myself for becoming so. I'm sorry. I'm still learning when to hold you close and when to let you go."

"Now's a good time for holding close."

He kissed her some more, and moved down to her neck. But when he started to fumble with the hook on her coveralls, she stopped him.

"What?" he asked.

"We can't. Everyone would hear us!"

"I built this bed; it won't creak. I can be quiet, so it's on you if they catch on."

She liked it when he got a little bossy like that, and let him do what he liked. She had been longing for his touch, and at last there was nothing stopping them from enjoying one another. As he pushed her down on the bed, Ellie whispered in his ear, "I think I talked Jones into joining us tomorrow." He paused, a strange look on his face. "At the clambake, I mean," she added to clarify. She hoped she had read him right, earlier that day when he'd seemed so intrigued by Jones.

Gabriel grabbed his belt as she reached for her contraceptive case.

"You'll have a harder time keeping quiet now," he hissed, sticking the folded leather between her eager teeth, but there could be no mistaking his enthusiasm after that. Ellie was quite glad he'd muffled her as he pulled her beneath him. She was no exhibitionist.

Ellie thought she might sleep afterward, but as usual she was wakeful once Gabriel fell asleep beside her. It was just too wonderful, lying beside her fiancé in their bedroom, letting a breeze so mild and cool it was almost autumnal brush over her naked body.

The thing was, eventually the sun would rise, and with it would come another day full of uncertainty. Perhaps they'd taken care of Hunter and his colleagues, but in the investigation that would surely ensue, who could say what would shake out—who would be questioned, what they would decide or discover. Her father . . . her brother . . . There would be much to explain. The lack of Lester's body alone would make things difficult . . . as would her father's unpredictability. It was strange to think how she had known him all her life, but she could not guess what he would do anymore. Neither could she anticipate what part her mother would play in all this.

And of course there was the question of Hunter's remaining followers—the men and women of Amityville, and from all over Suffolk County. She had seen them for what they truly were that day in the field—what they nurtured within their hearts. It wasn't Robert Frost who had been right; it was his neighbor—good fences did make for better neighbors. Now that she knew the true nature of her neighbors it would be harder for her to live here, in this place she loved so much.

Yet she did still love it. She always would. The people of this island weren't only those who had shown up at that rally in the field. Her friends lived here, too, as did plenty of strangers who had refused the clarion call of hatred and bigotry.

And the island was itself more than its people, with its forests home to willow and maple and pine and oak, sparrow and cardinal and robin, deer and fox and stoat and bat; its fields to bee and mouse, to wildflowers and crops. Its channels welcomed duck and its shores crab and sandpiper and turtle; under its adjoining waters thrived fluke and flounder and clam and crab and oyster and seal and more.

These thoughts made Ellie long for her notebook. It had been so long since she'd scribbled any poetry in its pages ... The last time had been just before that night on the bay when she'd run into Walter Greene. Practically a lifetime ago, or so it felt.

Gabriel slept heavily, his relaxed body a joy to behold. Even so, she slid out of bed quietly to leave him for a little while. She'd be back beside him soon.

Grabbing a pencil from the kitchen and the hurricane lantern, Ellie went out to the porch. The first cricket of autumn was chirping as she ducked under the mosquito bar and settled in.

She opened her notebook to a blank page, thinking of something SJ had said just before they'd set out to stop Hunter.

This is my island! Ellie wrote awkwardly with her left hand, the loopy letters odd and unfamiliar but nevertheless truthful and pure. *I love its shifting shore. I love the wetlands and the mudflats too* . . .

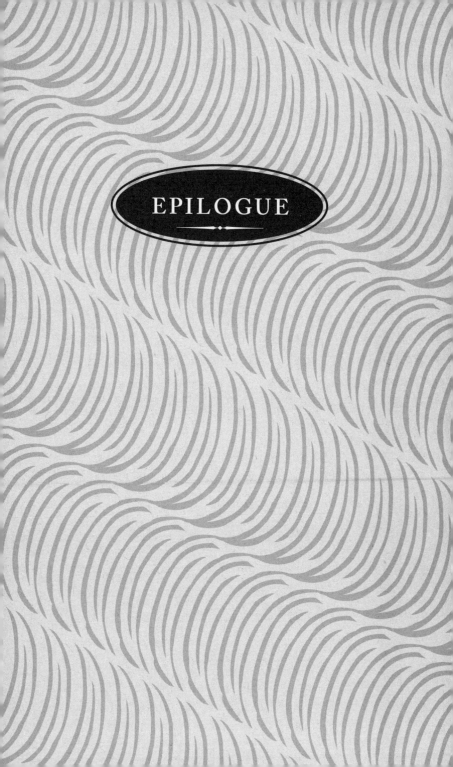

EPILOGUE

FROM

The Demon in the Deep
by G. Baker

AFTER A YEAR AND A DAY Susan stopped looking for Miss Depth, but it took longer than that for her to stop hoping her friend would return. She often caught herself glancing twice at white-haired women on the street, or in shops, but every time it proved to be only a passing similarity or a trick of the light.

It was difficult, wanting answers she knew she would never get. She understood so little of what she'd seen on the beach that day—what she had seen in her friend's house . . . and the only person who could tell her more was absent, gone as if she had never been, leaving a hole in her life Susan couldn't leave alone, like a little girl poking her tongue at the gap where a tooth ought to be.

Long after Susan had grown up enough to have weathered an unsuccessful romance, and then a successful one that made her a blushing bride and then a happy wife and mother of one, it occurred to her that perhaps it hadn't been her friend who had written her the note that she still kept folded in her Bible. Perhaps it had been the demon. But Susan couldn't figure out why she would ever want to summon the demon. She had seen what it could do.

Then one night Susan's husband didn't come home, and though upon his return he claimed he'd spent it at a friend's house after a business dinner kept him late, doubt crept in at the edges of his story. She kept thinking about it for long afterward; longed to know the truth.

She trusted him, but the temptation was there, to know for sure. She knew from experience that the truth was a funny thing. It had the capacity to destroy as much as heal.

It was still comforting, knowing she could learn the truth if she really wanted. But whether she ever would, that remained to be seen.

ONE MONTH LATER

FIN DIDN'T KNOW HOW she'd missed it, as many times as she'd read this book. G. Baker might have begun writing *The Demon in the Deep*, but she hadn't finished it. Something else had—something that wanted to draw in the curious with promises of seeing the truth. The message had been a flame, and young Delphine a moth . . . She'd even sought out the author herself, to receive the missing pieces of a puzzle she hadn't known existed.

Fin set the book down on the little table beside her favorite chair in the little solar of her house. The early mornings were getting a bit of nip to them as September rolled along, and it had been too cool to sit outside as she drank her tea. Now, though, the sun was up and the day was warming nicely. It was time to get herself together and go pick what might be the last of this year's beach plums.

She had asked for Ellie's mother's recipe before leaving Amityville for the little house she'd bought in East Hampton, right on the water. She'd picked it not just for its picturesque view, but for the good stand of beach plums that lurked in the bit of wooded area on the outskirts of the property. She'd already successfully canned some of her own jelly, though she had never done such a thing before in her life. It really wasn't so hard as she'd first thought.

She'd gotten a taste for seeing the truth of the world. It had helped her get this house at a fair price in spite of being a single woman, and had helped in her conversations with her lawyer regarding what it would take to obtain a divorce without losing anything, among other feats.

It took hours to get to Amityville either by car or by train, much less the city, but that was how Fin wanted it. She didn't want to see anyone; what she craved was solitude. Ellie had come to visit once, but Fin hadn't returned the favor. The sounds of the wind and the trees and the water were so soothing, and she preferred visitors that scurried and flew rather than marching up the walk in loud leather shoes.

It had been hard, to cultivate distance between herself and Ellie . . . She liked her friend so much. But that's why she'd done it. With their task of saving Long Island complete, her days were now a countdown until the demon took her for its own.

She'd preferred to say goodbye on her own terms. It wasn't as if the demon had told her how it would claim possession of her. Perhaps it would be all at once, and she'd be left a spectator in her own life once again . . . Or perhaps it would be a more gradual shift, until she was no longer sure what parts of herself were native and which were the demon. She'd tried asking, too, by eating a lot of the jelly all at once to try to gain an audience. But all she'd gotten for her trouble was a stomachache and the clear understanding that the truth was it didn't matter *how* it would happen, just that it indeed *would* happen, whenever the demon felt like it.

The important thing, Fin had decided, was to enjoy her remaining days . . . though it had occurred to her that it was already too late, and her mind was already more demon's than woman's. It was true that she'd never in her life wanted to buy a house far away from everyone she'd ever known or cared about to live with the gulls and the waves and her own thoughts. Or at least what she thought were her own thoughts.

One thing she felt certain of was that the choice to move out here had been hers and hers alone, for she'd made it the night they'd stopped Hunter. The demon had said it would take possession of her no sooner than ten days after she'd summoned it, and something told Fin it could not do so before that term was up. That's why she'd acted so quickly, contacting her lawyer and buying this house. She wanted to be sure *she* was the one doing every-thing, so when she changed her mind—*if* she changed her mind—she could take stock and assess whether it was really her deci-sion, or some outside impulse.

For now, it felt good, living where she wanted, in the manner she desired. For the first time in a long time, she was actually happy.

And it seemed as though the demon—her demon, not the one they'd thwarted—was happiest near the sea, for whatever reason. Maybe it would let her stay here. It had, after all, helped her save this place, and she did feel a deeper connection to the island ever since that night. Living here—knowing it was her choice—made her proud to say Long Island was her home.

As to whether she always would, that remained to be seen.

Acknowledgments

This book is dedicated to my grandmother, Harriet Elizabeth West Ketcham, whose poetry and love of the Great South Bay inspired the character of Ellie West; and to my mother, Sally Jane Tanzer, who took me to Amityville for a week or so every summer when I was a girl. Those library trips and long summer evenings we spent playing pinochle with my grandmother and grandfather are remembered here. There are, of course, a few others I wish to thank for their contributions to this book: my aunt and uncle Diane and Terry Ketcham in particular; Diane's book *Long Island: Shores of Plenty* (Windsor Publications, 1988) was a great help to me, as were our many trips on their boat, sometimes just out on the bay for a cruise, sometimes over to Fire Island to swim in the ocean. I'd also like to thank William T. Lauder, Seth Purdy, and Patricia Cahaney of the Amityville Historical Society, and my friends Andrew Liptak and Adam Scott Glancy for their help with other aspects of my research. Patricia's stories in particular added some excellent local flavor to the novel, for which I am very grateful, and Andrew and Adam actually know stuff about military history, which I really, *really* do not. Many thanks as well to my editor, John Joseph Adams, for believing in this book and helping me through a few rough patches in the writing of it; and my agent, Cameron McClure, who remains my artistic and emotional bedrock; my copy editor, Deanna Hoak; and of course my whole team at HMH. I am also grateful, as always, for the support (and forbearance) of my friends and family. You are all appreciated more than you can possibly know.

Keep reading for a sample from the next novel by Molly Tanzer!

Follow Miriam and Jane, two girls living in the north
of England during World War II, where they are
studying to be master *diabolists* . . .

CREATURES

OF

CHARM

HUNGER

Coming in 2020

1

HAWKSHEAD, ENGLAND

1945

MIRIAM TOOK A STEADYING BREATH before turning the knob of the old farmhouse's back door and stepping outside to feed the chickens and the geese. It was not the darkness, nor February's biting cold that made her hesitate, nor was it fear of predators that might be slinking through the gloaming—at least, not animal ones. Foxes and weasels did not frighten her; it was the threat of *who* might be out there, not *what*, that caused sweat to prick at her neck and under her arms even in the predawn chill.

She knew her fear was absurd. There were no Nazis prowling the yard. Nor were there any in the fields and rocky hills of Cumbria beyond the fence. No Nazis were hiding in the neighbors' barns or in the picturesque village of Hawkshead, down the lane. Here in the north of England she was safe, had been safe for years, and yet every morning she had to remind herself of that.

"Who's the real goose here?" muttered Miriam, as she let herself into the barn. The truth was, if Nazis ever *did* intrude upon their privacy, her "Aunt" Nancy, whose treasured flock pecked at Miriam's shoes, would know. Nancy was a diabolist—one of the most educated diabolists in the Société des Éclairées—and as the Société's Librarian, she had many wards to guard her home and the books therein. Not only that, but as her apprentice Miriam was not helpless either.

And one day, Miriam would summon a demon of her own.

Miriam rubbed at her numb and dripping nose before scooping up some grain to feed the poultry. She had been thinking quite a lot about demon-summoning of late, but that was for master diabolists. As an apprentice, she was limited to learning how to concoct potions, pills, and powders—armamentaria, as diabolists called them—with small amounts of diabolic essences. But, during all of her copious reading over the years, Miriam had naturally come across references to specific demons and the powers they granted their hosts.

Some demons let diabolists control others with a word, or heightened their senses, or endowed them with unnatural strength. Miriam was certain she would choose a demon like the latter—one that would help her move through the world with more confidence.

She'd tried and failed to overcome her fears. But in Nancy's laboratory, Miriam had created a potion that let her run more swiftly, in case she had to escape a dangerous situation. Putting a bottle of it in her pocket helped when she needed to go into the village, but it wasn't a real solution. Apprentice recipes, intended to educate, wore off quickly. Truly powerful armamentaria—the kind a master might make—needed more demonic essence than Miriam was capable of obtaining.

As she scattered grain on the ground, Miriam's mind strayed to a different farm where she'd fed poultry. Her aunt—her *real* aunt, Aunt Judith—had also kept geese, and goats too, on her farm outside Rotterdam. As a child, Miriam had loved to watch them play, especially the kids; she'd been less enamored with them when she'd hidden in that barn before fleeing the country. One goat had bitten her, tearing her dress. It had been so cold, but she hadn't any other clothes; she just had to make do until she'd crossed the border, but even then . . .

Miriam willed herself not to think about that. She couldn't risk having one of her attacks, not today. There was so much to do in anticipation of the arrival of another "aunt": Aunt Edith.

"All that happened a long time ago," Miriam said to the chickens and the geese as they nibbled at the grain she'd given them.

Edith was Nancy's sister. She too was part of the Société, though not one of its elected officials. The position of Librarian meant living in the Library, which was here, in rural Hawkshead, even though the Société itself was based in Paris. Why the Library was in Hawkshead no one knew, but it had been there in various forms long before the Société existed, and there it would remain.

Miriam liked Edith, but she didn't much like it when Edith came to visit, for a few reasons. Edith lived abroad and always brought news from Europe. That was hard—even when she had good news to share, it wasn't the news Miriam wanted.

It wasn't news of her parents.

Harder still was enduring the way Edith's visits affected Nancy's daughter, Jane. Jane always tended to put on airs when Edith stayed with them, and Miriam liked Jane much better when she was simply herself.

Miriam returned to the farmhouse, stepping over the furry bulk of their loyal dog, Hercules, as she ducked back inside. Nancy was standing at the AGA, frying bacon. The smell of it was mouth-watering. Partaking always made Miriam feel guilty, but her parents had implored her to "blend in" once she reached England—and as she'd discovered, eating pork products was a surprisingly large part of that.

"How are they this morning?" asked Nancy.

"Snug and warm and no longer hungry," said Miriam as she shed her coat and hat and slipped on her apron.

"I wish I could say the same," said Jane, as she bustled into the kitchen. "I'm starving!"

Miriam blushed when she saw Jane's perfectly coiffed hair—she knew how her own must look. Her "cousin" had obviously gotten up early to set herself to rights. Though only a scant half-year older than Miriam, these days Jane seemed so much more mature.

"No need to be dramatic, breakfast is ready," said Nancy, turning around with a tray full of bacon and fried bread, which she set down in the center of the scarred kitchen table. "My, Jane, look at you! All dressed up already. You still have to dust and sweep, you know."

"But I dusted and swept yester—"

"And it could do with another going over. This time, use the dust rag instead of talking to it as if it were Clark Gable."

Jane looked rather miffed at this remark, though it was true that for a while now it had been Jane's joy to see every picture she could at the theater in Ambleside.

Miriam had never gone with her. It was five miles to Ambleside, far too far for comfort. But in a way she felt she'd seen *Meet Me in St. Louis*, *Cover Girl*, and other films. Jane liked to talk them over after she returned, doing impressions of the actresses whom Miriam had seen only in glossy stills in Jane's magazines. Jane was good at impressions—so good she'd managed to sneak them into her everyday mannerisms after careful study of their expressions and movements.

"Edith is supposed to arrive around a quarter past two, so you've plenty of time to reapply that lipstick if it gets smudged. Yes, I noticed," said Nancy, who disapproved of cosmetics. Miriam thought this attitude a bit funny, given that Nancy was a master diabolist; most people would likely see diabolism as a far greater offense against nature than a bit of rouge.

Jane seemed to turn back into a little girl as she sullenly poked at her breakfast.

"You'll trip over that lip if you don't pick it up," said Nancy, but her teasing did little to mollify her daughter. "Oh, come now. What would Edith say if she saw you like that?"

"Mother!" That was another change—Jane had called Nancy "Mum" until lately.

"If you'd known Edie as long as I have, you wouldn't feel the need to make yourself up for her," said Nancy. "She was once your age, you know—and a lot wilder and more scabby-kneed than either of you."

"Scabby-kneed!" cried Jane.

Miriam stared at her plate. For some reason, Jane's horror at this comment exasperated her. Why should it surprise Jane that Edith had put away childish things, just like anyone else?

And anyway, diabolism was hardly the most polite profession. Master diabolists who had successfully summoned a demon saved their hair trimmings, their nail clippings, sometimes even their menstrual fluid or less polite effluvia—anything infused with the diabolic matter they regularly consumed. Such materials could be rendered for their diabolic essences to enhance the potency of armamentaria.

Squeamishness was not for the ambitious diabolist—in fact, some had been known to pull out a tooth or cut off a finger or a toe in the service of a particularly powerful preparation. Scabby knees weren't a patch on extracting one's own perfectly healthy molar.

But Miriam didn't say any of this. She took a deep breath and pushed her feelings down, as she always did, burying them deep.

"Oh yes. Edie played rugby with our brothers until the day she moved away," said Nancy.

"And she seems so civilized. I suppose there's hope for me yet," said Jane wryly, as she finally stabbed a piece of bacon with her fork.

Miriam looked up, glad she hadn't said anything. *That* was the Jane that Miriam preferred—sardonic and less serious about herself.

"Oh no," said Nancy, with an appraising look at her daughter. "There's no hope for you . . . or there won't be if you don't finish your chores."

Jane let out a childish sigh. Miriam smiled to hear it, but her stomach was still a tight ball of unhappiness. She knew that this moment—all of them together, just being themselves—would be the last of its kind for several days.

"Aren't you excited about Edith's visit, Miriam?"

Nancy's question caught her off guard.

"Of course I'm excited," she said quickly. "I've been wanting to ask Edith about her research into changing one's appearance by applying demonic residue via cosmetics." Nancy frowned again, until Miriam explained, "I think it might help me understand the theory behind the Fifth Transmutation." This was all true.

"Do you think so?" Jane was also a diabolist-in-training and was absolutely cracking at it. But where Miriam liked to think through the Art's theoretical aspects, Jane preferred its practical side. "I'd like to hear that too. The Fifth Transmutation is crucial when attempting Campanella's Substantive Exchange—and it's just so odd, what the *Grimoire Italien* says about demonic vapors and their impure properties being beneficial to the load . . . it's not clear if it means the load for the demon or the diabolist."

Miriam looked up from her plate. "The *Grimoire Italien*? Are you using the French translation of *Trasformazioni Della Materia*? In the original medieval Italian that passage is a bit clearer. The diabolist is more at risk, the benefit is on the side of the demon, but there's also a chance that . . ." Miriam trailed off as she saw Jane's face flush.

The learning of ancient languages was not among Jane's talents—which was nothing to be ashamed of, but Jane was sensitive about it.

Attuned to her position as an outsider in this house, Miriam always tried her best not to cause trouble or upset anyone. She appreciated this family and their acceptance of her more than she could say. After all, if such a thing were possible, she would be a part of it forever.

"Anyway," said Miriam, eager to smooth over the awkward moment, "I didn't realize you were reading that. The modern Italian translation is better and I have it in my room to compare with the medieval, since the medieval is a bother to read. It's barely even Italian, really—just medieval Venetian vernacular mixed with Latin."

"Thank you," said Jane, with a formality and poise learned from her favorite actresses. "I'd be pleased to look at it."

"*Later*," said Nancy, with a tone that conveyed exactly what they ought to be doing *now*.

Miriam began to clear the dishes; Jane too stood up from the table, but as she did a great yowl split the air and a slate-gray blur of wounded dignity streaked out the kitchen.

"Poor Smudge!" Jane, dismayed, hurried after the cat.

"You'd think one day he'd learn that sitting behind Jane's chair will only get him a pinched tail," said Miriam.

"Perhaps he enjoys the attention," said Nancy, as she wrapped the remainder of the bread in a cloth. "Speaking of enjoying things, I do hope you'll join us later? I think it'll be a lovely day for a walk, in spite of the cold, and quite a merry party once Edie arrives."

"Of course I'll come!" Miriam managed a smile, unsure whether the flutter of trepidation in her stomach was caused by her aunt's imminent arrival or the thought of hiking to the village.

"Good, good. Well, I'm off to the stacks for now. See you in a few hours."

"I will." Miriam longed to talk her aunt about unintentionally offending Jane; an adult's perspective would be welcome. But she held her tongue, turning her attention to the dishes.

Nancy squeezed Miriam's shoulder affectionately before sweeping out of the room. She too had something of the elegantly dramatic about her. And for both Nancy and Jane, it came out a bit more when Edith came to visit.

But even on a normal day the two Blackwood women carried a distinct glamour about them that Miriam ardently wished she possessed. But, it was not to be. No matter how hard she might try, she could never stop being completely herself: prosaic, drab, and afraid of every sound or shadow.